Defying Providence

Providence

Smallpox and the forgotten
18th century Medical Revolution

By

Arthur W. Boylston MD

ISBN: 1478232455
ISBN 13: 9781478232452
Library of Congress Control Number: 2012912765
CreateSpace Independent Publishing Platform
North Charleston, South Carolina

To My wife Anthea with thanks for all her help and support in making this book.

Preface

Defying Providence started as an attempt to answer the question "why did people give themselves smallpox". The practice was then called inoculation; it is now termed variolation. While researching what happened I discovered a revolution in medicine that took place in the 18th century. Perhaps its most powerful result was to free mankind from dependence on fate. An individual could defy providence and choose a safe way to prevent fatal smallpox. To get to that point, 18th century scientists invented powerful techniques to determine which treatments work and how infections spread. These are still used today.

I also uncovered what really happened before Edward Jenner could develop vaccination which would eventually lead to the eradication of smallpox; and how his biographer laid a false trail to protect his reputation. There were no milkmaids. Moreover, without inoculation the benefits of cowpox could not have been discovered

All this happened during the supposedly sterile 18th century when medicine was said to cause more harm than good. *Defying Providence* overturns several cherished myths. It will expand your views of the 18th century and raise your respect for the courageous men and women who gave themselves smallpox.

Contents

Prologue

December 1721

On a clear icy day a middle aged physician rides across the narrow neck of land connecting colonial Boston to the mainland town of Roxbury. Wrapped up against the freezing spray blown over the road from the tidal flats and the Charles River beyond, he has been summoned by a family to advise on the smallpox, now epidemic in Boston and the surrounding towns. The disease has already killed 13 heads of families in Roxbury and the town is terrified that there will be more deaths. He carries the usual medical kit of an 18th century country doctor, a selection of drugs and herbs, some of which are used to induce vomiting, some work as laxatives, others are blistering compounds, and he has his lancet for letting blood. He differs from his colleagues only by carrying a small tightly stoppered vial containing a few drops of thick creamy fluid.

Three thousand miles away as afternoon dissolves into the murky gloom of a misty Yorkshire evening a second middle aged physician is also riding to console a family afflicted with smallpox. Many children have died in the parish of Halifax and now a family wants help. He has long felt frustrated by the ineffectual treatments he has to offer his patients. He also carries a tightly stoppered vial containing a little creamy fluid.

Their vials contain smallpox. They are going to infect their patients with the era's most feared disease.

Between them they will help trigger the birth of modern medicine and change the world. They do not know of each other; they will never meet. Their work will eventually save millions of lives and alter the fate of North America. What they are doing will trigger the first flowering of scientific medicine. Both men are now forgotten. But both left accounts of their experiences and the hatred they faced as they tried to help their patients. Threatened with imprisonment and damned by many of their ministers, they persisted in believing that were doing much more good than harm.

Defying Providence is the story of inoculation for smallpox and its consequences. It demolishes a number of cherished myths.

A note on terminology is needed. In *Defying Providence* the word inoculation means just what it meant in the 18th century, the transfer of material from someone with smallpox to someone who had not had the disease. The word was derived from French for "transplanting" as in rose grafting. Later in this book the term vaccination will be used to refer to "cowpoxing", immunisation with cowpox instead of smallpox.

Defying Providence tells the story of the many men and women who wrestled with their consciences to turn inoculation from a primitive folk practice into the most powerful weapon against smallpox in the 18th century.

In order to convince themselves and their opponents that deliberately giving someone smallpox was safe and effective inoculators developed the first quantitative studies of a disease. They used their results to give patients a choice; await fate and have smallpox naturally, or defy providence and have it artificially. It was the first medical intervention that really was beneficial and it gave individuals the chance to control their own destinies. Now we would call this "evidence based medicine" which has become the cornerstone of modern medicine. Most textbooks claim that evidence based medicine began in 19th century Paris, but it really began 120 years earlier in England and colonial America.

When inoculation became generally available in the 1760's a humble country surgeon discovered that many of his patients could not be inoculated. He questioned them and found that they had all had cowpox. This was how Edward Jenner learned that cowpox prevented smallpox. He was not told by a milkmaid but heard it from a colleague. Furthermore, without inoculation the cowpox effect could not have been discovered. There were no

x

folk traditions; even Jenner says so. And milkmaids did not have especially beautiful complexions. Without inoculation no one would ever have accepted that giving people material from a sick cow could be beneficial. Many of the scientific and moral arguments against introducing an artificial disease had been won by the inoculators. In the beginning vaccination was identical to inoculation and many people could not tell whether they had been inoculated or cowpoxed. In time it would become clear that vaccination was safer and less trouble than inoculation, but it would never have got off the ground if inoculation had not been widely accepted.

Inoculation was the beginning of immunisation against infectious diseases, the most powerful and valuable of all medical interventions. It worked and proved to be both safe and to give lifelong immunity to smallpox. Without it Jenner could not have contemplated immunising with cowpox, and the development of vaccines might have been delayed for generations. When Louis Pasteur was feted for developing vaccines in the late 19th century he credited Jenner as the source of his inspiration. He should have acknowledged the inoculators. Isaac Newton once said that if he saw further it was because he stood on the shoulders of giants. Jenner and Pasteur stood on the shoulders of the inoculators.

Finally, it has become fashionable to say that medicine did nothing for mankind until the late 19th or even the early 20th century. The first half of the 18th century has even been called a medical desert. It wasn't. Two of medicine's most powerful tools were invented before 1730. By 1750 there was a safe way to avoid the dangers of smallpox the era's most feared disease.

Medicine is not often considered part of the Enlightenment, yet what could be more "enlightened" than the ability to choose your fate. Many individuals in the 18th century defied providence and chose a safe way to confront smallpox rather than wait for fate to decide their future.

Defying Providence tells the forgotten story of one of medicine's finest hours and the brave men and women who made it.

Chapter 1

A UNIVERSAL AFFLICTION

Smallpox is unique; it is the only disease that has been eradicated. Very few doctors now practicing have ever seen a case. In Europe and the Americas the disease was rare for decades before it was officially wiped out so that almost no one remembers what smallpox was like or the intense fear that it caused. Only polio in my lifetime has been able to induce the same extreme anxiety produced by an outbreak of smallpox in the past. To understand how the seemingly dangerous practice of deliberately giving your child smallpox came to be common practice it is necessary to remind ourselves of what smallpox was.

Smallpox is caused by a virus called *Variola major,* a member of a large family of viruses that infect most species of domestic animals. The name derives from the characteristic skin eruption of small blisters or pimple-like spots known as pocks. Some poxviruses are able to infect many different animals including elephants, rodents, and cows, while others can only infect one species; *Variola major* can only infect humans.[1] The origins and properties of smallpox virus are intimately related to the rise, and eventual elimination, of the disease that it caused.

Smallpox typically produced a distinctive rash of domed white pustules which were especially prominent on the face.

Although there were degrees of severity from individuals with only a few pustules to others whose whole skin seemed involved, it was usually possible for an experienced physician to make a correct diagnosis. Occasionally chicken pox could be confused with smallpox, but most of the time the prominent white pustules were a guide to smallpox. An almost unique feature of smallpox was the damage that it left behind when a patient recovered from the infection; many people were left with deep pitting scars on their faces, and some individuals lost the sight in one or both eyes. Such distinctive aspects of smallpox help to unravel its history. While some authorities have attempted to blame smallpox for calamities such as the plague that led to the collapse of Athens in the 4th century BC or the Antonine plague that seriously weakened the Roman empire, descriptions of those diseases written at the time do not mention the characteristic features of smallpox. The first unequivocal report of smallpox is found in China in a document written about 340 AD which refers to a disease imported in previous centuries along with prisoners captured along the Western border of China. It was called Hunpox or "prisoners" pox as a result.. *"Recently there have been persons suffering from epidemic sores which attack the head, face, and trunk. In a short time these sores spread over the body. They have the appearance of hot boils containing some white matter. While some of these pustules are drying up a fresh crop appears. If not treated early the patients usually die. Those who recover are disfigured with purplish scars which do not fade away until after a year. This is due to poisonous air. The people say it was introduced in the reign of Chien Wu when that king was fighting with the Huns at Nang Yang."*[2] These domed, white, pus filled pocks and the residual scars are not found in any other disease.

The next clear appearance of smallpox is in the writings of the Muslim scholars Rhazes and Avicenna who recorded an epidemic that destroyed an army that was besieging Mecca in the 6th century AD.[3], [4]Thereafter the infection spread rapidly to Cairo, across North Africa, and into Southern Spain carried by Muslim armies. Crusaders returning from the Holy Land brought the disease to Germany and France.[5]

Detailed clinical descriptions of many diseases by Hippocrates in Greece in the 4th century BC and by Galen in Rome in the 3rd century AD do not mention a disease with the salient features of smallpox, nor is there anything like smallpox in the Bible. However, there are a few hints that smallpox may actually be much older than I have indicated. In the Egyptian museum in Cairo the face of the mummy of Rameses V, who died in 1157 BC, is covered with a pustular rash which experienced clinical observers are convinced is smallpox.[6] Unfortunately electron microscopy to identify the virus has not yet been used to confirm the diagnosis, but it is possible that this is the oldest known case of the disease. Two other mummies from a similar time also have a suggestive skin eruption. However, there is no description of the characteristic features in any of the surviving Egyptian medical papyri, and there are no hieroglyphics describing a smallpox like illness on any of the ancient tombs or public monuments. Certainly there are no descriptions of the sorts of epidemic illnesses with exceptional mortality that characterize accounts of smallpox in China. Perhaps the disease was only an occasional visitor to Egypt and never established a permanent presence in civilized areas along the Nile, or perhaps Rameses caught it campaigning abroad? Unusually, Rameses V wasn't buried until several months after his death and it is possible that his smallpox-laden corpse killed off the first set of embalmers who attempted to mummify his body. If Rameses really suffered from smallpox, it is surprising that he did not trigger an epidemic which surely would have been noticed and linked to his death. If it really was smallpox it raises the difficult question of where it went for the next 1700 years. Sadly the disease that can be seen on his mummy will remain an unresolved problem until modern diagnostic techniques have established the nature of the infection.

Although Brahmin tradition and Hindu mythology suggest that smallpox was present in India well before the birth of Christ, there are no historical accounts of the disease there until about 1500 AD. Variola major could only infect humans and left its survivors immune so it required a large population with many new births each year in order infect new victims and survive. The dense population of the Indus valley would have been a suitable nursery for the virus and contact with migration between Indian and central Asia could have spread the virus to China. But the evidence is only indirect and also leaves the puzzle of why it did not spread to the Middle East before 600AD.

It is tempting to try to link the development of farming to the development of smallpox. Large amounts of stored grain supported increasing numbers of mice and rats, and a plausible scenario is that the virus transferred from mice to domesticated cattle or water buffaloes and infected humans at the same time. Once the virus had adapted to human infection and human to human transmission it could have spread along trade routes in East Asia.

The final stage in the spread of smallpox around the world began in 1520 when a slave belonging to a Spanish conquistador brought smallpox onto mainland South America.[7] Native Americans had no resistance to the virus and it slaughtered them in huge numbers. At the time a missionary commented that "*they died in heaps, like bed bugs*".[8] When everyone in a village caught smallpox at the same time there was no one to nurse the sick, to bring water or food so even individuals who might have recovered from the infection with a little support died. Contemporary accounts suggest that more than half the native population died. Epidemics occurred across the whole of the Americas as the virus spread and everywhere it had the same lethal consequences. Two contemporary accounts reveal the devastation caused when smallpox attacked Native Americans. Governor Bradford of Plymouth colony described the harrowing epidemic of 1634:

"*This spring also, those indians that lived about their trading house there fell sick of the smallpox, and died most miserably; for a sorer disease cannot befall them; they fear it more than the plague; for usually them that has this disease has them in abundance, and for want of bedding and linen and other helps, they fall into a lamentable condition, as they lie on their hard mats, the pocks breaking and mattering, and running into one another, their skin cleaving (by reason thereof) to the mats they lie on; when they turn them, a whole side will flay off at once(as it were) and they will be all of a gore blood, most fearful to behold; and then being very sore, what with cold and other distempers, they die like rotten sheep.*

The condition of this people was so lamentable, and they fell down so generally of this disease as they were (in the end) not able to help one another; no, not to make fire, nor fetch a little water to drink, nor any to bury the dead; but would strive as long as they could and when they could procure no other means to make fire, they would burn the wooden trays and dishes they ate their meat in, and their very bows and arrows: and some would crawl on all fours to get a little water, and sometimes died by the way and not be able to get in again....... For few of them escaped.... The chief Sachem himself now died and almost all his friends and kindred."[9]

This particular epidemic spread through New England and by 1636 had reached the Huron tribe just north of Lake Ontario. A Jesuit missionary reported *"terror was universal. The contagion increased as the autumn advanced; and when winter came, far from ceasing as the priests hoped, its ravages were appalling. The season of the Huron festivity was turned into a season of mourning; and such was the despondency and dismay, that suicides became frequent. The Jesuits, singly or in pairs, journeyed in the depth of winter from village to village, ministering to the sick, ... no house was left unvisited. As the missionary, physician at once to body and soul, entered one of these smoky dens, he saw the inmates, their heads muffled in their robes of skin, seated round the fires in silent dejection. Everywhere was heard the wail of the sick and dying children; and on or under the platforms at the sides of the house crouched squalid men and women in all stages of the distemper."*[10]

The disastrous consequences of smallpox were not confined to the Native Americans. The effect on small isolated communities of European colonists could be just as devastating. During an outbreak in Greenland in 1733 missionaries *"were almost everywhere shocked with the sight of houses tenanted only by the corpses of their former occupants, and dead bodies lying unburied on the snow. .. In one island the only living creatures they found were a little girl covered with the smallpox, and her three younger brothers. The father, having buried all the rest of the inhabitants, had laid himself and his youngest child in a grave of stones, bidding the girl to cover him with skins: after which she and her brothers were to live upon a couple of seals and some dried herrings til they could get to the Europeans".*[11]

However it arose, *Variola major* had some properties that are intimately tied to the way smallpox spread. Chief among these is that anyone who survived an attack of smallpox was immune for the rest of their lives. Therefore the virus could only become endemic, that is always present, in a society where there were enough individuals and births to generate a steady supply of new victims. Virologists estimate that a population of at least 200,000 people is required before the virus can establish a permanent base. In Europe only large cities such as London or Paris could sustain the virus. In 17th century London, for example, smallpox killed about three people every day in a typical year and about ten a day in a bad year.[12] But outside London, where most of the population lived in small towns and villages, the disease might be absent for many years. When it did arrive it spread as an epidemic until it had infected almost everyone who was susceptible before dying out.

The smallpox virus was remarkably tough, a characteristic that made it attractive to the Russians as a possible bioweapon (it could survive a bomb blast so it could be weaponised and still cause infection). Variola, unlike influenza virus or measles virus, for example, could survive on contaminated clothing or blankets for up to a year. Someone suffering from smallpox usually coughed up clouds of virus particles that settled on their surroundings. In addition, the scabs and pus from the pocks contained infectious virus. In the 18th century many people did not change their clothes for months at a time so that, if they had become contaminated with smallpox virus, they could spread the disease long after they had recovered from the infection. Anyone who came into contact with contaminated material was at risk if they had not had the infection before.

Local politicians frequently blamed smallpox outbreaks on tramps who had entered town with active smallpox or who had evidence of recent infection on their scarred faces. Itinerant peddlers could spread the disease because it was a common practice for the families of someone who had died to sell their bedding and clothes to peddlers who would then sell them at markets further down the road. Only a brief exposure to infected clothes was enough for a child to carry the virus home and start another epidemic. Smallpox would spread slowly outward from London following trade. It could strike sporadically; if no one susceptible to the virus happened to come into contact with an infected source then a town might be spared only for one further along the road to be attacked.

Seventeenth century observers were convinced that smallpox was becoming more common and more lethal.[13] Since clinical descriptions of smallpox are similar throughout the 16th and 17th century it is unlikely that there had been a change in the virus. As increasing numbers of the highly visible upper classes died in adulthood considerable speculation about the cause of this change in smallpox appeared. One theory blamed the increase on the diet of the rich who consumed large quantities of meat coupled with a heavy intake of wine causing an imbalance in bodily "humors". The alternative explanation was more pragmatic. Physicians were responsible. Only the rich could afford the fees of the London physicians whose extreme interventions employing excessive bleeding and purging (laxatives) were responsible for the increasing death rate.[14] The poor, who couldn't afford physicians, didn't die. No one realized that poor people died of smallpox in childhood.

The likely explanation for the increasing risk to the gentry is that the virus had become endemic in London. In the crowded rookeries where several families sometimes lived in a single room, the virus was always lurking somewhere, on the clothes of a passing footman, in the cough of a street monger; it was an unpredictable and unavoidable part of city life. When smallpox was always present the chances of an individual who had not had the infection coming into contact with a contagious case increased. Epidemics of smallpox spread slowly and were easy to avoid by leaving the infected area. Those with money lived a life apart from the generality of London's artisans and labourers. Children were taught at home and cosseted by handpicked servants who were often chosen precisely because they were immune to smallpox.

The great families had country estates where children played in rural isolation only returning to London during the fashionable season. Most never came into contact with anyone who was contagious, so that they entered early adult life at risk. But once they left the cocoon of childhood they were exposed to the swirling masses in the streets just like every other Londoner. Sooner or later they came into contact with smallpox.

Because smallpox spread surreptitiously it was difficult to avoid the virus. Unlike the plague, smallpox killed many members of Europe's Royal families. In England, the Stuarts, who succeeded Queen Elizabeth I in 1606 lost three potential monarchs to the illness in sixty years. The Protestant branch of the Stuarts died out when Queen Anne's only son died of smallpox opening the way for the Hanoverian succession and the constitutional monarchy that resulted. The Hapsburgs, who ruled the Austro-Hungarian, Europe's largest, lost five ruling heads or their heirs in a century. Promising royal princesses whose marriages might have played an important role in European politics were sometimes so scarred that they could no longer face life in public and retired to convents. Louis XV of France was known as "two noses" because of the lump of scar tissue smallpox left on his face. Unlike the plague, which killed few members of the aristocracy, smallpox killed the highest levels in society as frequently as it felled the lowest. The plague came in epidemics and spread in waves so that it was possible for someone with enough money to run away to a place that the disease had not reached and then to circle back around the advancing wave to areas where the epidemic had passed. Smallpox, once established, stayed, and was inescapable.

Chapter 2

SMALLPOX IN BRITAIN

The evolution of inoculation was largely determined by the behavior of smallpox in Britain and the medical community that tried to cope with the disease. In particular, the Bills of Mortality collected for London give one of the few pictures of the growth and spread of smallpox in the 17th and 18th centuries providing a background view of the environment in which inoculation developed.

Smallpox virus seems to have arrived relatively late in Britain.[1] One of the earliest well documented cases is that of Queen Elizabeth I in 1562 when the queen was 29 and had been on the throne for only four years. While numerous letters record the gradual increase in smallpox deaths thereafter, a number of factors make it difficult to measure the impact of the disease. Firstly measles and smallpox were lumped together as "flox" a term which seemed to mean "flooding" which could describe both diarrhea and the rash of smallpox as it "flooded" the face. Most of the numerical data derive from the London Bills of Mortality, the first attempt to quantify births, deaths, and the incidence of different diseases. London's local government was carried out by individual parishes, which were responsible for christenings and burials and provided relief for the poor within the parish boundaries. From 1603 the records for each parish were collected by the Guild of Parish Clerks and published every Thursday. The total for the whole year was published on the Thursday before Christmas. At first the Bills of Mortality gave only the gross figures for christenings and deaths, and sometimes the number of deaths due to plague, but by 1623 they included all the common diagnoses recognized at the time. Smallpox was still collated with measles and "flox". Finally, in 1652, it was recognized as a separate entity, and from this date it is possible to chart the burden of smallpox on London.

Each parish employed a "searcher" whose job was to view every corpse and record the cause of death. Searchers were usually old women, often with no other employment, and certainly no formal medical training. They were expected to inspect the corpse and record the most appropriate diagnosis. However, they were not above a little venality, and, if the family of the deceased was prepared to offer the price of a couple of tots of gin, the searcher would record whatever bland diagnosis was requested. At a time when most tradesmen worked from home, with a shop on the ground floor and the family quarters upstairs, it was bad for business if it became known that there was smallpox on the premises.

The searchers' job was made more difficult by the non-specific signs of fatal smallpox in infants. Typical smallpox, with its easily recognized rash of white domed pustules on the face and body, was unmistakable, but young children often died before the eruption appeared.[2] Often the only manifestations of smallpox were a high fever, rigors, or convulsions. Searchers would record these symptoms as the cause of death. Sometimes the only visible sign of smallpox was a type of bleeding into the skin known as "the purples", which was not recognized as a complication of *Variola major* until well into the 18th century. Many fatal cases went unrecorded.

The London Bills chart the steadily rising frequency of smallpox deaths. However, the vile London environment at the time complicates estimating the proportion of deaths due to the infection. In the stinking, sewage-laden streets of the capital, where coal smoke enveloped everything and the poor were often packed ten or more to a room, the death rate from many diseases was much higher than it was in the cleaner countryside. Children died from drinking contaminated water or from respiratory infections in their smoky airless courtyards. All the other noxious agents that killed its people diluted London's smallpox mortality. Even so, in most years smallpox killed about one in 14 of those whose burials were recorded, and in epidemic years it accounted for more than one in seven.

Ninety percent of the English population lived outside London. In these largely rural areas the impact of smallpox depended on the nature of the community and how frequently the virus appeared. If the disease only arrived every 15 years or so then there would be an epidemic which would infect almost everyone who had not had it before. Very young children, under the age of two, and adults over the age of twenty, were more likely to die than those in between.[3] Therefore the consequences of an epidemic mirrored the age structure of the community. More individuals in the most vulnerable age groups meant that the mortality was high. However, shorter intervals between epidemics meant that most of the susceptible people were in the golden interval between the ages of two and twenty when the disease was less fatal. In parts of the country, especially some of the northern cities such as Newcastle or Chester, smallpox seems to have been largely a childhood illness suggesting that either the virus had become endemic or that there were outbreaks at frequent intervals.

In the 18th century many young people left their isolated villages and farmsteads to better themselves in London. If they came from places where smallpox was rarely encountered, they carried their susceptibility and their increased risk of dying with them. In London, where the virus was ever present, they soon came down with the infection, so the figures for deaths in London contain two different groups: native Londoners, who were mostly children, and immigrants from the countryside, who were mostly young adults.

It is impossible to produce a really accurate estimate of the impact of smallpox on England because it varied from place to place and from time to time. In a small outbreak, random effects might produce a particularly high, or low, death rate. However, one fact seems clear; almost everyone caught the infection at some time. During epidemics, when reliable figures were sometimes kept, the mortality was about one in six. If all the unknowable variables, particularly those which led to underreporting smallpox deaths in childhood, are taken into account, then perhaps twenty five percent of the population died of smallpox in the early 18th century. At a time when half the children born did not survive to the age of fifteen, smallpox was responsible for about half of those deaths.[4]

Eighteenth century British physicians struggled to diagnose smallpox accurately and debated what the disease was and what caused it. In 1657 Thomas Sydenham, sometimes called the English Hippocrates, managed to distinguish between measles and smallpox. He also described two forms of smallpox. One he called distinct, where the pustules were spaced away from each other, and another which he called confluent, where the pustules ran together into a continuous sheet. Confluent smallpox was nearly always fatal, while the distinct form was rarely so which led to a little aphorism that there was one form of smallpox that a nurse could not kill and another that a doctor could not cure.

Sydenham also started a long running debate about the best treatment. He argued that the distinct form could be treated by what he called the "cold method". Traditional treatments, which he called the hot method, involved wrapping the patient in tight blankets, often coloured red, and placing them in a closed room with a roaring fire. On no account was the patient to be allowed out of the bedding and no breath of fresh, cool air should be let in. In his cool method Sydenham allowed patients with distinct smallpox to get out of bed, wear their own clothes, and even have the windows open.

Many doctors disagreed with Sydenham's cold method because they believed that smallpox was like fermentation in the blood. Fermenting juices like wine or beer often formed a thick scum on the surface, and the vats became warm and frothy. Doctors thought that the high temperature and bounding pulse of their smallpox patients showed that fermentation was occurring and that the pustules were like the surface scum. They argued that the disease process was creating a poisonous substance in the body and the pustules represented an attempt by the body to expel the noxious material. Survival hinged on the patient being able to get rid of all the poison before it could settle on the internal organs causing death. Hence the hot method was intended to encourage the foul matter to be expelled through the skin; a whisper of cold air might be enough to drive it back inside the body with fatal consequences.

Certain foods were thought to feed the poison producing smallpox. Meat, alcohol, and spices were particularly likely to stimulate the disease so treatment often consisted of a bland diet of bread and water with a few vegetables. Corrupt matter in the stomach and bowels were also believed to feed the disease, so both vomits and enemas were indicated. Whether or not to bleed the patient was hotly debated. The 18th century doctor was trying to save his patient by getting the poison out of the body as quickly as possible and removing any fuel that might feed the fermentation. In an extreme situation, when it appeared that the patient was likely to die, they could resort to something called "suppadena", wrapping lamb or pig kidneys around the patient's head and feet, in a desperate attempt to draw out just a little more harmful material. They believed that even a minute amount might make the difference between survival and death. Individual doctors developed their own secret mixtures of chemicals or liquids which they claimed were usually successful in treating smallpox. Such nostrums were given during the course of the disease but they were claimed to be particularly valuable if given before smallpox took hold.

Infections were especially a challenging for the 18th century doctor because there was no clear idea of specific infections and no concept of specific organisms that caused particular diseases. "Fever" was a general diagnosis that could develop into any one of many different disorders. A doctor could usually tell that his patient was suffering from a "fever" but could not tell which particular form the patient had until more distinct signs appeared.

Patients developing smallpox usually had a severe headache, backache, raised temperature, and felt dreadful for two or three days before the rash appeared. Would it be smallpox, some form of "continuing fever", a malignant fever, or something else? Physicians often called upon each other for second opinions at this stage, and it was at this stage that nostrums were thought to be especially useful. If the patient did not develop smallpox, but something more benign, the doctor claimed the credit; his treatment had altered the course of the disease down a safer path. Of course all these consultations and treatments cost money. For physicians smallpox could be a small gold mine generating payment every time a doctor visited a patient and for every extra nostrum prescribed. Only the very well off could afford a physician. Others relied on advice and a few treatments from an apothecary or just followed word of mouth from their neighbours.

The patient's experience of smallpox was extremely variable. A few were lucky and had only a few pocks on their faces and scattering elsewhere. Even 400 or 500 pocks were considered favourable and almost everyone survived. But as the number of pocks increased, the outlook became increasingly bad. In the confluent form the number of pocks reached tens of thousands.

One 18th century doctor left an account of the disease which conveys the full horror of severe smallpox: *"some of the bad symptoms attending which, are as followeth: purple spots, the bloody pox, haemorrhages of blood at mouth, nose, fundament, and privities; ravings and deliriums, convulsions and other fits, violent inflammations and swellings in the eyes and throat; so they cannot see, or scarcely breathe, or swallow anything to keep them from starving. Some looked as black as the stock, others as white as a sheet; in some the pocks run into blisters, and the skin stripping off, leaves the flesh raw, like creatures flayed. Some have a burning, others a smarting pain, as if in the fire, or scalded with boiling water: some have insatiable thirsts, others greedy appetites, and will crave food when dying. Some have been filled with loathsome ulcers; others have had deep and fistulous ulcers in their bodies, or in their limbs and joints, with rottenness of ligaments and bones; some who live are cripples and many blind all their days; beside other deformities it brings upon many, in their faces, limbs, or body, with*

many more grievous symptoms which the world had too great experience of, as being the attendants of that fatal distemper called the confluent smallpox".[5]

There were other symptoms as well. Smallpox patients stank. No one knows why, but the smell was described as truly revolting. In addition the patient's face swelled up as the rash started to appear so that many individuals were blind for a few days until the swelling went down. The ordeal must have been dreadful. Imagine Queen Elizabeth I wrapped in red blankets, laid in front of a blazing fire, her face swollen so that she could not see, her throat so sore that she could not swallow, and smelling so revolting that her courtiers could not stand to be the room with her. She was delirious for a few days, but in her lucid moments must have wondered whether she would live or die.[6]

Almost uniquely smallpox often left the patient with severe damage long after they had recovered from the acute infection. About one in one hundred lost the sight of one eye, and the disease accounted for about one third of all cases of adult blindness.[7] In young children it sometimes damaged a growing joint so that a limb became useless. Many of the blind beggars and cripples that occur in18[th] century literature were the victims of smallpox.

The 18th century has been called the age of smallpox. Fear of the disease permeated literature and private conversations. Mothers were advised not to count their children until they had had the smallpox since one that survived was worth two who still had it to come. Everyone caught smallpox and many died.

Chapter 3

A HEATHEN PRACTICE

The first hints that severe smallpox could be prevented began to reach Europe in the early 18th century.[1] English physicians who were members of the Royal Society became aware of a Turkish practice known as inoculation in a long letter written in Latin by a physician named Emanuel Timoni (or Timonius). Timoni was no stranger to London. He had medical degrees from Pavia and Oxford and had been elected to the Royal Society in 1703. His description of inoculation was written for the King of Sweden and several copies were in circulation around Europe by1714. Once translated it became clear that it was a detailed account of the practice of inoculation and its success in Constantinople. The commentary, read to the Royal Society by John Woodward on June 3, 1714 ran:

"The writer of this ingenious discourse observes, in the first place, that the Circassians, Georgians, and other Asiatics, have introduced this practice of procuring the smallpox by a sort of inoculation, for about the space of forty years, among the Turks and others at Constantinople.

That although at first the more prudent were very cautious in the use of this practice; yet the happy success it has found to have in thousands of subjects for these eight years past, has put it out of all suspicion and doubt; since the operation, having been performed on persons of all ages, sexes, and different temperaments….. none have been found to die of the smallpox.

…They that have this inoculation practised upon them are subject to very slight symptoms, some being scarce sensible they are ill or sick: and what is valued by the fair, it never leaves and scars or pits in the face." [2]The manuscript included a description of the method of inoculation. First, a young person with mild disease had to be found to act as the donor. Several pocks are pricked and the pus expressed, collected, kept warm, and transported to the recipient. A few small cuts or pricks with a three edged surgeon's needle were made, sufficient to draw a few drops of blood, and then the pus was mixed well with the blood as it rose from the wound. The arm was the most convenient place to make the incisions, and only a very small drop of pus was sufficient for each site. After the operation was over the site was covered by a walnut shell tied in place with a piece of linen.

While Timoni's testimony was intriguing, the fact that his manuscript had been transmitted by John Woodward cast doubt on its authenticity. His colleagues in the Royal Society considered Woodward a rigid, opinionated, bigot.[3] He once fought a duel with another distinguished physician over a disagreement about the correct use of laxatives in smallpox. No one entirely trusted him. But his information was too interesting to ignore, so the Fellows ordered the Secretary of the Society to write to William Sherrard, a highly respected Fellow who was then serving as consul in the Turkish city of Smyrna. Their request was that he *"please to send them the most exact and true account concerning this matter"*.

By chance Sherard was a friend of Jacob Pylarini a physician who had helped introduce the practice of inoculation among wealthy Greeks living in Istanbul. Pylarini told him that for many years Greek peasants had protected themselves from the infection but that the better off had not used it. In 1700 a wealthy friend who was terrified that his sons would die during the fierce epidemic then raging in the town had consulted him. Pylarini

sought out the old Greek woman who was thought to have introduced the operation forty years before and found her totally convincing. He advised his friend that the operation was safe and
gave lifelong protection against smallpox. Sherrard and Pylarini
had discussed the operation on many occasions when they were
both living in Smyrna.[4]

Sherrard's reply to the Royal Society gave the impression
that inoculation was old news. Christians in Constantinople had
accepted the practice for about sixty years and now regarded it
as a trivial part of growing up. Pylarini believed that inoculation
had been used in the Balkans and Caucasus for many years before
it had spread to Constantinople, and that all accounts indicated
that it was a valuable technique. Curiously, the Muslim majority
in Turkey would have nothing to do with it because they believed
that it interfered with Divine Providence. If Allah wanted you to
die of smallpox it was a sin to thwart his intentions.

Pylarini's short book, written in reply to Sherrard's request,
was published by the Royal Society in its Proceedings for
1716.[5]Fellows discussed inoculation on a number of occasions.
During one debate, Hans Sloane, soon to be President of the
Royal College of Physicians and President of the Royal Society,
doubted that the operation would always produce mild smallpox. He argued that he had observed that a patient with mild
smallpox sometimes transmitted a fatal form of the infection to a
contact. Just choosing a donor of the inoculum with mild disease
might not guarantee that the resulting reaction was favourable.[6]

Medicine was, and is, a very conservative profession.[7] The
theoretical basis for medical practice had been defined in classical times and was dominated by the belief that there were four
bodily humors whose interactions and balance controlled health
and disease. Ideas that didn't fit into this ancient framework
were anathema. An empirical approach to a new treatment by
testing it to see whether it worked was opposed if the treatment
didn't have an explanation in theory. Indeed, "empirick" was a
term of derision hurled at unqualified practitioners who claimed
that their treatments worked even if they could not explain why.
Experimentation without a logical basis was unacceptable, even

unethical. Very few new treatments had become established in the preceding two hundred years and those that did had to overcome fierce opposition from the medical establishment. Only "Jesuits bark", a source of quinine which was an effective treatment for malaria, had gained widespread acceptance and then only after decades of dispute.

London's physicians were the strongest upholders of established tradition. There were only about forty Fellows of the Royal College of Physicians who formed a tight clique limited to graduates of Oxford or Cambridge who had studied medicine, who could read Latin and Greek, and who were members of the Anglican Church. Firm defenders of orthodoxy, they monopolized the lucrative medical practice among the "quality", the wealthy upper classes who could afford to pay a doctor's exorbitant fees. A physician could lose his reputation, social standing, and income by advocating heretical views. And all of the medical Fellows of the Royal Society were also Fellows of the Royal College of Physicians so that even the most progressive members of the profession were constrained by tradition. Discussing inoculation was agreeable, actually performing it was not. Despite informed knowledge of the operation, no one attempted it.

However, a significant government appointment would soon lead to the first inoculations in Britain. In 1716, King George I's Prime Minister, Robert Walpole, offered the post of ambassador to Constantinople to an aspiring young politician, Edward Wortley Montague who accepted and began to plan for the move with his wife, Lady Mary. Beautiful, talented, vain, and rebellious she had been a figure in London society for the previous decade. Once in Turkey, Lady Mary quickly became aware of inoculation and the fact that it had been employed by many Europeans in the city.[8] Families even had inoculation parties where groups of children were gathered together and treated at the same time and then stayed and played together for about three weeks while the disease ran its gentle course. She was excited by the possibilities for she had every reason to hate smallpox. In her teens Lady Mary had been a famous beauty, but in 1714 she contracted smallpox. Although largely unscarred, she lost her eyelashes and for the rest of her life felt that some essential part of her attractiveness had gone. Many commented that her eyes, previously considered her most outstanding feature, now had a fierce, piercing quality. Worse, her beloved only brother had died of the infection, a financial as well as emotional disaster as the English dynastic system discriminated against women. The entire family estate was passed to the eldest son, and any property that a woman carried with her into marriage became her husband's to use as he wished. One of the few routes to financial independence for a woman was support from her brother, if he chose to help her. Equally, fathers required a son to maintain the family name and estate. With his wife already dead, and his only son also gone, Lady Mary's father had remarried and soon had a new heir.

When the Wortley Montagues arrived in Turkey they fortuitously employed Emanuel Timoni, author of the inoculation report, as their family physician. He soon explained the practice to Lady Mary and her Scottish surgeon, Charles Maitland, informing them that natural smallpox was particularly lethal in Constantinople, but that the inoculated form was gentle, with few of the distressing symptoms of the natural disease, and that the pustules dried without leaving scars or pits. Most importantly, once successfully inoculated, protection from the natural infection was complete. Only two weeks after arriving in Turkey Lady Mary wrote a glowing account of the practice to her childhood friend Lady Sarah Chiswell: *"The smallpox, so fatal, and so general among us, is here entirely harmless, by the invention of ingrafting. Every year thousands undergo this operation: and the French Ambassador says pleasantly they take the smallpox here by way of diversion, as they take the waters in other countries."*[9] But she doubted that it could be introduced into England because she believed that the medical profession would oppose anything that would threaten their lucrative practice in treating smallpox. Ironically, Sarah Chiswell was not convinced by her friend and died of smallpox in 1726.

In March 1718, while her husband was away negotiating with the Turks, Lady Mary arranged to have her five-year old son inoculated. As surgeon to the embassy, Maitland attended the operation and recorded the event:[10] *"About this time the ambassador's ingenious lady, who had been at some pains to satisfy her curiosity in this matter, and had made some useful observations on the practice, was so thoroughly convinced of the safety of it, that she resolved to submit her only son to it, a very hopeful boy of about six years of age, she first of all ordered me to find a fit subject to take the matter from; and then sent for an old Greek woman who had practised this way for a great many years: After a great deal of troubles and pains, I found a proper subject, and then the good woman went to work; but so awkwardly by the shaking of her hand , and put the child to so much torture with her blunt and rusty needle, that I pitied his cries, who had ever been of such spirit and courage that hardly anything of pain could make him cry before; and therefore inoculated the other arm with my own instrument"* The child had minor symptoms, favourable pocks, and recovered rapidly. Lady Mary was so impressed that she resolved to have her three month old daughter inoculated as well. However, the child's Armenian nurse had not had smallpox, and the risk of infecting her was too great so the operation was cancelled.

About the time that Lady Mary was setting off for Turkey, inoculation came to the attention of Cotton Mather, a Puritan minister in colonial Boston. Mather was already known to the Royal Society in London as, in 1713, he had written a series of ten letters, each outlining an unusual observation of a natural phenomenon, such as unusual weather patterns, which he sent to John Woodward at the Royal Society. The Society had begun to encourage correspondents in all parts of the globe to forward their unique experiences of the natural world to enlighten their English colleagues. Such submissions were read and discussed at the Society's weekly meetings and usually published in the Philosophical Transactions, the Society's journal. Sometime in 1716, William Douglass, newly arrived in Boston, gave Mather a bound copy of the Transactions for 1714 containing Mather's letters. Although delighted to see his works in print, it was the paper immediately following them that fired his imagination: Timoni's article. What most surprised Mather was that he had already heard of inoculation. He wrote immediately to Woodward: [11]

"I am willing to confirm to you, in a favourable opinion, of Dr, Timonius' communication; and therefore, I do assure you, that many months before I

met with any intimations of treating the smallpox with the method of inoculation, anywhere in Europe; I had from a servant of my own an account of its being practised in Africa. Enquiring of my Negro man, Onesimus, who is a pretty intelligent fellow, whether he had ever had the smallpox, he answered, both yes and no; and then told me that he had undergone an operation, which had given him something of the smallpox and would forever preserve him from it; adding that it was often used among the Guramantese and whoever had the courage to use it was forever free of the fear of contagion. He described the operation to me, and showed me in his arm the scar which it had left upon him; and his description of it made it the same that afterwards I found related unto you by your Timonius.

This cannot but expire in wonder and into a request of my Dr. Woodward. How does it come to pass that no more is done to bring this operation into experiment and fashion in England? When there are so many thousands of people that would give many thousands of pounds to have the danger and horror of this frightful disease over with. I beseech you, sir, to move it, and save more lives than Dr. Sydenham. For my own part, if I should live to see the smallpox again enter into our city, I would immediately procure a consult of our physicians to introduce a practice which may be of so very happy a tendency. But could we hear that you have done it before us, how much that would embolden us!"

Onesimus, a Guaramantee from southern Libya, cost fifty pounds when he was given to Mather as a present from his congregation at Christmas time, 1707. Mather's account leaves no doubt that the fateful conversation regarding inoculation had occurred before he had seen the report from Turkey. Personal testimony had a powerful impact on Mather because it provided evidence for the reality of the procedure. Onesimus's account indicated that this was not a fantastic story from some unknown distant land. The slave, and many of his compatriots, had actually experienced inoculation and he showed Mather the scars to prove it. Without Onesimus, Mather might well have ignored Timonius.

During 1716 the Pylarinus report was also published in the Philosophical Transactions and sometime before 1721 Mather saw it and had his high regard for inoculation confirmed. He was primed, but could not act. There was no smallpox in Boston.

Chapter 4

SMALLPOX COMES TO BOSTON

In April 1721, HMS Seahorse, accompanying a fleet from Barbados brought smallpox into Boston harbor. She was carrying infected crewmen who had been exposed to the disease during the epidemic then raging in the West Indies. Boston had stringent quarantine laws. Although ignorant of infection and micro-organisms, the colonists understood contagion and knew that dangerous diseases like smallpox were spread by contact. They had laws requiring any ship carrying disease to anchor far out in the harbor at Spectacle Island where the crew and cargo were to remain until certified safe by a doctor appointed by Boston's elected officers, the selectmen. Somehow the Seahorse escaped this stricture and landed at least two crewmen who soon developed smallpox. At least one of them died in town.[1]

The second line of defence against imported contagion was to isolate the diseased in a nominated house where they were attended by a doctor and nurses who were immune to the disorder. Armed guards were posted to keep the patient in and the curious out. All bedding and clothing was confined to the house for the duration. Only when a doctor certified that the danger was past could the recovered patient move freely about town, and his clothes and bedding would be fumigated first. Unfortunately this defence also failed. During their brief access to public places, the contagious crewmen managed to infect a few townspeople in the southern part of the town. The selectmen applied the quarantine laws and placed guards at the houses of those affected but it soon became clear that the disease had escaped. By the end of May the selectmen recognized that they were beaten; there were too many households with smallpox to isolate, so the guards were withdrawn. As a last gesture, the selectmen ordered the free Negroes of Boston to sweep the streets to remove the rubbish, which might otherwise generate a poisonous environment. In a world where disease was thought to be triggered by miasmas or changes in the atmosphere it was probably a rational attempt to remove a source of corrupt air. But the number of sick continued to grow, and the town was now at the mercy of epidemic smallpox. Benjamin Colman, one of the leading Puritan ministers recognized the scale of the impending disaster:

"Besides it now being nineteen years since the smallpox had been in town, it gave us a very dreadful prospect of distress and deaths, whenever it should come among us; all the children and all the young people born in the town or coming into it from the country within the long term of time having it before them." [2]About half the population of about 11,000 was at risk.

Faced with the prospect of the social and commercial disruption which followed an outbreak of smallpox there appeared to be nothing that anyone could do to prevent catastrophe except pray. Samuel Shute, governor of the Massachusetts Bay Colony, ordered the traditional day of humiliation intended to appease an angry God, but it too failed to halt the epidemic. As the disease began to spread, Cotton Mather, the town's leading Puritan divine, decided to try to persuade his medical colleagues to initiate inoculation to prevent the inevitable tragedy.[3]

In 1721 Boston was the largest town in North America. Its 11,000 people were crammed into the northeastern side of the cloverleaf -shaped Shawmutt peninsula. A man could walk from the north battery, looking across the mouth of the Charles River to Charlestown, To the town House, the civic centre, in fifteen minutes. Along the way he would pass wharves, boat building yards, master mariners' houses, and the warehouses of wealthy traders. Boston was a bustling port. It acted as the middleman in a booming three cornered trade between England, the North American colonies, and the West Indies. Manufactured goods and cloth came in from Britain. Locally bred horses and timber went to the Caribbean, and rum and molasses came back. So much traffic flowed through the port that it supported the third largest fleet in the British Empire bettered only by London and Bristol. A great wharf extended half a mile into the harbour providing deep water anchorage for large merchantmen and warships. At the top of Long Wharfe was the Town House, the commercial and political centre of the town, and just next to it lay the town dock where smaller boats delivered goods and brought wood and food into the city. The whole harbor was alive with small boats carrying goods to and from ships in the harbor and domestic essentials from the surrounding countryside. Dock Square was the focus of local commerce. Merchants based nearby had the pick of newly arrived goods and first access to news carried by arriving sailors. In the taverns around the Town House merchants and sailors exchanged gossip, opinion, and information.

In this bustling port Cotton Mather held a prominent position as the minister of the Second Church, known as Old North, a post he shared with his 84 year old father, Increase. His family was among the leaders of the Massachusetts Bay Colony founded in 1630, which was intended to promote and develop a new form of Protestant religion. Cotton's grandfathers, John Cotton and Richard Mather, had helped formulate the colony's religious laws, and Increase had played a leading political role in protecting the colony's charter during the troubled period after the Glorious Revolution in 1688. Throughout the preceding century the Mathers had led the colony through preaching and prayer and had defined the nature of the colonists' covenant with God, which formed the basis of Puritan society. Cotton was intended to succeed to this role and continue godly rule in Massachusetts. [4]

Puritans believed that educated ministers were essential to interpret scripture and guide sinners towards the path to conversion and grace. Harvard College had been founded to fulfill this role and young Cotton, aged eleven, was duly sent there to acquire the appropriate education for his exalted future. As the youngest boy in the college, probably the youngest to attend Harvard in the 17th century, he was bullied by the older, stronger students. Since college statutes forbade this, his father, a member of the board of overseers, demanded that the President of the college punish Cotton's tormentors, further increasing the boy's unpopularity. Suddenly the youngster developed a stammer, which terrified him as it threatened his preordained career. A Puritan divine was expected to preach for two or three hours at least three days a week and a speech impediment would have made this impossible. In despair he decided to study medicine as an alternative. From the hundreds of books he read during this troubled time he developed a lifelong interest in medicine and science. Eventually he mastered his stutter and resumed his preparations for the ministry, but retained a deep interest in unusual natural phenomena. He was fascinated by the manifestations of diseases and collected the first systematic catalogue of treatments used by the colonists.

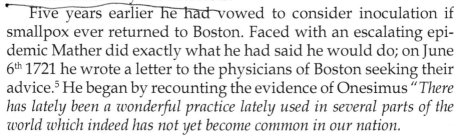

Five years earlier he had vowed to consider inoculation if smallpox ever returned to Boston. Faced with an escalating epidemic Mather did exactly what he had said he would do; on June 6th 1721 he wrote a letter to the physicians of Boston seeking their advice.[5] He began by recounting the evidence of Onesimus *"There has lately been a wonderful practice lately used in several parts of the world which indeed has not yet become common in our nation.*

"I was first instructed in it by a Guaramantee servant of my own, long before I knew that any Europeans or Asiaticks had the least acquaintance with it....I have since met with a considerable number of these Africans who all agree on one story that in their country, Grandy-mandy, many die of the smallpox: but now they learn this way, people take juice of smallpox and cutty skin, and put in a drop, then by'nd by a little sicky, sicky; then very few little things like smallpox and nobody die of it and nobody have smallpox any more. Thus in Africa where the poor creatures die of the smallpox like rotten sheep a merciful God has taught them an infallible preservative. Tis a common practice and is a constant success." Mather is using the Afro-American

vernacular to emphasize the immediacy of his information. He followed this testimony with a detailed summary of the paper of Timonius and a similar account of inoculation in Constantinople by Pylarinus. Finally, having presented his evidence for the practice, he appealed for support:

"I will only say that inasmuch as the practice of suffering the small-pox in the way of inoculation, has never yet, as far as I have heard, been introduced into our nation where there are so many who would give great sums to have their lives ensured for an escape from the dangers of this dreadful distemper; nor has anyone yet made the trial of it (though we have several Africans, as I now find, who tried it in their own country.) I cannot but move that it be warily proceeded in. I durst not engage that, the success of the trial here, will be the same that has hitherto been in the other hemisphere. But I am confident no person would miscarry in it but would most certainly have miscarried upon taking it in the common way. And I would humbly advise that it never be made but under the management of a skilful physician who will wisely prepare the body for it, before he performs the operation. Gentlemen, my request is that you should meet for a consultation upon this occasion and so deliberate upon it that whoever first begins the practice (if you approve that it should be begun at all) may have the countenance of his worthy brethren to fortify him in it."

There was no response from the physicians, so Mather decided to make a personal appeal to the town's leading doctor, Zabdiel Boylston.

"June 24, 1721

Sir,

You are in many ways endeared unto me, but by nothing more than the very much good which a gracious God employs you and honours you to do in a miserable world.

I design it as a testimony of my respect and esteem, that I now lay before you the most that I know (and all that was ever published in the world)

Concerning the matter, which I have been an occasion of its being pretty much talked about. If upon mature deliberation you should think it advisable to be proceeded in, it may save many lives that we set a great value on. But if it be not approved of, still you have the pleasure of knowing exactly what is done in other places

But see, think, judge; do as the Lord, our healer shall direct you, and pardon the freedom of, Sir

Your hearty friend and servant,
Cotton Mather."

This letter, and Boylston's response to it, would trigger months of uproar in Boston. Eventually the outcome of the debate would influence medicine in both Europe and America. Seventy five years later inoculation would save the newly born American revolution.

Chapter 5

A LUNATIC PHYSICIAN

Zabdiel Boylston was 41. Like all but one of the eleven doctors in Boston he was trained by apprenticeship and had no formal medical degree. His father, Thomas, was a self-taught physician in the small village of Muddy River, now the Boston suburb of Brookline.[1] Growing up in a doctor's household, young Zabdiel was effectively apprenticed from childhood. His father died when he was 15, and he became formally apprenticed to John Cutler, a Dutchman, who had experience of military medicine in both Europe and Massachusetts.

Zabdiel Boylston was a jack of all trades, part physician, part surgeon, and part apothecary; his shop was a cross between his consulting room and a business. Patients could attend for advice and a prescription, or could save the consultation fee by choosing their own medicines. His establishment was more a general store than a pharmacy, where he sold groceries, guns, swords, and spices, as well as medicinal herbs and patent medicines. Boylston had initiated the practice of advertising medicinal products in the local newspapers and was forthright about the high quality and value he offered. His home was above his shop and occasionally he used part of his house as a primitive hospital for patients who needed particular attention, or who had travelled a long distance to consult him.

Early in his career he developed a particular talent for surgery. His successful operations for bladder stone were publicized in the newspapers by the grateful families of those he treated. An audience of ministers and other doctors often attended his operations. One of his cases, described in 1710, is the first published record of an operation in North America.[2] In 1720 the husband of a woman on whom he had performed a mastectomy, a rare operation even in Europe at the time, provided the following testimonial:

"for the public good any that have or may have cancers – these may certify, that my wife had been labouring under the dreadful distemper of a cancer of her left breast for several years, and although the cure was attempted by sundry doctors from time to time, to no effect: and when life was almost despaired of by reason of its repeated bleedings , growth and stench, and there seemed immediate hazard of life, we send for Dr. Zabdiel Boylston of Boston, who on the 28th of July 1718 (in the presence of several ministers and others assembled on that occasion) cut her whole breast off; and by the blessings of God on his endeavours , she has obtained a perfect cure.

I deferred publication of this, least it should have broke out again. Edward Winslow

Rochester, Octob. 14th 1720.[3]

Boylston charged £35 for the treatment of Mrs. Winslow, a large sum equivalent to a whole year's wages for a chief mate on a sailing vessel. He was paid in installments over a period of years, but nine years later, when there were still nine pounds outstanding, he sued Winslow for the debt. Court records show that this was not unusual. Boylston sued more often than any other Boston practitioner; almost half of the suits filed by doctors were his. He always won. Although his fees for surgery were high, his usual charges were modest; one shilling to pull a tooth, one or two shillings to make a house call. Patients came from all over New England to seek treatment, and he often received referrals from the overseers of the poor. He was clearly a very successful doctor, much admired for his unique surgical skills. Boylston undertook these demanding and dangerous operations without ever seeing them performed by anyone else. Clearly he had courage, and perhaps a little arrogance, to undertake heroic measures without formal training.

Mather's invitation to consider experimenting with inoculation must have appealed to Boylston's audacious nature, but also raised a number of questions. Could deliberately transplanting smallpox really be beneficial? What were the dangers? He had Mather's account of the Timonius and Pylarinus texts as evidence for the utility and safety of the operation. He would surely have known Onesimus and have questioned him closely about his own inoculation, and there were other Negroes who could testify to the success of the operation. Reverend Benjamin Colman, Boylston's own pastor, wrote *"I will only add upon all a plain, but to me pleasing and informing discourse I lately had with a poor Negro, whom I found at work where I made a visit, and the gentleman of the house told me that the fellow had been inoculated in his own country. Whereupon I put several questions to him, in answer to which he told me, that he lived in a great town in his own country and when the smallpox came into it they did what they could to prevent the spreading of it; that the families that were first visited usually died among them; but when the sickness got into five or six houses so that the people began to despair of being able to stop it then all who had not had it went presently and received it in the way of inoculation (as we call it) and that not one more died of it thro' the whole town.*

We do not stay, therefore (said he) till the town be infected and people have many of them got the sickness within them and then go and take it; but the whole place takes it in a week and are well in a week (I use some of his words here giving the true sense of what he said to me). He went on to answer the questions put to him and told me "That he never knew of any blains or boils following the practice in his country ; that as to himself none had troubled him any more than what others are subject to; & that he never heard of any bodies having it again in his country; but to prove that his country men think themselves as secure from it as any of us may do he told me , that sometimes when young men among them wanted to go a trading two or three hundred miles off but were afraid because they had not yet had the Small-pox it was common for them to enquire where it was & go to the place & be inoculated &

then go and trade anywhere without fear. When I asked him (what I did not at all suppose he could inform me in) how his countrymen came into the knowledge of this way of giving the smallpox? and how long had it been among them? he told me that he knew nothing of those things he supposed it was long before he was born and no doubt but GOD told it to poor Negroes to save their lives: for they had not the knowledge and skill as we have."[4]

Zabdiel Boylston considered the evidence of the slaves and the written descriptions of inoculation from Turkey for two days.

"June the 26th, 1721. I began the experiment; and not being able to make it upon myself (such was my faith in the safety and success of this method) I chose to make it (for example sake) upon my own dear child, and two of my servants.

I inoculated my son Thomas, of about six, my Negro man, Jack, thirty six, and Jackey, two and a half years old."[5]

Years later Boylston said that he was driven by the desire to save his children from the horrors of smallpox. The memory of his own severe illness in the epidemic of 1702 and the dreadful effects on his patients convinced him to try inoculation. He was aware that his visits to the sick during the impending epidemic made it probable that his own children would become infected since he would certainly be exposed to smallpox and would almost certainly carry it home on his clothes.[6]

Five years later Boylston wrote an account of his experiment revealing his fears as he watched his son and servants.

"They all complained on the sixth day; upon the seventh the two children were a little hot, dull, and sleepy, Thomas (only) had twitchings and started in his sleep....the children's fevers continued, Tommy's twitchings and starting in sleep increased.... Yet as the practice was new, and the clamour, or rather rage, of the people against it so violent, that I was put into a very great fright; and not having any directions from Dr. Timonius or Dr. Pylarinus concerning this practice I had nothing to have recourse to but patience, and therefore waited upon nature for a crisis (neither my fears nor the symptoms abating) until the ninth (day); when early in the morning I gave him a vomit, upon which the symptoms went off, and the same day, upon him and the black child, a kind and favourable smallpox came out... after which their

circumstances became easy , our trouble was over, and they were soon well."[7]

On that day Zabdiel Boylston straddled 1200 years of medical practice. The vomit he prescribed was based on classical Roman medical theory that it would eliminate some of the smallpox poison; but inoculation was the first instance of specific immunisation to avert an infectious disease, which is still the cornerstone of preventive medicine.

Boylston's neighbours observed his experiment because he let the children play in his garden on Dock Square, and Colman noticed that Tommy's troubles were probably due to his playing in the gutter where he got both wet and cold. Later Tommy's difficult course would be attributed to his childish misdemeanour, but at the time it was terrifying. For a few days Boylston thought he might have killed his child. The neighbours were outraged, with good reason, because Boylston had introduced smallpox into a part of town from which it had been absent. Before he performed the operation on his family all of the cases of smallpox were south of King Street, the main dividing line between North and South Boston. Now the infection had been introduced into the more densely populated North, and he was putting their lives at risk. Everyone soon knew what Boylston had done. His garden was overlooked by his neighbours and he had made no attempt to keep the children indoors. Most Bostonians believed, and prayed, that smallpox might pass them by if only it could be contained in other parts of town. No one knew what the chances of avoiding the disease during an epidemic were because no one had asked the question. When the Boston epidemic was over, the town records revealed that more than 9 in 10 of those who were not already immune to smallpox had caught the disease.

His first experiment convinced him inoculation was beneficial *"it was plain and easy to see (even in these two) with pleasure, the difference between having the smallpox this way, and that of having it in the natural way."* His servant Jack had only a few pocks near his incision, which led the doctor to conclude that he had had the smallpox before.

On July 12, as soon as the boys were well, Boylston inoculated 39 year old Joshua Cheever, who almost ended the inoculation experiment before it had really begun. He seemed well, and Boylston was on the brink of concluding that the inoculation had failed, when, on the ninth day, a fire broke out in a nearby house and Cheever rushed with others to put it out. Returning home *"wet with water and sweat he became very ill and full of pain"*. The next morning the doctor feared that he was developing the confluent form of smallpox. Cheever got the full treatment; he was bled a large amount, given a vomit, and blistered. *"Fortunately his symptoms eased and a kind, distinct form of smallpox appeared.... and his pains, and our fears were soon over"*. Had Cheever died, the violent opposition of the townspeople would certainly have forced an end to the experiment. Despite the good end results, the worrying symptoms shown by Tommy and Cheever caused the doctor great anxiety. Two days after inoculating Cheever he operated on another neighbour and his own Negro servant Moll, who was Jack's wife and Jackie's mother. Moll, like her husband, did not develop any of the symptoms or the rash of smallpox so he concluded that she had also had the disease before.

Fear and anger spread through the town. Many Bostonians thought that a lunatic physician was spreading a lethal infection and putting everyone's lives in danger. While Boylston continued to operate, opposition mounted. He was called before the selectmen of Boston to explain himself on two occasions in the three weeks after his first inoculations. Continuing public outrage led him to publish a brief account of his experiments in the Boston Gazette on July 17th, in the hope that he could calm the storm. He began *"I have patiently born with abundance of Clamour and Ralary, for beginning a new Practice here (for the Good of the Publick) which comes well Recommended by men of Figure and Learning"*. After a brief account of the success of his experiment on the children in his own household he summarized the evidence from Turkey and promised to give further proof of the value of the process in the future.[8] His piece only inflamed the situation.

Mather lamented in his diary *"At this Time, I enjoy an unspeakable Consolation. I have instructed our Physicians in the new Method, used by the Africans and Asiaticks, to prevent and abate the Dangers of Small-Pox, and infallibly save the Lives of those that have it wisely managed upon them. The Destroyer, being outraged and the Proposal of any Thing , that may rescue the Lives of our poor People from him, has taken a strange Possession of the People on this Occasion. They rave, they rail, they blaspheme; they talk not only like Ideots but also like Franticks, and not only the Physician who began the Experiment, but I am also an Object of their Fury; their furious Obloquies and Invectives"[9].*

Boylston had continued with his practice despite the opposition of most of the town. Now he was summoned before the selectmen, certain lawyers, and the town's doctors. At 4pm on July 21 Boylston faced his accusers; the issue was the safety of inoculation. He was allowed to present his evidence reiterating the Turkish practice, the evidence of local Negroes, and his own experience. He had seven patients under inoculation who had not yet developed symptoms (Cheever's fever would begin that night) and he invited the town's doctors to inspect his patients and follow their progress. Only one accepted. When pressed about the safety of inoculation he could only reply that all medical interventions, even such widely used treatments as bleeding or laxatives sometimes went wrong. He thought that inoculation was no more dangerous that any of the other procedures available at the time.[10]

The most damning evidence against inoculation was the testimony of Dr, Laurence Dalhonde, a Frenchman who claimed that he had personally witnessed fatal consequences following the operation, and that he knew of cases where inoculation had failed to prevent subsequent smallpox. Dalhonde's written evidence was presented in French and translated by William Douglass, the only doctor with an M.D. degree in town. Dalhonde made three claims: first, that while he was serving in the French army he had witnessed thirteen soldiers who were inoculated, of whom four had died, six had been very ill, and three who had been totally unaffected. Second, that while in Flanders he cared for a Captain Hussart, a dragoon officer, who had had severe smallpox and yet claimed to have been inoculated several times ten years before. Thirdly, at the battle of Alamanza he had witnessed the inoculation of two Russian soldiers and when one of them had died six weeks later the autopsy findings revealed ulceration of the lungs which was attributed to "corruption" spreading from the inoculation site. Douglass argued that Dalhond's evidence indicated that inoculation was both dangerous and useless. It also tended to spread the disease and caused it to remain longer than necessary in the town. After a full debate the selectmen accepted Douglass's position and issued the following proclamation:

At a meeting by Public Authority in the townhouse of Boston, before his Majesties Justices of the Peace and the Select-men; the practitioners of Physic and Surgery being called before them, concerning Inoculation, agreed to the following conclusion.

A resolve upon a debate held by the Physicians of Boston concerning Inoculating the SmallPox, on the twenty first day of July, 1721.

It appears by numerous instances, that it has prov'd the death of many persons soon after the operation, and brought distempers upon many others which have in the end proved deadly to 'em.

That the natural tendency of infusing such malignant filth in the mass of blood, is to corrupt and putrify it, and if there be not sufficient discharge of that malignity by the place of incision, or elsewhere, it lays the foundation for many dangerous diseases.

That the operation tends to spread and continue the infection in a place longer than it might otherwise be.

That the continuing the operation among us is likely to prove of most dangerous consequence." [11]

At this point only 17 Bostonians had died of smallpox and the selectmen hoped that the disease would go away. They misguidedly believed that it was still possible to escape the epidemic. Beleaguered, Zabdiel Boylston returned to his house and abandoned inoculation for the moment.

Chapter 6

AN ILLITERATE
CUTTER FOR THE STONE

The day after Boylston's humiliating defeat by the selectmen a vicious diatribe spread across the front page of the Boston Newsletter[1]. Inoculation was attacked as a wicked and felonious action. The author claimed that many doctors knew of the procedure but had rejected it because of its well known dangers. In fact the article claimed all Boston's doctors had rejected Mather's request that they consider the operation, except for a "certain cutter for the stone". This was a particularly nasty insult because genuine doctors would not perform the operation since it had a high mortality. An ancient part of the Hippocratic Oath pledges "not to cut for the stone, but leave it to specialist operators". The writer thought that Boylston was so illiterate (he could not read Latin) that he was unable to read the acknowledged authorities on the treatment of smallpox and had therefore subjected his own child to a rash, unjustified experiment. The writer alleged that young Tommy had actually been dangerously ill and that his father had resorted to the most extreme forms of treatment, even placing kidneys on his head and feet, to save his life. The doctor's ignorance was so extreme that he had no idea how to manage patients with smallpox and it was dangerous to employ him to treat anyone with the disease. Boylston's brief newspaper article explaining what he had done and why was labeled a "quack bill" implying that he was a quack because he had advertised his treatment which a respectable doctor would never do. A further charge was that, by inoculating at his house in Dock Square, he had introduced smallpox into the commercial centre of Boston, surely a criminal offence of which the town's lawyers should take note.

To further increase the terror of inoculation the author stated that inoculated individuals sometimes developed "plague sores", the swollen, draining lymph glands that were characteristic of bubonic plague, then the most feared of all infections. He rounded off his attack by claiming that Timonius and Pylarinus had been misrepresented by Mather and Boylston and that they had actually stated that dangerous complications and deaths were common, not unknown, after the operation. He signed himself W. Philanthropus, from the Greek *philo*-lover and *anthropus*-man implying that he was acting as a friend of humanity.

Philanthropus put forward a paradoxical argument, one which would affect debates about inoculation for years. On one hand he said that inoculation was a dangerous practice because it could spread smallpox, on the other hand he argued that the disease that resulted was not smallpox but some other form of eruptive fever resembling measles or possibly chickenpox. If the rash that appeared was only measles or chicken pox then inoculation was useless because the only justification for it was that it would produce immunity to smallpox. Oddly, no one pointed out this contradiction and the confused argument merely meant that the ordinary citizen had no way of judging what the risks and benefits might be.

Everyone in Boston recognized Philanthropus as William Douglass the town's only "real" doctor. A Scot, he had studied at Edinburgh and received an M.D. degree from Leyden University, the leading medical school of the day, before seeking his fortune in the New World.[2] Ironically he had presented Cotton Mather with the volume of the Philosophical Transactions which contained both Mather's letters describing unusual natural phenomena and the Timonius paper, which had stimulated Mather's determination to experiment with inoculation.

Douglass had ended his piece by challenging the ministers, as a matter of conscience, to say whether inoculation amounted to doubting Divine Providence. Did it not thwart God's plans? This attack on Boylston infuriated the Puritan ministers and led to a rapid escalation of hostilities. Benjamin Coleman, Boylston's pastor, drafted a rebuke which appeared in the Gazette on the last day in July.[3] Calling Boylston a "cutter for the stone" was unfair. His God given talents had saved many lives. Even reputable operators were looked down upon because the high mortality associated with the operation meant that the surgeon was little more than a butcher. Would the townspeople have tolerated insults such as "illiterate" or "ignorant" if they had been aimed at Boston's other leading doctors? They would not accept seeing Boylston spat at in such terms. While the ministers conceded that Boylston might have been a little rash they urged that all concerned should treat each other with charity and humility and accept that all were good friends to each other and their country.

Had the ministers ended their letter at that point they might not have provoked the months of controversy that followed, but they closed their document by asking how Douglass, or anyone else, could question the judgment of men of piety and learning such as themselves who had given the issue serious thought and concluded that inoculation was safe. In their opinion the practice was a God-given benefit and that they should trust God in giving them such a valuable means to avoid the horrors of smallpox. There was nothing more complicated or ingenious in the operation than there was in bleeding and many other common treatments for disease which depended on trust in God's Providence. By denouncing their support for inoculation Douglass had strayed into their territory. Matters of moral judgment were for ministers, not doctors.

Shortly after this letter appeared another witness came forward claiming to have previous experience of inoculation. One

John Forehand, *"at the order and direction of the selectmen"*, testified that he had been told of a disastrous experiment with the operation in Greece. Some of those treated had lost the use of their limbs, others had swelled up and died, and others had caught smallpox, all of which suggested that the practice was both dangerous and useless.[4] The ordinary citizen of Boston must have found the situation deeply confusing. Puritan ministers, who might have been expected to argue that smallpox was God's judgment and that fate could not be avoided, were supporting a new practice that made smallpox less threatening. The town's doctors, who might have supported a practice that spared their patients lives, were against it. What evidence there was in favour of inoculation was derived from the accounts of slaves and heathen Muslims, and that testimony had been rejected by men who claimed to have witnessed disasters.

At just this moment the opponents of inoculation gained a valuable ally. John Franklin, a printer, had lost his contract to print the local newspapers and, assisted by his 16 year old brother Ben, established a new journal. Unlike "The Gazette" and "Newsletter" which published commercial information and European news, "The New England Courant" would publish opinions, debates, and speculative articles alongside the usual list of ships entering or leaving port. The brothers gave their journal the motto "Jack of All Trades". The first issue carried two articles attacking the ministers and the practice of inoculation on the front page. John Checkley, a long standing opponent of Cotton Mather contributed a short poem satirizing the ministers:

"Who like faithful shepherds take care of their Flocks,
by teaching and practicing what's Orthodox,
Pray hard against Sickness, yet preach up the POX!"

William Douglass, writing on behalf of a Society of Physicians, continued his attack on the ministers. [5] The development of the Society of Physicians was ominous, they soon adopted the name "Physicians Anti-Inoculators" for the sole purpose of blocking the advance of the new technology, Douglass pointed out that, despite the concerns of the townspeople, contradicting the opinion of the doctors, in opposition to the selectmen, and in spite of the eye witness evidence that inoculation was dangerous, *"six gentlemen of piety and learning, profoundly ignorant of the matter"* had concluded that they understood the complexities of small-pox better than anyone else and advocated inoculation. The only reason that anyone should accept their views was that they were men of "piety and learning". But if their personal traits were the only reason why they should be believed, why shouldn't any-one else with an education have a view? Douglass thought that they should confine themselves to religious matters and not ven-ture into areas where they had no expertise. The ministers had set themselves up as judges of a man's qualifications to practice medicine and had given high praise to a mere "quack advertise-ment". One might think that they believed that Boylston was as important a figure in medicine as the acknowledged great phy-sicians working in London. Boylston's religious or moral attri-butes were theirs to decide, but not his medical skills. Believing that inoculation was no more dangerous than bleeding was an "infatuation" and such infatuations were likely to become epi-demic diseases of the mind just as smallpox was an epidemic of the body. In a word, the ministers were insane.

Douglass's letter was accompanied by another from James Stewart who picked up the theme of a possible relationship between inoculation and plague.[6] He appealed to the towns-people to reject the operation to preserve their health from an even greater danger than smallpox. He attached a letter from Marseilles describing the plague epidemic afflicting the town:

"Father abandoned the child, and the son the father, the husband the wife, and the wife the husband, and those who had not a house to them-selves lay in the streets and pavements. All the streets were filled with cloathes and household goods, stewed with dead dogs and cats, which made an insupportable stench". Did it make sense to risk importing this disease which had never afflicted North America?

While the ministers and Douglass exchanged insults, Zabdiel Boylston waited on the outcome of the seven patients whom he had inoculated before his confrontation with the selectmen. Although Cheever caused him a brief period of anxiety, they all did well and had only mild, discrete smallpox. Convinced by his own observations that the operation was indeed safe he resumed using it. Almost immediately he had another near catastrophe.[7]He inoculated Mr. and Mrs. Webb, a rather frail couple in their late sixties who developed the usual mild form of the infection. But their daughter Esther only came for her own treatment after nursing her parents through their illness. Four days after the procedure she developed full blown confluent smallpox. Boylston had *"hoped that she had not taken the infection from them. But we were soon convinced of that error"*. He recognized that when a person developed smallpox in less than seven days after inoculation they had actually contracted the infection naturally, and now he also realized that inoculated patients were capable of transmitting the full natural illness to their contacts. He would need to take greater care to make certain that his patients did not spread the infection, and he would not leave many days between treating members of the same family. Esther received the full range of treatments before she recovered, and Boylston later mused that he would have been accused of her murder if she had died. Inoculation was too new for Bostonians to understand the subtle difference between natural and artificial smallpox; they would have concluded that he had killed her.

Douglass now published a crude satire in "The Courant".[8]In it he suggested that inoculation should be used to kill off the Eastern Indians threatening northern New England. He likened this approach to a military campaign where a mixture of *"negro yaws and confluent smallpox"* would be spread by inoculators. A bounty of 10 pounds would be paid for each Indian who survived long enough to spread the infection to his own village, but only 5 pounds would be paid if the Indian died before transmitting the disease.

Four of the men inoculated in July placed a testimonial in the newsletter saying that they had all had mild disease and recommended the practice as safe and effective.[9] Douglass hurried to reply.[10] Their testimony should be considered like the ancient fable about the fox which lost its tail and encouraged all his friends to join him so that the calamity became universal and spared the fox from teasing. He argued that the men were actually extremely lucky and that their symptoms had been much worse than they claimed. He alleged that abscesses in the bowels and groin would occur frequently, that some would become paralyzed, and that they would be in a sorry state similar to that of patients with terminal syphilis even if they survived. Like syphilis, inoculation would at first seem successful and only years later would the complications appear. And it did not prevent future smallpox. Douglass was supported by a letter from a Dr Herrick who reported that while he was a ship's surgeon he had met sailors who claimed that they had been inoculated and subsequently caught smallpox. He was ready to come into Boston to swear the facts on oath.

Opposition among Boston's populace continued. The inoculator and his supporting ministers were reviled on all sides. Mather expressed his agony *"The town is become almost a hell on earth, a city full of lies, and murders, and blasphemies as far as wishes and speeches can render it so: Satan seems to take strange possession of it in the epidemic rage against that notable and powerful and successful way of saving the lives of the people from the dangers of smallpox. What can I do on this occasion to get the miserable town dispossessed of the evil spirit which has taken such horrible possession of it?"* [11] He came to believe that the Devil had attacked him because he was preventing his harvest of souls. Sinners who escaped smallpox might repent and escape forever.

Mather was put into agonies of doubt and despair when his younger son, Sam, asked to be inoculated. His Harvard roommate had died of smallpox and the boy was terrified that he would be next. But Mather could see that if Sammy died his position in Boston would be destroyed. All those who had attacked him would now be able to say that his foolishness had killed his son. After agonizing for days he was persuaded by his father to have the boy inoculated in secret. Boylston was disgusted and recorded that it was the only time that he had been asked to inoculate surreptitiously. Sam did well, but his father's diary reveals his anxiety that the boy had severe smallpox and was going to die, while Boylston's account reveals that his course was favourable like all his other patients.[12]

Chapter   7

A MORAL DILEMMA

S o far the debate had centered on the safety of inoculation and whether it provided immunity from smallpox. While these were important questions they could be answered in time and with experience. But now a formidable moral opponent appeared. At the end of August "The Courant" published a long letter from the Rev. William Harris, renowned as the most conservative of the Puritan ministers[1]. He led the First Church and theologically was often allied with the Mathers against the liberal Benjamin Colman and Thomas Prince in issues regarding church membership and the correct forms of the Sabbath services. Yet despite his religious affinities with the Mathers he raised serious doubts about inoculation. He found it *very strange, believe me Sir, that there would be so many, who blest with a sound and vigorous Constitution, should be desirous to bring upon themselves a Distemper, of which they themselves are afraid, and from which so many flee, that they should be so discontented when God brings it upon them, yet can be well satisfied to bring it upon themselves, after this new Fashion."*

In his letter he raised a series of religious and moral issues in the form of questions to which he supplied well thought out answers. Was self infection lawful? No, he answered, because there was a chance that you would die and that would make you guilty of "self murder" and that was sin under the sixth commandment. Was it unlawful to produce on oneself a lesser illness to prevent a greater one? Yes, one could not be sure of catching smallpox and one could not be sure that it would be mortal if one did. Therefore it was unacceptable to give oneself a disease that one might avoid all together and which might be less severe that the inoculated form. He rejected the attempts of other Puritan ministers to expose the inaccurate reports and outright lies spread by the anti-inoculators on the grounds that they were themselves only expressing opinions. They had no evidence that the reports of disastrous consequences were untrue. In Harris's words," *If one died after inoculation who was to blame? If one spread smallpox to a neighbor following inoculation, and the neighbor died, who was to blame?* Harris argued that in both cases the one inoculated was as much to blame as the inoculator.

The sixth commandment required self love and self preservation he argued. One must avoid pain and insecurity because they were a threat to life, and it would be sinful to neglect remedies if they were beneficial. However, epidemic diseases were sent as judgments from an angry God and required a different sort of medicine. Epidemics were the most severe punishments that God could send and therefore required great humiliation and strict observance of the duties of repentance. Man could only prostrate himself before his angry God and plead for forgiveness. Inoculation failed to help man meet the judgment of the Lord. It was an invasion of the Divine realm to give oneself smallpox. By making the disease less severe it interfered with Divine justice, it defied providence.

"In short I affirm it unlawful for a person in health upon any account to receive a less infection to avoid a greater, because our blessed Saviour, the great, the Skillful Physician says, he that is whole needs not a physician, but he that is sick may apply to them". Man must wait for God's appointed time.

For Calvinist Protestants the argument was that inoculation interfered with God's preordained plans for one's soul. Your fate was fixed at the moment of birth and it was sinful to try to avoid divine judgment. Harris's arguments were persuasive to devout Puritans. How could Mather reply?

Mather chose to reverse many of Harris's assertions in a pamphlet with a long winded title which begins *"Some Account of what is said of Inoculating or Transplanting the Smallpox."*[2] Strangely Mather is not listed as the author and the title page of the piece says that it was published by Zabdiel Boylston. However, G.L. Kittredge, the most distinguished of Mather scholars has clearly shown that most of the writing is Mather's and only a small part was written by Boylston.[3] The first two thirds of this piece reviews the evidence from Constantinople and the testimony of Boston Negroes as well as reporting Boylston's results up to the middle of September when he had treated 31 patients who had all survived. The last four pages give Mather's considered replies to Harris's questions.If the sixth commandment required you to protect yourself from disease or death, then inoculation was a moral requirement because it was less dangerous than the natural smallpox. Mather argued that the lesser relative risk outweighed the absolute prohibition on taking a risk. In his view one was always at risk of the fatal illness and therefore obliged to take steps to lessen the threat. If one acted in good faith and one did by some chance die, one was not guilty of "self murder". Inoculation was like taking steps to protect one's own house when a neighbour's house caught fire. If your neighbour's house is on fire, is it a presumption upon divine providence to prevent the fire spreading to your own house when you cannot be certain that the fire will spread? *"Pray sit still, my neighbour, your house is not yet on fire; the Almighty can preserve it"* This was clearly ridiculous. Any sane person would look after the safety of his property. So why didn't the same argument apply to any form of preventive medicine? In short, Mather argued that people had a duty to be inoculated. But the conservatives replied that it was foolish to set fire to your own house to try to preserve it, which to them was what inoculation amounted to.

Mather relied heavily on the argument that inoculation was a gift from God rather than an entirely human intervention, although some of his opponents suggested that the operation was actually the work of the Devil trying to lure mankind into disregarding divine Providence. The Devil would have people trust in inoculation rather than in God to protect them during an epidemic. But Mather maintained that God had indeed given man a magnificent gift by giving him a means to avert the worst aspects of smallpox. Opposing inoculation was opposing God's own mercy and might be seen as blasphemy.

Some sense of the atmosphere in Boston is found in a letter Mather wrote to London in early September, 1721.

I must say I never saw the Devil so let loose on any Occasion. A lying Spirit has gone forth at such a rate that there was no believing any Thing one heard. If the inoculated Patients were a little sickish, or had a Vomit given them, it was immediately reported, that they were at the point of Death, or actually dead. While the Patients lay blessing and praising Almighty God for showing them this easy way to escape a formidable Enemy, it was confidently reported That they bitterly repented of what had been done upon them, and would not on any terms be brought into it if it were to do again. When the Patients had their incisions either actually and perfectly healed in some, or within a day or two of it in others, it was confidently reported, That they were perishing under terrible Ulcers, and had their Arms or Legs rotting off.

Then the People would assert, that here were persons on the very Spot who underwent the inoculation in England a great many years ago; but afterwards had the Small-pox in the common way; and they said they would bring these persons to us. A few minutes after, they would assert that it was never practised in England; but there was an act of Parliament which made it a Felony; and they said they would produce the Act to us. But never any Patient had so many Pustules of the Small-pox as there were lies now daily told and spread among our deluded People."[4]

Boylston and Cotton Mather tried to rebut the mob in their pamphlet, one of only two pieces written by Boylston during the epidemic. Mather stressed the evidence that inoculation was successful, relying heavily on the testimony of his slave Onesimus and evidence collected by Benjamin Colman from several other Africans. They all agreed that the practice was well known and widely used particularly when an epidemic of smallpox broke out or when traders were to embark on a long journey when they might encounter smallpox en route. He set out their testimony in broad dialect to emphasize that these were their own words, not his. Furthermore, it was acceptable for Christians to learn about new treatments from Africans and Mohammedans. Had not the colonists learned of tobacco and treatments for rattlesnake bites from heathen Indians? The minister then argued that inoculation was like any other medicine; it might fail sometimes, just as vomits or purges might kill a patient, but on the whole these medicines worked as expected. In what way was inoculation different from any other preventative medicine?

Boylston outlined his clinical observations and pointed out some of the mob's idiotic beliefs. "*I have made my experiments with all the disadvantages that can be imagined, on old and young, on strong and weak, on male and female, on white and black, and in the worst season of the year; and on greater numbers than I judge proper, (considering the unaccountable rage of unadvised people) to mention; But more than twice seven, I can assure you, and it has succeeded well in all, even beyond expectation*". He acknowledged that some of his patients were a little sicker than he had expected from the Turkish accounts, but all his patients had recovered, and their symptoms were easy to manage. Mostly the symptoms were mild, pocks few, and the malignant secondary fever non-existent. No boils or abscesses had occurred and "*to form a cry of Plague on this occasion, as if the practice would bring the plague: this is so excessively ridiculous that it is a wonder that any people can think it*". Besides, swellings, sores, and abscesses were a recognized consequence of many diseases and didn't indicate that the plague had developed. They sometimes occurred as a consequence of natural smallpox and were never linked to an outbreak of plague. The charge was mindless scaremongering. Most of his patients would gladly undergo inoculation again because the resulting symptoms were only those of mild smallpox. "*Indeed, for anything that yet appears, here is a discovery, that is the greatest blessing to mankind, and should be thankfully received…Many lives might be saved, and the health of the town much sooner restored, if the practitioners and the people in the town would come more into this practice*"

Their pamphlet changed nothing. Mather remained disturbed by the deep animosity of the town. Boylston was threatened as he went about his rounds. Sixty years later one of his daughters recalled that her father would reassure them when they feared for him with expressions of pious calmness and trust in God. She recalled that the family *"trembled whenever he left the house for fear that he would be sacrificed to popular fury, and never visit it again"*.[5]

Checkly and Douglass continued their assault on Cotton Mather. Together with the other anti-inoculators they met at Richard Hall's tavern to exchange ideas and plan further attacks. Mather's right to use the letters FRS, signifying Fellowship of the Royal Society, was questioned. Fellowship was a prestigious honour and gave credence to Mather's qualifications to speak on scientific matters, but if his opponents could show that he was a fraud his position would be undermined. It would also strengthen the anti-inoculators' argument that ministers should stick to religion and should not meddle in affairs where they were unqualified. Mather's claim to an FRS was supported by a letter from Richard Waller, the secretary of the Royal Society, saying that he had been elected by the Council and membership of the Society in 1714.[6] However, the rules required that Fellows take an oath and sign the membership book before membership was complete and the cleric, who had never left New England, had not done this so the official membership lists did not include his name. The anti-inoculators placed the list on a wall at Hall's and invited Mather, or anyone else who might be interested, to inspect it to confirm their claim that he was not entitled to the grand title he used. At stake was his right to pronounce on scientific issues. The Anti-inoculators argued that ministers were not entitled to speak on medical problems, which were strictly the territory of doctors. However, the minister's membership of the world's most prestigious scientific society gave him the aura of an expert in science as well as religion. If Mather was fraudulently claiming to be a Fellow of the Royal Society then no one needed to pay any attention to his medical pronouncements.

Chapter 8

DISASTER

Despite the fury of the town and the outspoken opposition of Douglass and his colleagues, inoculation continued to grow. By September Boylston was inoculating most days and had treated 58 people by the end of the third week when he suddenly stopped operating. Yet the epidemic continued to grow; by mid October about one in four Bostonians had the disease,[1] yet an apparently valuable method of avoiding the worst consequences of the infection had almost disappeared. What had happened? Almost certainly the pause was caused by the death of one of Boylston's patients, Mrs. Sarah Dixwell, the well known wife of the town clerk, who died twenty four days after her operation.

This was not supposed to happen. All previous accounts suggested that inoculation was safe. What had gone wrong? Boylston's case notes outline her progress. *Mrs. Dixwell was a fat Gentlewoman of a tender Constitution, she became frightened into the Practice, as most of the others had done; not only by living with the Infected, but passing some days by the Door wherein lay a Corpse ready for the Grave, which died of Confluent Small-Pox, the stench whereof greatly offended and surprised her with fear of being infected: However, she went the usual Time of nine Days before Eruption, and broke out full of a distinct sort;*

but being of a very moist Habit, they fluxed in her Face, about the 7ᵗʰ day: she had a sore Throat, was often restless, and by Turns had a Difficulty of Breathing, her Fever and Thirst being yet moderate: the eleventh her Pox began to turn; the 13ᵗʰ her face became crusty; and the 14ᵗʰ the Scabs began to fall off, and she appeared more comfortable; her Incisions grew wider, and run plentifully. All this while we were in good Hopes of her doing well. This afternoon her two Children were brought to her, just recovered in the natural way, which gave her great Joy, but put her Spirits in too great a Motion; and the Weather changing cool she took some cold, for that Evening she was taken with hysteric fits, which held her about two Hours; but upon the use of an Anodine and some Anti-hysterics, she became quiet, and rested some Hours that Night, and seemed refreshed in the Morning, and held it good part of the Day: but the Evening returning, brought on her fits, together with new Fevers; upon which I bled her and repeated her Blisters, and used many other means, but to no Effect: The Fits and Fevers followed her close until the 17ᵗʰ of Eruption, and the 26ᵗʰ from Inoculation, when she died.[2]

The major figures in the inoculation controversy interpreted her death to suit their prejudices. At the time Boylston thought that she must have had a second, coincidental infection, which caused her fits and fever. Later he began to think that the sore throat and blocked breathing indicated that she had actually caught natural smallpox and that her demise was due to the natural infection, not inoculation. Cotton Mather denied that her death was related to inoculation in any way. He needed to believe that the procedure was completely safe because it came from God, so his explanation was that she had died of a completely unrelated disease, just as many of his parishioners died suddenly of unexpected fevers. But for Douglass she was a stroke of luck. Here was the first evidence that inoculation was the dangerous procedure that he had said it was. Within days he had written to his friend Alexander Stuart, a Fellow of the Royal Society, in London.[3] What did he think of this crazy new practice? He presented a terrible catalogue of deaths, deformed limbs, and lingering disasters, which he claimed had been covered up by the inoculators. He acknowledged that only one of about sixty individuals inoculated had actually died, but implied that there were many suppressed horrors that would only become known in time. He intimated that some patients had died in secret following inoculation, and implied that Boylston had deliberately concealed their fate. Douglass's paper was read to the Royal Society on November 16[th,] 1721. It was the first news of the Boston experiment published in London.

In the next month, between the last week of September and the last week in October Boylston inoculated only five people. Then just as suddenly as it had ceased the demand for inoculation reappeared. During the last week in October seventeen individuals came forward. Inoculation's revival coincided with the appearance in Boston papers of news from London that the Prince and Princess of Wales had sponsored a trial of inoculation on a group of prisoners who had all done well and had mild smallpox.[4] The combination of royal approval and apparent success made it acceptable again.

Now there was a distinctly different social mix of patients. Before most of Boylston's inoculees were members of Mather's church "Old North" or had been members before a congenial split in that congregation when the meeting house became too small for the growing North End. These were Mather's neighbors and friends who had followed his and his father's spiritual guidance for most of their lives. The new patients came from socially prominent families who belonged to the Third Church, known as "Old South" whose fathers held positions granted by the Governor and were therefore members of the "Royalist" political faction as we shall see in the next chapter. These individuals were also members of some of the richest families in town.

For the first time there was also a group from the nearby town of Roxbury including their young minister, Cotton Mather's nephew, Thomas Walter. He and his companions became central figures in the most violent episode during the inoculation controversy. On November 12 someone threw a lighted hand grenade into the room where they were sleeping. Fortunately the fuse fell out and no one was hurt. But the event terrified Mather, who was convinced that the devil himself had inspired the attack. While Mather and the Boston papers were outraged by the attack, no harm was done. Despite his near miss, ThomasWalter recovered from his inoculation safely and returned to Roxbury.

Roxbury was a town of about 1500 people seven miles from Boston on the other side of the neck of land connecting Boston to mainland Massachusetts. Zabdiel Boylston had close relations with the town. His father had paid a large sum towards the costs of building the meeting house and young Zabdiel and his family had worshipped there. At least one of his nieces, Rebecca Abbott, lived there while another niece, Mary Lane, and his sister in law, Sarah Boylston, sought to escape the epidemic in Boston by living with her. Boylston inoculated them, the first patients he treated outside Boston. When they and Thomas Walter and his companions all recovered after having mild inoculation smallpox they triggered a rush of people demanding treatment.

Although opinion in Roxbury had initially opposed the operation, when the first thirteen heads of families who caught natural smallpox died the atmosphere quickly changed. With first hand evidence that the procedure was safe seventy seven people including several whole families took up the operation. Boylston enjoyed the support of a fellow doctor in Roxbury, the first doctor to join him in inoculating. Philip Thompson, uncle of Thomas Walter's wife[5] inoculated a further 35 people bringing the total in Roxbury to over one hundred, a substantial portion of the population.

Boylston would eventually publish his case book, which is sometimes called the first clinical study in America. Among the details of his patients he tells of the Dorr family in which he inoculated nine individuals including the father and the family's Indian servant. He had only one nurse to look after all of them so he put them together in one room and even put three in one bed. "Here *was a melancholy Sight indeed! I had often three or four, but never nine in a Room together; the poor Children. with their Sickness, and the Winter's Cold, proved forward, one crying another coughing,: one wanted Drink, another to do its needs : one to get up, another to go to bed, and so on; so that together with opening and shutting the Door, the jingling of the warming-pan, Fire-shovel and Tongs, there was scarce a Minute in the 24 hours that was still and quiet."* Mr. Dorr was so upset by the pandemonium he "needed bleeding and extra medication".[6] Boylston seems to have had difficulty finding adequate nursing care for his patients. He complained that on one occasion he had only one nurse to look after four men, and she was a drunkard.

Meanwhile the Mathers and their allies continued to exchange insults and charges of blasphemy, impiety, and arrogance with William Douglass. Isaac Greenwood, one of Cotton Mather's acolytes, began a series of dialogues charging Douglass with vanity and jealousy.[7] He claimed that Douglass had intended to introduce inoculation himself and was only angry because Boylston did it first. Worse, he claimed that Douglass had committed a serious breach of medical ethics by continuing to treat his patients, and charging them fees when it was clear that they were beyond hope of recovery. When a patient was clearly dying the honest doctor withdrew admitting that he had nothing more to offer. Despite all the invective nothing changed.

The epidemic of 1721 was unusual in that it ran an explosive course. By mid October the peak had passed, and by early December there were few cases of smallpox in Boston. While Boylston continued to operate, more of his patients came from outside the town, and he had not inoculated anyone in Boston after early December, when he was approached in mid May by relatives of the Chief Justice of Massachusetts, Samuel Sewall, who sought inoculation. Boylston obliged them and was rewarded by another torrent of abuse. Since smallpox had been gone for months the selectmen were outraged and banished the patients to a quarantine island in the harbor. Boylston was forced to concede that he would now cease inoculating. William Douglass could not resist having the last word. He crowed in the "The Courant" of May 21st *"Last January inoculation made a sort of exit, like the infatuation thirty years ago after several had fallen victims to the mistaken notions of Dr. Mather and other learned clerks concerning witchcraft. But finding inoculation in this town, like serpents in summer, beginning to crawl abroad again last week, it was time, and effectively crushed in the bud by the Justices, Select men, and unanimous vote of the town meeting."*[8]

After just under one year, from June 1721 to May 1722, the Boston experiment was over.

Chapter 9

FATHERS AND SONS

Most modern interpretations of the events of the summer of 1721 emphasize the dangers of inoculation, the wisdom of Douglass, who was the only "official" doctor with a university degree in Boston, and the brave but rash decisions of Mather and Boylston. This view is simplistic because it ignores many factors which acted to promote or retard the introduction of inoculation. To understand what was really happening during that dangerous year we need to explore the individuals and their motives who tried to block the operation, and the factors which led a small group of individuals to undergo the new and possibly dangerous procedure. In particular the role of politics as a factor driving the explosion of opposition has been ignored.

Behind the controversy which exploded in Boston lurked Elisha Cooke Jr. He formed the link between Boston's doctors' rejection of Cotton Mather's request that they consider inoculation, the selectmen banning Boylston from continuing with the experiment, and the vociferous outrage of William Douglass. Elisha Cooke Jr. was not only the leader of the selectmen; he was also a doctor, and a shrewd and powerful politician with a long standing hatred of Cotton and Increase Mather. By some accounts he was also the wealthiest man in town. Cooke's influence on the events of the summer of 1721 injected colonial politics into what has previously seemed a medical controversy.

Boston had been divided into two informal political parties or factions since the charter controversy which began in 1691, King James II had revoked the Charter of the Massachusetts Bay Company that formed the legal basis for life in the colony in 1683. Under the old charter Massachusetts had enjoyed an unprecedented degree of local autonomy, including the right to elect their own officers, among them the governor, judges, and both colony-wide and local representatives. The town meeting, a much prized aspect of New England politics, was the starting point for the political framework. Although Puritan ministers could not vote for public officials, and could not stand for office themselves, they controlled the political process through the requirement that candidates had to be members in good standing of one of the town's churches and have the support of their minister.[1]

In 1688, Increase Mather, Cotton's father and co-minister at the second, or Old North, Church, was sent to London to negotiate for the restoration of the charter. In 1690 Elisha Cooke Sr., a prominent merchant, was also sent to London to participate in the discussions around the governance of New England. Mather made no progress and eventually, in 1691, when William and Mary were co-regents, agreed to a new charter which made Massachusetts a royal colony with a governor appointed by the crown. The royal prerogative gave the Governor the right to appoint judges, magistrates, and customs controllers as well as other lesser officers. When it became known that the new Governor, William Phipps, had recently become a member of the Mathers' church, Cooke became convinced that this was an attempt by Mather to retain his political power by his influence over the governor. When Mather packed the new General Court, the house of representatives of Massachusetts, with men from the North End of Boston where his congregation was concentrated, Cooke refused to be associated with the minister or the new Governor and travelled back to Boston on a different ship."[2] A recent historian characterized this episode saying "*vehement opposition to both Phipps and the Mathers came from the outraged group led by Elisha Cooke that believed*

Increase Mather had betrayed his covenanted duty by accepting a charter providing for a royally appointed governor… it seemed to him, and other Bostonians that Mather had packed the General Council with men from North Boston, in a bid for personal control".[3]

From the charter debacle two factions emerged; one supported the royal Governor and one still longed for the old charter with its rights and privileges. Although they formed only an informal grouping, royal appointees such as judges, legal officers, indeed anyone holding an office under the crown, tended to support the Royalist faction along with most of the Puritan ministers whose religious beliefs included a commitment to the importance of hierarchy and a clear subordinate relationship between governed and governor. Just as the Puritan religion was based on a strict relationship between God, ministers, and heads of families, so political stability required a similar subordinate relationship with the King at the top, his appointed ministers, and the public. Old charter supporters viewed the rapacious behaviour of royal appointees with alarm and disliked the Puritan ministers for meddling in civic and financial affairs when they were not qualified to do so. Now Increase Mather's political machinations came back to haunt him. In the first election for the General Court, held after the new charter was installed, all his appointees were thrown out, and almost no one from the North End was elected to the Court for decades. Adherents of the Old Charter faction were a majority among Boston's electors and the representatives that they selected, and through their influence in the General Court, could annoy the Royal Governor by refusing to grant him a reasonable salary. The governor in turn could manipulate the Court by vetoing its officials if he did not agree with their views. Elisha Cooke Sr. was elected speaker of the General Court and rejected by the governor on more than one occasion. He was also stripped of his position as a judge.[4]

When Cooke Sr. died in 1715, his son, Elisha Cooke Jr., inherited the mantle of unofficial leader of the "Old Charter" or "Popular" faction. In 1717 Cooke and two of his cronies were elected selectmen, an event which horrified Cotton Mather. He tried to persuade them to modify their views, which he considered divisive, but failed. His antipathy for the Cooke faction is revealed in his diary entry when one of them, Oliver Noyes, died suddenly *"There is a wicked party in this country who fill the land with strife and sin, and who are drawing the people into continual snares, and into such actions and follies as are a blemish unto us , and threatens to bring horrible oppression and slavery upon us….except the hand of our glorious Lord in some wonderful way deliver the country from two or three men …the country in the ordinary way must be ruined,.*[5] Mather absolved himself of feelings of revenge and personal malice and then prayed that the Lord deliver the country. *"Within these few hours GOD has in a marvelous manner, and at a critical moment smitten with apoplexy one who has been and would still have been the greatest hinderer of good and misleader and enchanter of the people that there was in the whole House of representatives"*[6]

Elisha Cooke Jr. created the first political "machine" in the colonies. The town meeting still had the power to elect the Boston selectmen, and they in turn had the power to set local taxes and to grant licenses to sell alcohol. The selectmen could influence the appointment/election of the town's taxing officers who could award tax abatements; an obvious way of rewarding political support. Supporters would receive lower assessments than their holding warranted or, in some cases, the taxes simply were not collected. Alternatively raising the tax assessment for Popular party supporters could give them the right to vote because it was based on an individual's taxable worth. In 1719, Elisha Cooke Jr. was elected moderator of the selectmen and the beginnings of the famed "Boston caucus" were in place. Although the caucus was a major feature of Boston politics after about 1740 its roots lie in the relationship between Cooke and the process of choosing who would be elected to public office in 1720. Cooke and his cronies would control Boston politics for a generation after the inoculation controversy. The same individuals appeared year after year as selectmen, assessors, or delegates to the House of Representatives. When a vacancy appeared a "promotion" from the ranks of the assessors became common. Such relationships were unknown before 1717 when Cooke assumed power.[7]

However, Elisha Cooke Jr. was more than just the leader of the selectmen. He was the wealthiest man in Boston and he was one of the town's doctors. When Cotton Mather presented his petition to Boston's doctors suggesting that they investigate inoculation, he was asking for support from a man who hated him and his political machinations. Cooke's loathing for the Mathers had been inherited from his father, and both men had been humiliated by the Royal Governor on many occasions. Cooke Jr. had the support of another doctor, William Clark, who served several terms as a selectman and as a representative to the General Court during the period 1719-1725, suggesting that he was a member of Cooke's nascent caucus. Thus two of the town's most influential politicians with deep anti-Mather convictions were also leading Boston doctors. Mather's attempt to introduce inoculation would have struck them as another example of ministers meddling in affairs beyond their calling. Controversy between the ministers and the "Popular" party over banking methods, markets, and the use of potential naval timber, among other issues, had pulled the ministers into defending positions far removed from their core religious roles. If successful, inoculation might even restore the flagging popular influence of the Mathers, and the other Puritan ministers. *"What was really at issue in 1721-22, in the minds of the participants, was not the long range vectors of science over credulity, but a more pressing question of prestige and authori*ty".[8] The sons of the two men who started the charter debate now faced each other over inoculation. When Zabdiel Boylston was called before the selectmen and lawyers of Boston to explain his conduct, he was facing men who opposed inoculation on political grounds as much as ones of public safety.

William Douglass presented most of the evidence against inoculation at the hearing, and published his broadside attack on Boylston within days. Curiously, this letter to the *Boston News Letter* was dated July 20, the day before the actual meeting of the selectmen.[9]. Did he know the outcome before the case had even been presented? To prepare his translation of Dalhounde's evidence Douglass probably had access to this information before the hearing so he may have colluded with Cooke before the fact.

What lay behind Douglass's attack on Boylston? Was there more than just concern for the safety of the procedure? If so

Douglass's behavior is less that of a genuine physician interested in what is best best for patients and takes on a more personal tone. Since Douglass was the main voice of opposition to inoculation it is important to understand what drove him to his extreme language and his intemperate opposition to the ministers as well as Boylston.

There are at least two motives that could have driven Douglass to his extreme position. Both involve his professional standing and his income. On the one hand his professional standing was threatened by Boylston whose activities might limit his practice, while on the other hand he stood to enhance his position as a reputable doctor by forming an alliance with Cooke and his medical allies. In mid 1721 Douglass had been settled in Boston for less than three years and was still in the process of establishing his reputation. He held the only university MD degree in Boston, which he had obtained from the Dutch University of Utrecht.[10] At the time medical schools in the Netherlands were considered to be the most advanced in Europe and many British students chose to finish their medical education there. In letters to his friend Cadwallader Colden, Deputy Governor of New York, Douglass had disparaged his local colleagues as ignorant and unskilled. [11] He would have expected to have the leading position in Boston medicine because his degree allowed him to call himself a "physician". In 18th century England a Physician was the top of the medical totem pole. Below him were apothecaries who sold drugs and herbs and who could give medical advice but only if they did not charge a fee for it. Further down were surgeons who carried out the distasteful manual tasks such as giving enemas, draining abscesses, or treating superficial leg ulcers. Below this recognised hierarchy was group of practitioners ranging from "wise women" who often had considerable experience of traditional folk medicines and obstetric problems to quacks, mountebanks, and outright charlatans. An individual could choose to consult based on the practitioner's reputation and fees. Not surprisingly Physicians charged the most. Douglass clearly thought of himself as the pinnacle of Boston medicine.

Doctors of any type were uncommon in Massachusetts in the 17th century, so the minister, usually the best educated man in town, was the established source of medical advice. Gradually, self-taught "doctors" like Zabdiel Boylston's father, Thomas, began to treat illnesses and injuries as well. A few surgeons with European experience settled in Boston and surrounding towns and they were able to take on apprentices and teach them the necessary skills. By the time Douglass settled in Boston there were about eleven "doctors" in the town who held the title as a courtesy, even though they had scant formal training. Most of them engaged in trade as well as medical practice by importing drugs and herbs from England.

Historians often interpret Douglass's position as that of a modern physician with a detailed knowledge of science and therapy, while Boylston is often portrayed as a sort of country bumpkin without university education, classical languages, or worthwhile training. However, Boylston was actually a formidable figure in Boston medicine. He had served an unofficial apprenticeship with his father in their village, Muddy River, now part of Brookline. Thomas Boylston was a successful doctor/farmer who could afford to make the largest contribution from the residents of Muddy River towards the building of the enlarged meeting house where the villagers worshipped. He was also a military surgeon and served with the militia during King Philip's war, the bloodiest war between the Native Americans and colonists in the 18th century in which 800 settlers and at least 3000 Indians were killed. When his father died, Zabdiel was apprenticed to John Cutler, a Dutchman who had experience as a naval surgeon in European service and also as a surgeon in King Philip's war. [12] In England apprenticeship with a surgeon was a common form of medical training , and there were only a handful of university educated "physicians". In the English countryside, where ninety percent of the population lived in small towns, villages, or on farms, the surgeon/apothecary provided much of the medical care. Fifty years after Boylston finished his apprenticeship, Edward Jenner trained in a similar way with two apothecary/surgeon brothers named Ludlow in the small West Country market town of Chipping Sodbury. Boylston's training would have fitted him for rural practice in England in the early 18th century.[13]

By 1721, Boylston was the most accomplished surgeon in Massachusetts, possibly even in the whole of North America. He had performed the first recorded invasive operations. His successes were recorded in the Boston newspapers. Numerous referrals from the guardians of the poor testify to his high reputation with the town's political elite. Among his patients was Chief Justice Samuel Sewall who had called on Boylston to disembowel the corpse of his wife prior to burial and the wealthy Stoddards who had consulted him over the care of their children. In 1721 he had been in practice from his house in the centre of town at the top of Dock Square for almost twenty years. Far from being an illiterate country amateur, Zabdiel Boylston was Boston's leading doctor.

For William Douglass, Boylston was a serious professional challenge. He despised Boylston for his lack of formal education and for the fact that he ran a store selling hardware as well as drugs and herbs, as well as practicing medicine. Carrying on "trade" was beneath the status expected of a doctor. But Boylston had an established medical practice and regularly treated Boston's leading citizens who Douglass felt should consult him.

In his correspondence with his friend Cadwallader Colden, Douglass revealed that his primary motive for settling in Boston was that he believed that he would make more money than he could in England. So far his work was largely confined to "strangers", merchants, ship captains and other travelers who passed through the bustling port.[14] It must have galled him to see the wealthy merchants of Boston seek medical advice from men he considered untrained amateurs.

On July 28th, 1721 Douglass wrote that he had successfully treated a complicated case of smallpox and his hands were full. He claimed that he had a large share of the smallpox work and seven or eight thousand cases were expected during the epidemic, which might last for a year or two. This was his great opportunity; he would "seize the day". Thousands of patients represented a large income and his reputation would be enhanced.[15] However, Boylston threatened his position. If he established inoculation as an alternative to natural smallpox then he would have cancelled Douglass's advantage. Furthermore, if Boylston proved able to treat his inoculated patients successfully then he, not Douglass, would reap many of the professional benefits because he would be called to manage difficult cases. This rank amateur would have stolen Douglass's trade. Therefore he had good reason to try to demolish Boylston's reputation before it swamped his own. Although some historians have interpreted Douglass's stand as an attempt to preserve professional standards, it is important to note that there was no "medical profession" in the early18th century. The various forms of "doctoring" were trades just like saddle making or book selling. Douglass was trying to protect his income from a competing tradesman, not upholding the honour of his profession. There were no recognized professional standards to defend. Patients chose to obtain their medical care through recommendations from respected figures such as the clergy, their own assessment of the severity of the illness, and hence the necessity for an expensive doctor and fee they could afford. Many people "self-doctored" in that they decided what was wrong with them and then bought what they thought were the appropriate medicines from an apothecary.

Douglass needed to advertise his superiority to the "illiterate" Boylston. He also could make very powerful allies by attacking Boylston and the ministers since his views dovetailed with those of the "Old charter" faction headed by Elisha Cooke Jr., which included most of the other medical practitioners in Boston. If he were allied with them against Mather he could expect their support by referrals and recommendations. Approval from socially prominent doctors such as Cooke or Clark would significantly boost Douglass's status and his income. Thus his attacks on Boylston were intended to counter the threat to his reputation, while his attacks on the ministers gained him the support of the town's most important politicians. Cooke, who was a leader, but not an articulate spokesman, had found a fluent ally in his war with the Mathers. Cooke was *a leader rather than an exhorter of men, who, while he might cause others to write, himself had no vocation for authorship*. [16]

Amidst all the controversy and outrage, who had the courage to undergo a new and possibly dangerous procedure? Zabdiel Boylston published his case notes in 1726 making it possible through the use of church and town records to reconstruct the progress of inoculation. Although the episode is usually known as the Boston inoculation controversy, less than half those inoculated were actually Bostonians, with over one third coming from the nearby small town of Roxbury. Among Bostonians the influence of Cotton Mather was an important factor in making the choice to undergo inoculation as 60 of the 94 who joined the experiment were members of Mather's church. His influence was even more pronounced at the beginning of the inoculation saga when three quarters of those inoculated by Boylston were members of Mather's congregation and lived within a five minute walk of the Old North Church, his meeting house. Despite the support given by Benjamin Colman, Boylston's pastor, only a few members of his congregation at the Church in Brattle Square volunteered for the operation; nor were many of Boylston's neighbours inoculated. Thus proximity to Cotton Mather and an established relationship with his spiritual leadership played an important role in determining who would agree to be inoculated in Boston.

Several factors seem to combine to explain the popularity of inoculation in Roxbury. Perhaps the most powerful was the devastating impact of smallpox on Roxbury which had killed thirteen heads of families, about one in ten of all heads of families, when the disease reached the town.[17] For Puritans this was particularly tragic since husbands were expected to act as moral guides to their wives and children as well as being the bread winners.[18] Without a husband, a family was morally rudderless as well as impoverished. Another factor was the leadership of the town's two ministers: Thomas Walter, who volunteered to go into Boston to test the operation before it was recommended to the whole town, and his father Nehemiah, the long serving minister of the First Church in Roxbury. When the 48 year old Nehemiah was himself inoculated along with two more of his children and his son Thomas's wife it sent a strong message in support of inoculation to the whole community. Even here Cotton Mather probably played a powerful role as Nehemiah Walter was married to Mather's sister and Cotton had acted as a mentor to Thomas during his early days in the ministry. Furthermore Boylston had grown up in Roxbury and some of his family still lived there.

One further indication of the important role of ministers in persuading their members to accept inoculation comes from Charlestown, a town about the same size as Roxbury, located roughly 200 yards across the bay from Boston. Business of all sorts was carried out across the narrow channel and many Boston families had relatives there. Yet despite the presence of one of Boylston's nieces, who did agree to be inoculated, only 20 Charlestown residents, members of only three families, took up the new procedure, and they were all close relatives of families who had already been inoculated in Boston. Lack of interest in inoculation was not due to opposition from the town's minister, but may have been due to his absence. He, his wife, and some of his children, had died at the start of the epidemic and there was no minister to promote inoculation in contrast to Roxbury and the North End of Boston where the ministers played a leading role in the acceptance of the new practice.

Mather, as an overseer of Harvard College, may also have been instrumental in the decision by a group of 15 students and two of their tutors to be inoculated. By the time the epidemic had ended all four of the faculty and about 17 students had been inoculated and tutor Thomas Robie had begun inoculating others in Cambridge.

Tracing all 244 individuals that Boylston inoculated reveals two extended family networks as well as the religious links outlined above. One family is centred on Cotton Mather and the other are relatives of Jerusha Minot Boylston, Zabdiel's wife. Thirty-one patients link to Mather and 33 link to Jerusha, but ten of these are her own children and servants. Finally the two extended clans link to each other through the Rev. John Webb, who was related to Mather, and his wife, Sarah Broomfield, who was related to Jerusha Boylston. Good news of successful inoculations may have spread through family contacts making it much easier to agree to the operation. In this respect Jerusha Boylston may have been a pivotal figure since all her children had been inoculated successfully during the first weeks after her husband began inoculating, so she could give personal testimony to the ease with which they had passed through inoculated smallpox.

Although these extended family networks seem strange to a modern eye, Puritans took the biblical adage that a man and woman became one flesh when they married seriously. Both sets of relatives became part of the family and the relationship persisted even after one partner died. Judge Samuel Sewall, for example, corresponded with at least 48 "cousins". *"Sewall could claim such a multitude of relatives because he recognized kinship with persons far beyond the limits we would today hold within the family pale"*.[19]

Just as individuals who were inoculated can be shown to share family, meeting house, or political links with each other, so can many of those who refused the operation. No member of the town government or their families was inoculated, and no members of the First Church, Elijah Cooke's church where the Rev. Harris, who had done so much to develop the moral arguments against inoculation, was minister, were inoculated. Elijah Cooke's political influence on the town's elected officials seems to have been an important factor in discouraging their participation while several members of the opposing faction the "Royalists" underwent inoculation.

American writers have usually concentrated on the bravery of Zabdiel Boylston for continuing to inoculate in the face of strong opposition. This is fair, but Cotton Mather is often relegated to the sidelines, credited for suggesting the operation and for persuading Boylston to take it up, but not given much credit for promoting the practice. Identifying the church and political affiliations of Boylston's patients suggests that Mather played a dominant role as chief persuader-the opinion leader. Boylston could only inoculate someone who asked for the operation. He was the operator, but Mather was the influential force.

The opponents of inoculation very nearly succeeded. The first adopters, the ones who showed that the operation was safe, came from only 3 families. Six were Boylston's own family, four were Webbs, and six were Langdons who were all members of Mather's congregation, as were the other five individuals. Political opposition nearly killed the project before it got going.

Chapter 10

PRISONERS AND ORPHANS

As HMS Seahorse carried smallpox into Boston harbor Lady Mary Wortley Montague sent for Charles Maitland, the Scottish surgeon who had been part of her husband's entourage during his ambassadorship in Turkey. Now back in London, she wanted him to inoculate her five year old daughter, also called Mary, who had not been inoculated in Istanbul because her nurse had not had smallpox. Maitland was reluctant, perhaps fearing for his professional reputation if he undertook a potentially dangerous practice. Eventually he persuaded Lady Mary to allow three physicians to witness the procedure and the child's course. In late April young Mary became the first person inoculated in England.[1]

Among the witnesses was James Keith. He had already lost two of his sons to smallpox and was anxious to preserve their sole surviving brother. He prevailed upon Maitland to inoculate the boy who did well.

While Boston was seething with anger over Boylston's audacious practice, events were moving slowly and quietly in London. Lady Mary extolled the success of her daughter's treatment among her society friends, and inoculation became a topic for polite conversation, but nothing appeared in the press[2] The court became interested. Sir Hans Sloane, president of the Royal College of Physicians, recollected that the operations of little Mary and young Keith had coincided with a severe bout of smallpox affecting Princess Anne, the oldest daughter of the Prince and Princess of Wales. The child was so ill that Sloane thought that she might die. Fearing for their two younger daughters the royal parents had consulted with him about whether the girls should be inoculated. Sloane was familiar with inoculation; he had participated in the discussions of inoculation at the Royal Society, but felt that tales from abroad and the good results in only two children were insufficient evidence of the benefits to justify recommending the operation for two such prominent children. He sought advice from a physician named Terry, who had practiced medicine in Turkey, who reassured him that the practice was always successful and never dangerous.[3] But by then Princess Anne had recovered and the threat to her sisters had receded. Inoculation seemed promising but no doctor would risk his reputation and livelihood on foreign rumours and good luck with two children. After all, natural smallpox was sometimes a very mild illness. Perhaps Lady Mary had been lucky.

In early June a group of physicians, probably led by Sloane, decided to pursue the issue. They petitioned the King through his legal advisers asking him to grant a reprieve to two condemned prisoners in Newgate prison *"upon condition that they will suffer to be tried upon them the experiment of inoculating the smallpox"*.[4] George I's advisors agreed that the lives of condemned prisoners were his to dispose of in any lawful way he chose, and thought some good might come from the experiment. In mid-June prisoners were offered remission of their sentences if they agreed to be inoculated.

Six prisoners who swore that they had not had smallpox were selected:[5,6]

Mary North, 36, had been tried on March 3, 1720 for shoplifting. Despite her defence that she was a lunatic, and her attempt to act crazy in court, she was convicted and sentenced to the new punishment of transportation, removing criminals to the American colonies rather than hanging them. A year later she was one of the first people convicted of returning from transportation without permission and sentenced to hang.

Ann Tompion, 25, alleged to be the best pickpocket in London, stood trial with her brothel keeper husband on October 12, 1720 for stealing 11 guineas from a woman they had lured into travelling down the Thames with them. Although their defence was based on the testimony of several whores in Tom Tompion's employment, Ann was convicted of theft.

John Cauthrey, 25, was convicted of the theft of three wigs from his master. Potentially a capital crime, since they were worth more than 5 shillings, the jury seems to have been moved to lenience and found that he was guilty only of theft to the value of 4s 10p, thereby reducing the sentence to transportation. Alone among the Newgate volunteers he was not facing the gallows.

John Allcock, 20, was charged with theft, animal theft, and grand larceny. In the space of a few days he had stolen a horse from Sarah Powell, a Holland shirt, silk handkerchief, and cravat from Charles Blanchard, and a pair of silver spurs from a Mr. Barlow. When apprehended he confessed and returned the stolen property, but was still convicted on all three charges.

Richard Evans, 19, was indicted and convicted for stealing 14 yards of Persian silk and a riding hood from the shop of Samuel and Richard Dickens.

Elizabeth Harrison, 19, confessed that she had stolen the huge sum of 62 guineas from her mistress. Tempted by the cash, and with access to the key to the trunk where the money was kept, she could not resist pilfering small amounts until the whole sum had vanished.

Throughout July preparations for the experiment were underway at Newgate. The King granted official remissions, changing the volunteers' sentences from death to transportation so long as they agreed to continue with the project. The Prince of Wales and his wife, Princess Caroline of Anspach, became official sponsors of the trial and gave it unparalleled stature. Several physicians and surgeons employed by the royal couple accompanied by their apothecary visited the prison and arranged to move the volunteers into more favourable accommodation.[7] The condemned cell, where they had lodged, was a stone walled room below ground, with an open sewer running down the middle of the airless room. Lice were so thick on the floor that they crunched whenever the prisoners walked around. The stench was legendary. Jail fever (typhus) was rampant. In this disgusting hole filled with the shouts and cries of the inmates many prisoners did not survive long enough to trouble the hangman.

The legal machinery moved forward. On July 4 they were given conditional pardons. On July 21 they were reprieved. If they went through with the operation they would be freed. Eventually, on Wednesday, August 9, 1721 the experiment began.[8] Maitland made incisions in both arms and the right leg of each prisoner and rubbed smallpox pus into the cuts. Sir Hans Sloane, President of the Royal College of Physicians and Vice President of the Royal Society, supervised operation along with John Steigherthal, the King's personal physician. About 25 physicians, surgeons, and apothecaries, among them many famous members of the Royal Society, witnessed the affair. One German observer noted that the prisoners shook with fear when Maitland took out his inoculation knife because their fellow inmates had told them that they were actually going to be bled to death.[9]

Mary North suffered from the "vapours" as she frequently did, but otherwise the prisoners had no symptoms. On Saturday Maitland felt that the wounds were not sufficiently inflamed and suspected that the inoculum he had used was defective because he had kept it overnight before he instilled it. He found a fresh supply and regrafted five of the prisoners in their arms. There was insufficient material to treat Evans a second time. But the surgeon had been unnecessarily pessimistic. The original incisions showed signs of infection the next day and on the seventh day after inoculation the first blemishes appeared on the convicts' faces.

It now emerged that Richard Evans had lied. He had had smallpox the previous September while in prison, and had pretended that he had not had it in the hope of escaping execution. Maitland noted that he had no symptoms at any time and that his inoculation sites did not become inflamed. This was an important piece of evidence that inoculation really did produce smallpox since it was well known that natural smallpox produced immunity to further infection. The failure of inoculation to have any effect meant that immunity worked in both directions. It also confirmed the accounts of Timonius and Pylarinius that inoculation had no effect on someone who had already had smallpox.

Despite the presence of their pustules, the five prisoners who developed smallpox remained healthy until, on the 10th day, Alcock added to the experiment when he used a pin to prick open his pocks believing the folk myth that this would prevent them forming scars. Maitland was annoyed. He had no idea what would happen to the boy as a result of his foolishness. Although Alcock was the most severely affected of the prisoners, he had only about sixty pocks, a trivial number compared to the hundreds or even thousands on a patient with natural smallpox. Maitland continued to observe his charges carefully, noting that all were progressing well and that the pocks duly dried up and dropped off , just as they would after a mild case of natural smallpox. Even Alcock's healed normally. On the sixth of September, the prisoners having recovered, the King completed his part of the bargain and they were all released. Evans, who could have been hung for lying, was forgiven.

Maitland admitted that he was surprised by the favourable outcome of the experiment since the prisoners had been given no special preparation. They had a very unfavourable *"habit of the body, and circumstances"*, not the least of which were the foul conditions in Newgate prison. During their illness an eminent "Turkey merchant" came to inspect the prisoners and their incisions and eruptions. He commented that the results were just like those he had observed in Constantinople, reinforcing the view that inoculation in England was as safe as it was in Turkey.[10]

Unaware of the tumultuous events in Boston, Charles Maitland went back to his life as a country surgeon. When the Newgate experiment was finished he returned home to Hertford, about thirty miles from London, where there was a particularly virulent outbreak of smallpox in progress. On October 2nd he inoculated two year old Mary Batt, daughter of a neighbour, Thomas

Batt. She had a very mild course, but produced an unexpected result when six of the Batt's servants, who were fond of cuddling and kissing little Mary, developed "the right natural smallpox". While three had the distinct sort, three had confluent disease and severe symptoms. Two recovered, but one maid, who would not follow her doctor's advice, died.[11]

Maitland's surprise at these secondary infections indicates that he had not considered whether inoculated smallpox could be contagious just like the natural, dangerous infection. Like Boylston, he had not appreciated the importance of taking steps to prevent the spread of smallpox after inoculation. However, this episode confirmed his belief that the mild disease following inoculation was truly smallpox, a crucial finding for later debates.

Ten days after inoculating Mary Batt he inoculated Joseph and Benjamin Heath. Three year old Benjamin had mild smallpox, but poor Joseph, *"being a fat, foul gluttonous boy, who would not be confined to the rules and directions I had strictly charged his mother with, as to diet and keeping warm"*, had severe symptoms before the pocks came out and many pustules when they did appear.

"What a difference there is to be observed between these two boys. The reason of it seems to be plainly this: the younger, who had the favourable kind, was of a clean habit, moderate appetite and easily governed during the whole process. The elder was not only, as I have said of a gross, foul constitution, but likewise had a voracious appetite, always eating and filling his belly with the coarsest food; as cheese, fat country pudding, cold boiled beef, and the like...nor was there any care taken to restrain or keep him within in cold, windy, frosty weather; he once wet his feet in the water..." [12]

Maitland's attitude towards Joseph's troubles was typical of 18th century medical thinking. Good health required a balance between four humours, which were in turn influenced by diet, weather, and physical circumstances. To a large extent health was the responsibility of the individual whose daily activities could affect the humoral balance. Disease was something you brought upon yourself and it was your responsibility to correct the problem and restore your own health. Doctors were an incidental part of the process and could be dispensed with if an individual took the right therapeutic measures. Maitland thought that Joseph Heath's problems stemmed from his intemperate diet which upset his internal equilibrium. Since he was a child he was only partially responsible for his condition, and the surgeon wondered whether he should have taken greater care and given more preparative treatment as a precaution before inoculating. Possibly a bland diet for several weeks, bleeding, or purging, or perhaps all three would have eased his symptoms. The Heath's four month old baby caught natural smallpox from her brothers, further supporting the identity of inoculated and natural disease and the risk of contagion.

Sir Hans Sloane was convinced by the Newgate experiment that inoculation resulted in mild smallpox. However, there was no evidence that inoculation conveyed immunity from natural infection, and without immunity the procedure was pointless, so Sloane and Stiegherthal decided to test whether Elizabeth Harrison really was immune.[13] They paid for her to accompany Maitland home where she was put to work nursing a servant with smallpox. When a boy at the local school came down with the severe form of the disease she was ordered to sleep in the same bed with him throughout his illness. After ten weeks of continual exposure to patients with the most extreme forms of the disease she had not contracted the infection. Maitland accepted that this proved that Harrison's inoculation had produced immunity because she would surely have caught the disease after this much time had she not been immune.

The medical evidence seemed conclusive, at least to those who wanted to believe it. Inoculation transferred true smallpox, not some other disorder, and it resulted in immunity just like the natural disease. However, Princess Caroline was not yet ready to try the operation on her own children. She wondered whether the fact that the Newgate patients were adults might have made a difference to the positive result. Would the procedure be as successful when children were inoculated?[14] To find out she ordered that a list of all the orphan children in the care of St. James's parish, Westminster, be prepared so that they could be inoculated at her expense.[15] And she asked Maitland to stand by to carry out the operation. But something happened which delayed the experiment. The likely explanation for the Princess's attack of cold feet was the arrival of a letter from Boston reporting the death of Mrs, Dixwell.[16]

In February 1723, when Maitland finally published his account of the Newgate experiment and the subsequent inoculations of the Batts and Heaths, and Elizabeth Harrison's immunity, he claimed that he had been ready to print it in November but had been delayed by the Princess's unwillingness to proceed. At the end of November an extract of the evidence presented to the Boston selectmen found its way into the London newspapers.[17] Dalhonde's damning testimony was prominent; so was the news that Boylston had been ordered to abandon the procedure. All the news available in London pointed to catastrophic results of inoculation in Boston.

As winter wore on the picture became cloudier. Cotton Mather sent an account of Boylston's experiment that was entirely enthusiastic.[18] Mrs. Dixwell's death was not thought to be due to her inoculation. Also Reverend Benjamin Colman's very personal description of the relative gentleness of inoculated smallpox compared to the natural disease was in print. He had even leant over to smell inoculated patients and confirmed that they did not have the disgusting stench associated with the real disease. He likened the comparison as being *"From a Place of Horror into a Garden of Pleasure"*.[19] Another Puritan minister, based in London, Daniel Neal added a historical account of the Boston experience to Colman's book pointing out that with over two hundred patients and only three or four deaths the Boston experience was much larger that that in all Europe and worth considering.[20]

But William Douglass once again muddied the waters.[21] He wrote another pamphlet to Alexander Stuart reiterating his views that Boylston and Mather were lying and concealing the true consequences of their experiment from the public. They had defended their behaviour by citing the testimony of Negro slaves, and everyone knew what liars they were. Douglass claimed that the inoculators were making it impossible to give any reasonable assessment of inoculation by their actions. It seemed a shame that potentially valuable information was lost, however, Douglass did concede two crucial points. Some of the patients did develop smallpox and it was nearly always mild. Furthermore no one inoculated had come down with smallpox during the ensuing six months suggesting that it provided short term immunity. Perhaps it would be useful for slave merchants to protect their cargoes while at sea, he suggested.

Maitland did perform a few private inoculations in December 1721[22], and then, at the end of February 1722, inoculated six parish orphans under the patronage of the Prince and Princess of Wales. An official announcement on March 10th invited *"the curious may be further satisfied by a sight of those persons at Mr. Foster's house ….where attendance is given every day from ten to twelve before noon, and from two till four afternoon"*.[23] Two weeks later a further official statement was released *"clearing up all doubts relating to the inoculation of the smallpox"* suggesting that the opposition press and gossip mongers were spreading fanciful accounts of undeclared catastrophes.[24] Anti-inoculation sentiment seems to have been widespread. Lady Mary recalled that some of her fashionable acquaintances cut her dead, others encouraged their servants to chastise hers for allowing their mistress to mistreat her children, and sometimes total strangers hissed at her in the street.

The long delayed inoculation of the Westminster orphans, which Princess Caroline had announced in November, was planned for late March. However, when she learned that the children were half-starved and sickly, as were all orphans in the care of parish authorities, she consulted Sloane. His opinion, that it was safe to inoculate them, persuaded her to carry on with the trial. The children, like all the other London guinea pigs, had mild smallpox and recovered without mishap.

Chapter 11

PHYSICIAN OF HALIFAX

W hile Maitland fretted over the delay, a second English physician began to inoculate 200 miles north of London in the Yorkshire dales. Thomas Nettleton M.D. was born in Dewsbury, West Yorkshire, and studied medicine at Utrecht, a leading Dutch medical school favoured by British students. He obtained his degree for a thesis on "Inflammations" and returned home to begin practicing in the parish of Halifax.[1]

West Yorkshire in winter is a cold windy place. Low hanging mist, rain, sleet, and snow sweep across the moorland. Days are short; there are only about eight hours of sunlight on the few clear days. In December 1721 Nettleton found himself facing an outbreak of epidemic smallpox in this bleak countryside.

"Having too often found with no small grief and trouble, how little the assistance of art cou'd avail in many cases of the smallpox, I was induced to try the method of incision or inoculation which came so well recommended by many physicians from Turkey and which had lately been practised in London. This I thought was sufficient to justify the Attempt"[2]

Unlike Zabdiel Boylston, who had Mather's support and encouragement, or Charles Maitland, who on drew his Turkish experience and the support of Hans Sloane and the royal family,

Nettleton would embark on inoculation alone. Among his first experiences was the sort of clinical dilemma that disturbs any physician

"The eighth and ninth (cases he inoculated) *were in a family where they had four children, none of whom had had the smallpox. I was called to the eldest, who was seized in the natural way with the most malignant sort I ever saw, attended with the worst symptoms that could be, insomuch that he died on the fourth day, all full of purple and livid spots. The parents were very desirous that any means might be used to preserve the rest; but here I was in great doubt and perplexity how to act. I knew very well that if I should venture to make the incision, whatever should happen would be charged against that, and it was not improbable, but some of them might have already taken the infection, in which case it was uncertain what the event might be. On the other hand, if it was omitted, I did very much fear they might all die, such instances having been known, and the contagion, which has got among them, being of such destructive nature. Wherefore I was willing to run the risk of my reputation, rather than the children should all perish."*[3]

He put his career on the line and proceeded with the operation.

Based on his observations of only six patients he knew that the inoculation would not produce any symptoms for at least seven days. He warned the parents that he could not guarantee success if the children were already infected and went ahead. As he feared, three days later one of the children developed the same hemorrhages shown by her brother and died on the seventh day. Her brothers developed smallpox on the eighth day, typical of inoculation, and survived.[4]

In all he had successfully inoculated 40 people and noted that none of his patients had caught natural smallpox even though they often nursed other family members or neighbours during the epidemic.

Nettleton's lonely campaign was made more difficult by the reaction of his neighbours in the parish of Halifax. It met with *"the vigorous opposition from many honest and well meaning persons"* who believed it *"an unlawful and unwarrantable practice"*.[5] Opponents were in the great majority, and, like the Boston anti-inoculators, spread rumours of dreadful consequences. The physician regretted that these misrepresentations had caused many to refuse inoculation for themselves or their children who then died unnecessarily. His motive for introducing the practice was, *"so far from knowing that it was a crime, I always thought the duty of our profession to do whatever we could to preserve the lives of those who commit themselves to our care."*[6] Eventually Nettleton's courageous care for his patients would provide one of the foundations for the complete vindication of inoculation. He wrote a description of his experiences with inoculation to a friend, William Whitaker, who passed the letter to James Jurin, secretary to the Royal Society. Nettleton provided an independent confirmation of the utility of the procedure under circumstances that differed greatly from the controlled experiments in London.

By the end of March 1722, over seventy individuals had been inoculated in England and there had been no deaths. The Princess consulted Sloane, who, ever the politician, equivocated. *"I told her Royal Highness that by what appeared in the several essays, it seemed to be a method to people from the greatest dangers attending that distemper in the natural way…but not being certain of the consequences … I would not persuade nor advise the making of trials on patients of such importance to the public. The Princess then asked me if I would dissuade her from it; to which I made answer that I would not. "*[7] Caroline ordered Sloane to seek permission from the King. *"I told his majesty my opinion, that it was impossible to be certain, but there might be dangerous accidents not foreseen: To which he replied, that such might have happened to persons taking physic in any distemper".*[8]

On April 17 1722, Princess Amelia, 11, and Princess Caroline, 9, were inoculated by the King's Huguenot surgeon, Claude Amyand, with help from the more experienced Maitland. Since the girls knew Amyand and would be more comfortable with him, he made the actual incisions while Maitland pinched the skin where the incisions would be placed and supplied the pus. Sloane and Steigherthal supervised the affair and were responsible for the children's care during their ensuing mild illness.[9]

This should have been the end to any debate concerning the acceptability and advisability of inoculation. The royal Family was the final arbiter of lawful practice and fashion. The King's own physicians and surgeon had approved the procedure. No higher authority existed. However, one of Maitland's patients, the four-year-old son of the Earl of Sutherland, died four days after the princesses' operation. Sutherland, a well-known politician, had himself died four days before his son, so the family was said to have had been cursed by the father's actions and more disasters were forecast. General anxiety concerning the princesses followed until it was clear that their course was benign. But this death, which was widely reported, cast a pall over inoculation and reinforced fears of its safety.[10]

Amyand inoculated his own two children on the same day that he operated on the royal daughters, and on the following day he operated on the six children of Lord Bathurst. A few days later he treated the Marquis of Middlesex, son of the Duke of Dorset, followed by two children of the Earl of Berkeley.[11] Maitland inoculated nineteen others in the month following the royal experiment. But in mid-May a second tragedy occurred. One of Lord Bathurst's footmen, a "strong hail young man" of nineteen died after being inoculated. He had been exposed to the Earl's inoculated children, and was treated to prevent his catching the natural infection from them. Opposition, slow to develop in London, now rose, and an "inoculation war" began fuelled by newspapers with opposing political views.

Chapter 12

WHIGS AND TORIES

Two deaths following inoculation opened the door for opponents of the royal family to use the practice to attack the government. English politics at the time was divided into two camps; Whigs who were largely supporters of the Hanoverian King George I and were often religious dissenters who disagreed with Church of England practices, and Tories who believed that the rightful King was Charles III, the son of King James II who had been deposed in the Glorious revolution of 1688. They were often "high flying" Anglicans who supported religious practices very similar to those of the Roman Catholic Church and were "non-jurors" because they could not take an oath to support the King. Whigs naturally supported inoculation, at least in part, because it was sponsored by the Prince and Princess of Wales and had been approved by the King. The ensuing row threatened to destroy the reputation of inoculation. But attempts by its supporters to counter their critics not only rescued inoculation, but led to the first flowering of scientific medicine.

The first critic to publish was Legard Sparham, a surgeon, who produced a pamphlet opposing the operation, "*Reasons against the Practice of Inoculating the Smallpox*," at the end of May 1723.[1] His rambling text revolved around two ideas: that rubbing poison into

a wound was dangerous, and that the disease produced by inoculation was not true smallpox and therefore could not protect against
further infection. He misinterpreted Nettleton's experience, con-
centrating on the few, mild complications which had occurred,
rather than the much more frequent successful outcomes. When
trying to point out the irrationality of inoculation he wrote *"Nor
can reason justify the contrary; for the condition of this matter, thus
infused, will always be the same; that unless we suppose some singular
virtue to remain in the blood as a proper antagonist, it would be absurd
to think them secure from a second infection"*. Had Sparham been a
cleverer man, or had he been able to overcome his prejudices and
accept the evidence that inoculation did produce protection, he
would have discovered the science of immunology. Immunity is
indeed due to "proper antagonists" in the blood.

Sparham thought inoculation an outlandish, calamitous innovation. It was similar to the South Sea Bubble, rampant stock
market manipulation that had ruined the fortunes of many members of society in 1720. Now people were "bubbling" their health,
not their money. He compared the idea of preventing a severe
disease by introducing a trial episode to a soldier asking to be
shot to prepare himself for battle. Sparham even suggested that
Nettleton's letter was a fake concocted by London pro-inocula-
tors to counteract criticism. He claimed that the physician did
not exist and his report was entirely fictitious. Sparham's booklet
was presented to the Royal Society where it received a unique
reception; it was not discussed, and the author was not thanked.[2]

Shortly after this appeared, on July 8th, the Reverend Edmund
Massey spoke from the pulpit of St. Andrew's Church, Holborn,
giving his religious objections to inoculation in *"A Sermon against
the dangerous and sinful practice of inoculation"*.[3] Starting from the
supposition that the devil had inoculated Job with smallpox when
he tormented him with the plague of boils, Mr. Massey argued
that this showed that inoculation had come from the Devil and
was therefore a diabolical, sinful practice. He chose to consider
two points *"For what causes are disease sent among mankind?"* and
"Who is it that has the power of inflicting them?" In addressing the
first of these questions he decided *"disease is sent either for the*

trial of our faith, or for the punishment of our sins." In either situation, preventing disease interrupts God's plan. Without the miseries of smallpox, he argued, faith could not be tested. Without the horrible consequences of infection our sins go unpunished; a catastrophe as unpunished sins lead straight to hell. Without threat of punishment, what vile, lascivious practices might we all indulge in? To the second query he replied *"God sends disease"*. Therefore it is a sin for man to claim God's prerogative by artificially transmitting smallpox. *"I shall not scruple to call that a Diabolical Operation which usurps an authority founded neither in the laws of nature or religion, which tends in this case to banish providence out of the world, and promotes the increase of Vice and Immorality."* He thundered a condemnation of all who supported inoculation *"I hope the time is coming that these Spreaders of Infection will be distinguished from those of the Faculty who deserve honour, and not permitted to mingle with them, as the Devil among the sons of God left like the Disease-giving Practitioner"*

The minister also tried to demonstrate that inoculation contravened the commandments. Lascivious thoughts were banned under the seventh commandment barring adultery on the grounds that anything that tends to promote a sin is as evil as the sin. Just so inoculation, which he perceived to be *"voluntary and causeless wounding, mutilation, etc."* and therefore barred by the sixth commandment against murder, which also covers all forms of physical injury. He finished with another blast at the physicians *"let the atheist, and the scoffer, the heathen and unbeliever, disclaim a dependence upon Providence, dispute the wisdom of God's government and deny obedience to his laws; Let them inoculate and be inoculated whose hope is only in and for this life!"*

Edmund Massey's use of the church of St Andrew Holborn to preach his anti-inoculation tract was a clear signal that high church Anglicans opposed inoculation. The minister in charge of St Andrews was Henry Sacheverell, a notorious high churchman who had instigated riots when he opposed the religious policies of the Whigs.

As Massey became the main theological opponent, so William Wagstaffe emerged as the most significant medical critic of inoculation. A fellow of both the College of Physicians and the Royal Society, and a well known wit, he was physician to St. Bartholomew's Hospital, the most ancient of the London hospitals. He spelt out the conservative view of inoculation in "*A Letter to Dr. Friend shewing the Danger and Uncertainty of Inoculating the Smallpox*".[4] He began by appealing to the Englishman's innate sense of superiority "*Posterity will scarcely be brought to believe that an experiment practised only by a few ignorant old women, amongst an illiterate and unthinking people, should on such slender experience, so far obtain in one of the Politest Nations in the world*". Wagstaffe also produced some sound critical arguments against the operation. Current medical theory held that the distinction between mild and confluent smallpox lay in the state of the patient's blood. Since this was an unknown variable, the inoculator could never be certain that he would always produce the milder form of the disease. Also, the correct dose of smallpox matter could not be determined. Wagstaffe asked how one could compare material derived from two different pustules and two different donors? Since a minute quantity of "pocky matter" seemed effective, how could the inoculator be sure he was not using a hundred times too much material with consequent fatal results? Experience and time might resolve these concerns but they certainly argued against general use now. Any doctor who used the wrong dose would be guilty of a crime if the patient died.

Wagstaffe compared inoculation with the experiments on blood transfusion carried out by Richard Lower in the 1660s. He had successfully injected blood from one dog into another, but when he injected mercury or hydrochloric acid, the dog dropped dead. Wagstaffe argued that this showed that injecting foreign materials into the circulation was likely to be harmful. The only experience of injecting a disease that he was aware of concerned a transfusion between a mangy dog and a healthy one. This exchange produced an astounding result; the healthy dog did not develop mange, but the mangy dog got better. The unexpected outcome was eventually explained by reasoning that the benefits of the transfusion had resulted from bleeding the sick dog and had nothing to do with the healthy transfusion, reinforcing the idea that transferring disease by inoculation might well have unforeseen results. But these were experiments on animals. No one had even considered trying to transfer disease between humans, and it was unwise to do so since the results of the animal experiments were ambiguous. Physicians had enough to do in curing diseases without also spreading them.

Another objection was that the disease that was produced by inoculation was not true smallpox but some other form of "eruptive fever". Immunity could only develop if true smallpox was transmitted. Wagstaffe claimed that only about a quarter of Nettleton's patients had developed what seemed to him to be unequivocal smallpox. The rest, he thought, might have had chicken pox or some other kind of "pimples". Since the microbial nature of specific infection was unknown, the idea that one disease sometimes produced another was not far-fetched. Indeed, Wagstaffe cited a number of clinical cases from his own practice. *"there are examples, for instance, where a gonorrhoea has given a true pox, and where a pox, on the other hand has given a mere gonorrhoea"* In this case he seems to have ignored the possibility that the patient involved might have had both diseases and transmitted only one. He had other examples, however, which led him to believe that infection in general could be transmitted, but that the exact disease which resulted might not be the same as the original.

Fevers were thought to be a general type of disease and might evolve into any of several related conditions. When first confronted by a patient a physician often had only the presence of a fever and a sense of discomfort to guide his reasoning about the likely course of the disease. Fevers were undifferentiated until a characteristic rash appeared, and many believed that there was more than one possible outcome to a fever, and that the nature of the illness could be manipulated by treatment. Smallpox was not necessarily smallpox until the typical eruption appeared, so it could be argued that it was possible that giving an inoculum from smallpox might induce a different sort of fever, which evolved into a different disease. Wagstaffe supported his views with his own account of the Newgate experiment, denying that the prisoners had developed the real eruption of smallpox. He was certain that inoculation was producing something other than smallpox and therefore it could not prevent subsequent natural infection. After studying the various favourable reports in circulation he was able to pick out contradictions between them. Where some accounts said that the prodromal symptoms were very mild, Nettleton's account said that they were exactly like natural smallpox. The Turkish description said that the process was completely safe, yet Maitland and Boylston had had fatal cases. Some suggested that inoculation could not produce contagious disease, but Maitland's experience with the Batt family clearly showed that it was infectious and could be deadly. He also challenged the view that inoculation was safer than natural smallpox by claiming that the true mortality of natural smallpox was only about one in one hundred in London.

Wagstaffe reprinted all the negative information about inoculation that had arrived from Boston. He detailed the evidence that Dalhounde had given where it had been claimed that many previously inoculated individuals subsequently came down with the natural disease. He even said that he knew of one example in London where a child, who had been inoculated and had an eruption, had developed natural smallpox three months later. If true, this case showed that inoculation was not always protective and therefore not worth the risk. The whole issue was clouded by contradictory claims suggesting that the authors were actually doing different things. Which was the "real" inoculation, he wondered.

Picking up another theme first expounded by Douglass, Wagstaffe suggested that inoculation could transmit others diseases such as tuberculosis or syphilis, or even madness. Every surgeon knew that making wounds, as in bloodletting, sometimes led to an infection at the incision, and sometimes this produced an abscess or even a systemic infection. Why might the inoculation incisions not have the same ill consequences?

Reverend Edmund Massey's uncle, Isaac Massey, the apothecary to Christ's Hospital, the well-known charity which supported orphan children and trained them for military or domestic service, joined his nephew by attacking Maitland's morals claiming that at the time of the Newgate experiment he had seen the surgeon extolling the virtues of inoculation in Child's coffee-house where he seemed to be interested in employing the operation, regardless of its success, because he hoped to make a fortune from it.[5] He charged that Maitland really meant to say *"have patience with my Doctrine of Inoculation till I have rais'd a Fortune and am become Sir Charles, then let 'em damn both It and Me"."* *"And had it not been for some unlucky Miscarriages, the Inoculators would have had the best chance for full Practice and full Pockets, that ever fell into the Hands of so small a Set of Men"*. Maitland's claims that inoculation was always safe and effective were *"very like a Quack Doctor's printed Bill, whose Pill, or Bolus, is always Safe and Salutary; a noble preservative, and an infallible Cure: Fear not then, Gentlemen, venture your money and your Children, trust to inoculation with all its uncertain Effects, it will be a safe Preservative"*.

The apothecary argued that the practice should be made illegal. Smallpox usually caused abortion when a pregnant woman became infected, and he speculated that inoculation would be used as a means of inducing abortions to destroy unwanted pregnancies and would amount to the mortal sin of murder. He was also concerned that, because the operation was sometimes fatal, families might use it to eliminate unwanted children. He cited instances where a step-parent had killed off the child of a previous marriage to promote their own offspring. Even natural families might want to prune weak or scrofulous children to advance a healthy sibling. Since inoculation was more fatal to the weak and infirm, what better way to select for stronger heirs than by poisoning unfavoured children with smallpox?

Isaac Massey claimed that giving a disease to a healthy child was similar to carrying out dissection on criminals who were not quite dead. This revolting image was completely irrelevant, but he used it to argue that at least the criminal in this case would be dying and some good might come of the operation, whereas the inoculated child was completely healthy and no good could come from its death. At present *"Inoculation was so weakly supported by evidence or theory that it would be better known as Incantation."* The range of fantastic complications was truly terrifying: syphilis, scrofula, murder, abortion, live dissection, other unnamed but ghastly consequences; how could anyone undertake such a dangerous operation?

But amongst his list of horrors Massey made one telling criticism. Inoculation statistics were flawed because they did not compare like with like.[6] Most of those inoculated were healthy children, while most of those who died of smallpox were already ill, old, or very poor. Many who died had not had the benefit of good care during their illness, whereas the inoculated got the best possible support.

The inoculators found themselves under fire from senior churchmen and doctors on both moral and medical grounds.

Chapter 13

THE SUPPORTERS FIGHT BACK

Wagstaffe's damning appraisal drew a swift rebuttal from the inoculators.[1,2] The operation's incensed supporters rubbished Wagstaffe's letter. The most extensive critique was published by John Arbuthnot, an accomplished mathematician, renowned satirist, fellow of the Royal Society and the Royal College of Physicians, and formerly Queen Anne's physician.[3] He particularly attacked the flaw in Wagstaff's argument that allowed that inoculation might prove to be beneficial, but that only time and many experiments could prove it to be. How could anyone gain the necessary experience if inoculation were banned? How could any young physician learn anything if he was not allowed to practice and also not allowed to learn from his experienced colleagues? By advocating the seemingly reasonable line "wait for more experience" his opponent was actually making inoculation impossible, and also making all medical advances unlikely. That was absurd.

Those with direct experience of inoculation suggested that Wagstaffe had never observed patients through their whole course, so that his comments on their clinical state following the operation were bogus. Arbuthnot was particularly scathing about Wagstaffe's misreporting of the state of the Newgate prisoners.

He had seen them every day and was in no doubt that they had smallpox. By relying on hearsay, rather than personal observation, Wagstaffe was more than wrong; he was negligent. Samuel Brady, Physician to the garrison at Portsmouth, pointed out that all of the patients he had inoculated in Portsmouth had symptoms and progressed through the disease just like patients with natural smallpox. Nettleton had been misrepresented by Wagstaffe. He had actually stated that his patients had experienced an eruption and a sequence of symptoms identical to mild smallpox. Arbuthnot claimed that Wagstaffe was acting on "reports" rather than personal observation, and that such a prominent physician really ought to know better. By denying what many who had attended the Newgate experiment had stated was true, ie that the pustules which followed inoculation were the same as the pustules of real smallpox, and that the symptoms, although few, were identical to those experienced during a mild case of the natural infection, Wagstaffe was making a fool of himself.

There was another contradiction in Wagstaffe's argument which the supporters of inoculation seized upon. At one point he argued that inoculation did not produce smallpox, and therefore it was useless, but at another point, he argued that the disease was smallpox, and therefore was dangerous to both the inoculated and their contacts. Which did he believe? Asked Arbuthnot. If he were any kind of experienced physician he would have recognised the symptoms as genuine and realised that the operation produced true smallpox.

Arbuthnot turned the Boston letters back on Wagstaffe when he seized on the phrase "*the effects seem less mortal, and the symptoms easier*" in one of Douglass's letters as evidence that even an outright opponent saw the benefits of inoculation.[4] The Boston trial of inoculation had been communicated by well-respected sources such as Cotton Mather and Benjamin Colman, and, with over two hundred cases, the Boston experience was significantly greater than that in England, and therefore carried great weight. Inoculation's opponents could only cite the death of Mrs. Dixwell to support their claim that the practice was dangerous, and the Boston ministers had disputed that she actually died of smallpox. They held that she had died of epilepsy after her inoculation-induced disease was over. If there were many others who died of inoculation, as Douglass alleged, where were their bodies? "*Under a dung heap*?" perhaps.[5] But then why didn't the physicians of Boston who had opposed inoculation, and who had attended the dying not make these cases known? Surely some of these phantom dead would have come to light? Despite all the attention thrown onto inoculation in London, its opponents could only name three who had died: William Spencer, Lord Bathurst's footman, and Sarah Dixwell. . Where were the mysterious "others" whose names weren't known but whose rumoured deaths discredited the operation? Raising these questions exposed the opponents' dependence on supposition and hearsay; they had no factual evidence for their claims. All reports, even Douglass's grudging admission, favoured inoculation, therefore Wagstaffe's position resulted from bigotry; he had made his mind up, was incapable of recognising the truth, and would stretch to any argument to discredit the practice.

Several physicians pointed out that his arguments against inoculation could just as easily be applied to any new medicine and, in effect, meant that no medical advances could ever occur. He was arguing in exactly the same way as his predecessors in the Royal College of Physicians had argued when they had opposed the introduction of "Bark" (quinine) for malaria. Now it was widely used, and very beneficial. But this medicine had originally been discovered by savage Indians and promoted by Jesuits, even worse than the heathen Mohammedans and the "old Greek lady" of Constantinople who introduced inoculation. Time and careful observation was the way to answer any questions about doses or methods of proceeding with inoculation, not a blanket ban, which would deny humanity the benefits of this method of preserving a great many lives and preventing much misery. Wagstaffe had argued that only further experience could reveal the value and dangers of inoculation, but he had argued that no further tests should be performed. How was experience to be gained if not by actual inoculation? He had contradicted his own argument.

Arbuthnot's pamphlet finished with a series of signed testimonies, probably collected by Maitland, which refuted specific examples used by Wagstaffe to support his argument. He had cited the case of Mr. Degreave's daughter whom, he alleged, had a successful inoculation followed by natural smallpox three months later. Maitland published an affidavit from Mr. Degreave. His daughter had the smallpox once, not twice, and in his view it was a delayed response to inoculation.[6] Anti-inoculators cited her case as an example of successful inoculation failing to produce immunity, but her father affirmed that he had observed her every day for the first three weeks and that she did not develop an eruption. She had remained slightly unwell for eleven weeks and then a true mild smallpox eruption appeared. Some confusion had arisen from the fact that she also had scabies, (the Itch), which produced a rash, but she had caught this from her brother and it had been successfully treated. The claims that she had two episodes of smallpox were false. Although rare, such cases of a delayed response to inoculation had featured in the reports from Constantinople so the child was not unique.

The post mortem reports on both the Spencer boy and Lord Bathurst's servant were also published. The child was found to have had hydrocephalus and was known to have had convulsions during life. Since he died during an epileptic fit, it was likely that this resulted from his previous condition and not from inoculation. Lord Bathurst's servant had died with pneumonia and confluent smallpox. However, an exact record of the clinical events revealed that he had been exposed to the Bathurst children several days before inoculation, and that his clinical symptoms had begun before the seventh day after the operation suggesting that he had a natural, not inoculated, infection. Finally, Artbuthnot appended recent letters from Mather and Nettleton who reported success in over 300 cases.

While the attack on Wagstaffe was intense, Arbuthnot's reply to Rev. Massey was scathing. As Arbuthnot said, "the charge against the inoculators is heavier... in as much as immorality is a greater fault than bad practice in physic".[7] Inoculation's supporters set out to ridicule the poor minister. Did the Devil really produce the first inoculation on Job? Well then where did he get the pus, since smallpox was unknown in biblical times? Job was also singularly unlucky, most patients recover from the disease in two to three weeks, but the poor man had suffered for years. Yet Job was also very fortunate because he had confluent smallpox without the usual distressing symptoms such as sore throat, shortness of breath, or delirium.

Charles Maitland also published a letter replying to Massey who had charged the inoculators with great cruelty to the prisoners in Newgate because no known system of justice forced felons to suffer a horrible disease. To this Maitland replied that *"they preferred it to hanging"*. The minister seemed to have invented a new religious maxim *"do not do good, lest evil come of it"*. If removing the fear of mortal smallpox tended to encourage lascivious behaviour, so must all medicine. At least all effective medicine; treatments that were not beneficial would be acceptable to the minister. Maitland commented with heavy sarcasm *"Could I then by one pleasant dose cure a distemper, I ought not to communicate the dangerous secret, but deprive mankind of so valuable a discovery lest some senseless clown should be encouraged to drink a pot of ale more than he might otherwise."* [8]

All those who wrote supporting inoculation agreed that Mr. Massey had been intemperate and uncivil, even unchristian, in his invective. Massey attempted a reply but was reduced to whingeing that he had not intended the Job text as anything more than a metaphor. His explanation did not ring true, and only found credence among those who already opposed inoculation.

Although the supporters and opponents split along party lines, there is one curious exception[9]. John Arbuthnot, the most eloquent supporter of inoculation was a Tory. He published his long tract under the title "Mr. Maitland's Account"[10] and his name does not appear anywhere in the document, yet he is universally considered to be the author. Arbuthnot may have preferred anonymity to protect his standing among fellow Tories. If many of his wealthy patients were professed or secret Tories his espousal of inoculation might have disgusted them and led them to seek another physician.

Chapter 14

THE CALCULUS OF PROBABILITY

One claim made by Wagstaffe and Isaac Massey triggered the most significant result of the whole inoculation controversy. Both claimed that the mortality from smallpox was much lower than people thought. Wagstaffe argued that the recent London Bills of Mortality showed that the death rate was about one in one hundred, and Massey claimed that there had been no deaths among over one hundred boys under his care. Was smallpox really less dangerous than commonly believed?

Was inoculation really safe?

Amidst the storm of controversy how could anyone prove that inoculation was beneficial? Both sides held strong opinions but there were few facts available, and these were disputed. Even the most basic information about smallpox was missing. No one had ever determined what the chances of dying from it were so there was nothing to compare with inoculation.

John Arbuthnot, Cotton Mather, and Thomas Nettleton, [1, 2, 3] among others had argued that only experience could give a reliable picture of the merits of inoculation. By experience they meant what we would now call evidence, that is the results of inoculating a large number of individuals to determine exactly what happened. Such "experience" could then be compared with the evidence of a large group of patients suffering from natural smallpox. In 1714 a French mathematician, Jacob Bernoulli, had published the "law of large numbers", which stated that it was possible to predict the composition of a mixture of different coloured pebbles if enough samples had been taken. It would be possible to predict *"how much more likely one disease is to be fatal than another-plague than dropsy....or dropsy than fever – and on that basis make a prediction about the relationship between life and death in future generations."*[4.] If enough experience was collected it would be possible to determine the likely outcome of a case of smallpox. But Bernoulli's theorem had never been tested and no one knew how to apply it to a realistic problem such as smallpox. To many of the general public and most ministers of religion the idea that it was possible to calculate the chances of living or dying seemed blasphemous. Only God could know such things. His intentions were not predictable.

In November 1721 James Jurin was elected Secretary of the Royal Society. It was an auspicious conjunction of man and moment. Jurin was both a mathematician and a physician.[5] An acolyte of Newton's, he was interested in attempting to apply mathematical analysis to medicine. He had studied mathematics at Cambridge and worked as a headmaster at a school in Newcastle, where he was one of the first followers of Newton to offer a series of public lectures on applications of mathematics to practical problems encountered in coal and lead mining. Almost any machine could be explained in mathematical terms, and enthusiasts like Jurin offered to explain the principles to all comers, even those with no prior mathematical knowledge. His espousal of Newtonian mathematics, and the implications for understanding the forces that underlay natural science alienated the Jacobite-leaning Northerners so he left abruptly and returned to Cambridge to study medicine at the relatively old age of 31.

After receiving his medical degree Jurin maintained his mathematical interest by joining the "iatromechanicals", an informal group of physicians who tried to apply mathematics to physiological problems such as the strength of the contraction of the heart or the flow of blood in tubes. His career was promoted by his maternal uncle, Caleb Cotesworth, who was a socially prominent physician and member of the Royal Society. Although a newcomer to the overlapping circles of medicine and science in London, Jurin's many friends among mathematicians and natural philosophers from his Cambridge days gave him easy access to this august company. Within two years he had been elected a Fellow of the Royal Society, within five he had been elected its Secretary.

Jurin had arrived at the centre of British scientific life at a crucial moment. The Secretary was responsible for the Society's correspondence with a far flung network of reporters. Some were traders who reported unusual phenomena witnessed on their travels. Some were obscure colonial backwoodsmen who provided information about rattlesnakes and native remedies for snakebite. But others were the leading scientists of the age. Antoni van Leeuwenhoek, who had invented the compound microscope, sent his first views of the microscopical world to the Royal Society. Along with his drawings came his commentary, written in Dutch. It was part of the Secretary's job to arrange for the translation and publication of these seminal works.

The Secretary was responsible for the publication of the "Philosophical Transactions", the Royal Society's journal, where papers presented to the weekly meeting of the society were printed, along with any of the many letters that poured into their offices which he thought would be interesting to the journal's subscribers. The Society tried, with mixed success, to act as a focus for scientific works published in foreign languages. Many scientific treatises were still written in Latin, and many interested natural philosophers could not read them. By translating them into English the Society made them accessible to a wider audience. The Transactions became essential reading for anyone interested in the natural sciences. Mather and Nettleton both learned of inoculation from the translations of Timonius and Pylarinus published there in 1714 and 1716.

Inoculation was an issue that aroused enormous interest within the Royal Society. While most Fellows believed that it was beneficial, there was no conclusive proof. Thomas Nettleton had written to a friend, William Whitaker, in London, in early April 1722 presenting the positive results of his first forty inoculations.[6] His letter added to the weight of evidence in favour of the practice just as the decision to inoculate the Princesses was taken. Whitaker had shown the letter to several members of the Royal Society, among them James Jurin, who recognised its value and offered to publish it in the Transactions. Jurin wrote to Nettleton requesting more information, and the physician reported that he had inoculated another 15 individuals with the same success as before.[7] This letter, whose significance will become clear, is attached to the version of his letter to Nettleton intended for the Philosophical Transactions. It appears almost as an afterthought and confusingly is dated June 16th 1722, while the main part of the letter on the same paper is dated April 3rd 1722. It appears that Nettleton prepared his manuscript of the Whitaker pamphlet dated April 3rd as Jurin had requested, and tacked on the second letter at the end. In this second letter he revealed his motivation for beginning the practice, despite the objections and opposition of many of his neighbours.. *"I had, as well as all others who have been engaged in the Practice, with sufficient Sorrow and concern, been called to many in the Small Pox, whose Cases were so deplorable, as to admit of no relief. And therefore I coul'd not but be very thoughtful about this Method, which promised to carry many Persons thro' that cruel Distemper, with so much ease and safety. I was so far from knowing that it was a Crime , that I always thought it the Duty of our Profession, to do whatever we could to preserve the Lives of those who commit themselves to our care; And I knew no reason why we ought not, with all humble thankfulness to Almighty God , to make use of any means which his good providence shall bring to light conducing to that End. ..But when we had the account in the Publick Papers that it had by their Royal Highness's Command been done with success in London, I could not be satisfied without trying it here. I was soon convinced that it was of great use."* [8]

Nettleton suggested that the way to prove that inoculation was safe was to determine the mortality of natural smallpox and compare it to the mortality of inoculation. *"Sir, I doubt not that when you have collected a sufficient Number of Observations for it, you will be able to demonstrate, that the Hazard in this Method is very inconsiderable, in proportion to that in the ordinary way by accidental Contagion…I have made some enquiry hereabouts, and I shall take the freedom to transmit the Accounts to you because I believe that you can depend upon their being taken with sufficient care and impartiality".*[9] In Halifax, Rochdale, and Leeds, three substantial West Yorkshire towns, he found that there had been 1,245 cases of smallpox and 270 deaths, approximately one in five. None of his sixty inoculated patients had died. In this letter, dated June 16, 1722, Thomas Nettleton arguably produced the first example of scientific medicine. There are no earlier examples of a quantitative comparison between a treatment and a disease or, as in this case, two ways of contracting an illness. Jurin had the letter read to the Royal Society meeting on June 21 and had it published in the next issue of the Philosophical Transactions.

William Wagstaffe had claimed that the rate of mortality on smallpox was only about one percent, so that inoculation had no role in preventing death from the disease.[10] To refute Wagstaffe's claim, John Arbuthnot had attempted to calculate the death rate from smallpox from figures available in the London Bills of Mortality.[11] Over the 12 years between 1707 and 1718 about one in twelve burials was due to smallpox. However, this was only a crude approximation since the bills included many burials of stillborn babies and children under the age of one who had little chance of catching smallpox. He reasoned that since about one in four children born died before they were one year old, the real mortality rate in smallpox was about one in ten of those over the age of one who were able to catch the disease. Since not everyone caught smallpox, the true rate of mortality was probably greater; if only half the population caught smallpox then one in five of them would die.

John Arbuthnot was one of the first (possibly **the** first) to suggest that experience, by which he meant evidence, obtained by sampling from a population, might reveal the characteristics of the whole population. In 1692 he introduced his translation of text by Christiaan Huygens on the mathematics of determining the odds at games of dice with an example.[12] Whereas the chances of a particular result in gaming could be calculated from knowing the number of dice and the number of spots on each die, some probabilities could only be determined following experience, that is, evidence obtained by taking a sample from the group in question. He suggested that it would be possible to determine the probability that a young woman was a virgin or that a London man about town had had gonorrhea if he asked a large enough sample of the relevant group. He implied that if a sample of girls showed that only one in three was still a virgin then it was likely that only one in three of all the girls in London were virgins. Unfortunately he never published the results of his sampling. Arbuthnot would use this principle to try to make a more accurate estimate of the risk of dying after inoculation compared to the risk after natural smallpox. He had seen the figures recently sent to the Royal Society by Thomas Nettleton and appended Nettleton's paper, published in the Philosophical Transactions, to his own pamphlet. He estimated that the mortality from natural smallpox was about one in ten, and, so far, there had been no deaths from inoculated smallpox in Nettleton's hands. Thus "experience" showed that there was a marked difference in the chances of dying from natural as opposed to inoculated smallpox.

When Arbuthnot cited Nettleton's letter of June 16th as evidence, supporting the view that Wagstaffe had miscalculated the mortality of natural smallpox and that inoculation was the safer option, he produced one of the first examples of what is now known as "evidence- based medicine", the concept that numerical evidence rather that tradition or opinion of a single individual doctor in a handful of cases should determine the choice of medical treatments. Clinical trials to ascertain the value of particular treatments had been conducted throughout the twentieth century and "evidence- based medicine", which became fashionable in the late 20th century, was the idea that *all* treatments should be determined after fair trials whose results were widely publicised. Historians of evidence- based medicine usually trace its origins to mid nineteenth century France,[13] however, Arbuthnot, in 1722, is using numerical evidence obtained by Nettleton to argue the safety of inoculation compared to natural smallpox. Not only did he refute the arguments of Massey and Wagstaffe, he declared that "*Mankind in all those Matters* (medical and surgical) *govern themselves by the strongest Probabilities; and that these are on the Side of Inoculation, I shall plainly demonstrate*".[14]

Genevieve Miller and Angela Rusnock, historians of inoculation, have identified Nettleton's letter as the first use of quantitation in medicine.[15], [16]However, it is subtly more than that. Arguing from evidence rather than opinion or established practice for a particular treatment is still a controversial area in modern medicine. Even now, in the twenty first century, evidence-based medical practice is resisted by some doctors and the pharmaceutical industry.

Arbuthnot's treatise became part of the swirling pool of information both for and against inoculation. Quantitative evidence was a new way to determine probability or authority. Previously opinion, often the collected views of a group of acknowledged authorities, was the most common method to determine the best choice when two or more alternatives were available. Such authorities would argue from custom and established principles not from "experience". An observation needed to fit into an accepted theory before it could itself become accepted as a fact. Language, rhetoric, and the ability to frame a logical argument were more powerful than experience as ways to assess the probability of an argument being correct. Testimony was also an important part of determining the truth of events. For example, Maitland included signed witness statements from his patients and other witnesses to support the truth of the accounts of inoculation which he gave in his pamphlet.[17] Testimony of the original participants was essential to give a true picture of what had occurred. During the inoculation controversy, many false accounts of individual catastrophes appeared scattered among the genuine reports of disasters. Testimony was essential to separate reality from fiction, and was particularly useful when the outcome contradicted expectations.

Thomas Nettleton sent a third paper to London on December 16th 1722.[18] As secretary of the Royal Society, Jurin had been flattered by Nettleton's acknowledgement that the Philosophical

Transactions had been the source of his inspiration and asked him to confirm the crucial role of the Royal Society in his experiments. *"The obliging acknowledgement you are pleased to make of the knowledge received from the Philosophical Transactions was very agreeable to the Society and would be more so if you should think proper to mention it in the account which is to be made publick"*[19] Nettleton was pleased to agree. Jurin had also asked for further details of his progress. Nettleton spelled out his understanding of the inoculation controversy and the method by which it could be resolved:

"It is to me perfectly indifferent whether the thing is received or exploded. There are two propositions advanced by favoureres of the practice concerning which the public seems to require more full satisfaction. That the distemper raised by inoculation is really the smallpox and it is much more mild and favourable and far less mortal than the natural sort"[20]. By now no one seriously disputed that inoculation produced true smallpox. Nettleton asserted that all of the symptoms were exactly like those of the distinct form and that the number of pustules varied between patients and with them the severity of the illness, just like the natural disease. *"In short as this distemper is raised by an engraftment from the smallpox, as it has the same appearance, and is capable of producing the same infection there seems to be no room for doubt of it's being the true and genuine small pox. And if that be allowed it will follow from thence that those, who have been inoculated , are in no more danger of receiving the distemper again, than those who have had it in the ordinary way."*[21]

He pointed out that some of his patients had shown no effect following the operation and that in these cases the person had already had smallpox, indicating that immunity was the explanation. He also noticed that a few of his patients had eruptions that were so mild that it was hard to know whether they had actually been successfully inoculated. None of these individuals had caught the disease during the current epidemic despite being exposed to patients with natural smallpox and therefore even this very slight illness seemed sufficient to induce immunity.

"As to the latter proposition, that the ingrafted small pox is far less dangerous than the natural, the truth of this I suppose can only be found by making comparison so far as our experience will extend." He had

scoured West Yorkshire and adjacent Lancashire and reported 3405 cases of natural smallpox and 636 deaths. *"I am very sensible you will require a great number of observations before you can draw any certain conclusions".*[22] This letter was read to the Royal Society on December 20th 1722.

Jurin had clearly been thinking about the problem of smallpox mortality as well.[23] He accepted Nettleton's suggestion that larger numbers were required before the safety of inoculating could be demonstrated conclusively and set out to determine whether inoculation could be demonstrated to be less dangerous than natural smallpox. Neither the overall risk of dying from smallpox during one person's lifetime nor the risk of dying once you had caught the infection were known. He had made calculations similar to Arbuthnot's from the London Bills of Mortality and concluded that the chances of dying from smallpox were about one in eight. However, he recognised that there was a superior way of determining the risk which was to do as Nettleton had done and collect "experience", which could lead to a "calculus of probability". Jurin used "experience", by which he meant quantitative evidence, to develop his investigation into the value of inoculation. He recognised that there were many kinds of information that he could collect. What choices he made would determine the outcome of his project. With great insight into the pitfalls of complexity, he chose the simplest possible options. He would try to answer only three simple questions: what was the mortality rate with inoculation, what was the mortality rate of natural smallpox and were there any unequivocal examples of smallpox following successful inoculation? He neatly avoided all the problems of trying to measure complications or severity of symptoms which would have been almost impossible to determine for the natural cases. Any two physicians might disagree over whether a particular patient had severe smallpox or not, but not over whether the patient was dead. Death was an unarguable endpoint, an event that was not open to differences in interpretation or opinion. Jurin also avoided a possible point of contention when he chose not to try to determine whether a death was really due to inoculation. He would accept that, for his purposes, all deaths were equal.

Although he did record and publish the details of deaths following inoculation, he left the conclusions regarding the relevance of inoculation to the reader, and scored them all in the "dead" column. Thus freed from criticisms of selective reporting or biased interpretation, his simple mathematical comparison would be difficult to refute.

James Jurin had a clear idea of what he was trying to achieve. He needed to show that inoculation was both safe and protective against further smallpox. *"If these two points are effectually settled, there would, I suppose, be an end of the dispute, at least among physicians. For if either of them be fairly determined in the negative, the practice of inoculation must on all hands be given up. And on the other hand, if the test of experience should plainly declare for the affirmative side of both these questions, I doubt not but that every gentleman who has the honour to serve his country in the capacity of a physician will have integrity and humanity enough to declare himself honestly and openly in favour of the practice. At least he will consider whether it will be for his reputation, when his friend and his patient shall put his life, or the lives of his children, into his hands to amuse himself with theological disputes and scruples whether it be lawful to save them."*[24]

Jurin was not a completely unbiased observer. His intellectual circle centred on the Royal Society, which had already decided in favour of the operation. However, he was fair in presenting both positive and negative results and there is no evidence that he selected his results or suppressed fatal cases to make his point. Inoculation was such a controversial topic at the time that it seems likely that any death following inoculation would have been reported either to Jurin or in the press. Therefore the number of deaths that he records is likely to be accurate. Likewise his figures for deaths following natural smallpox were derived from careful house to house investigations, or from published bills of mortality. It is possible that some successful inoculations or some very mild cases of smallpox went unrecorded, but if these cases had been reported, they would only have increased the apparent safety of inoculation and slightly decreased the mortality rate of the natural disease; the overall conclusions would have remained the same. Although Jurin supported the practice it still needed to pass scientific scrutiny, and a mathematical analysis of the outcome of inoculation would be a powerful tool for convincing doubters.

In England the basis of knowledge was slowly changing from a world of words and arguments to a world of quantities and numbers. Jurin's motive was to provide the numbers that would refute the arguments of those who opposed inoculation. *"For if the practice of inoculation be really found to be a means of preserving life, it will not be easy to make the world believe that it is criminal to use it."* [25]

Jurin added the Yorkshire survey results to figures supplied by Dr Whitaker from Chichester and Dr Williams in Wales, which showed that 856 of 4626 natural smallpox cases had died. Therefore the rate of mortality from smallpox during the current epidemic was between one in five and one in six. He published these figures in his first pamphlet on the topic *"A Letter to the Learned Caleb Cotesworth F.R.S. of the College of Physicians, London, and Physician to St. Thomas's Hospital, containing a comparison between the danger of the Natural Small Pox and that given by Inoculation"* which was read to the Royal Society on Jan 23, 1723 and subsequently published in the *Philosphical Transactions* next to Nettleton's third letter.

Confusingly these two crucial papers are in Volume 32 number 374 dated November – December 1722 which completely muddles both the timing and the relationship between the two documents. Using both the dates on Nettleton's letter and the minute books of the Royal Society it is clear that Nettleton's letter reporting his quantitative investigation of natural smallpox was read to the Royal Society about a month before Jurin read the paper which became his first publication reporting quantitative information. Most of the results he published were derived from Nettleton's letters.

Jurin's pamphlet was very well received by his intellectual peers leading him to make annual assays of the progress of inoculation. On December 11th 1723 he published an advertisement asking anyone, anywhere, with experience good, or bad, of inoculation, to write to him at the Royal Society.[26] Jurin asked for details of the patients and a complete record of the outcome. Initially this caused a problem because many high-born patients wished to preserve their privacy, and many of Claude Amyand's female patients were sensitive about their ages, so Jurin accepted that the study would be anonymous. Names would remain locked away in the files of the Royal Society, only numbers, and not personal details, would be revealed. This proved acceptable, and information began to flow in to the Royal Society from around Britain.

Jurin's first report of the response to his invitation, published in 1724, produced the remarkable finding that inoculation was in use throughout the whole of England less than 24 months after the Newgate experiment.[27] There were inoculators in Carlisle, near the border with Scotland, and in Portsmouth and Southampton on the south coast. While the bulk of the patients were inoculated by Maitland, Amyand, and Nettleton, there were small numbers in 15 widely separated towns. There were also at least 36 operators; most were surgeons, surgeons supervised by physicians, or apothecaries, but at least two inoculators were medically unqualified women. Mrs Roberts, of Leicester, had performed the operation 5 times, and Mrs. Rudge, near Shaftesbury, had treated six including three of her own children. The technical simplicity of inoculation favoured its wide dissemination.

Claude Amyand sent in brief descriptions of his first sixty inoculations which give us a snapshot of what inoculated smallpox was like.[28] For reasons not entirely clear, he, and the other inoculators, had abandoned the Turkish practice of making a small scratch with a needle into which the smallpox matter was placed. He used a lancet to make a short incision through the skin just above the elbow. Sometimes incisions were placed in both arms or one arm and one leg and smallpox matter was rubbed into all of them. He also says that he placed an "issue", a small deep hole in the arm which was normally used to drain off poisons from the blood. Most of his patients were the children of nobility, including his own two grand children, and Sir Hans Sloane's granddaughter. After a gap of seven to nine days his patients began to feel unwell and about two days later the characteristic rash appeared. All his patients had the "distinct" form of the disease but the number of pocks that appeared varied from 50 or so to "too many to count". This was still much better than the thousands that appeared on someone with the "confluent" form of the illness.

Amyand's incisions proved a problem. A large smallpox pustule developed where the pus had been applied. Although this dried up and fell off when the other pustules matured, the incisions continued to "run", that is leak fluid, for six to eight weeks after the operation. In a few cases the incisions became infected and a few children developed multiple abscesses, probably from bacteria which entered through the incisions. Such abscesses were a well known complication of smallpox so that their appearance did not cause great alarm and all but one child recovered. Amyand noted that none of his patients, apart from the two who died, had developed any of the nasty symptoms of severe natural smallpox, such as a severe sore throat or confluent pustules Although his descriptions sound terrifying to us, the results were so much less severe than the natural disease that they were considered a great improvement. The two children who died both *had* been ill with complicated diseases for many months before their inoculation. Amyand was annoyed that in one case the family had withheld the information that their daughter had suffered from several episodes of jaundice in the previous two years. Had he known, he said, he would have refused to inoculate her.

Jurin's correspondence network produced another very startling piece of information. Self-inoculation had been practised in parts of Wales for at least a century. Dr Perrott Williams reported that the custom was known as *"buying the pox"*.[29] A few scabs were bought from a patient recovering from smallpox; three pence for ten is the only known price. Some held these in their hands for *"some considerable time"*; others rubbed a raw spot on the back of one hand and applied the scab to the wound. Several elderly citizens testified that, in the time they had known of the practice, which was certainly longer than 70 years, no one had died from this procedure and no one had contracted smallpox a second time. In most instances those involved were older children or teenagers who took it upon themselves to organise the event. This bizarre practice was fully confirmed by Richard Wright, a local surgeon.[30] Haverford West is a port in West Wales, so it is possible that returning sailors had brought news of the practice back from Africa or the Levant, but the origin of this practice is unknown.

In his account for 1724, published in 1725, Jurin added the figures from 14 English and Welsh towns to the results communicated by Cotton Mather so that he now knew of 14,559 individuals who had had natural smallpox, of whom 2351, roughly one in six, had died.[31] There had been 474 inoculations in England and nine deaths equating to a death rate of about one in fifty. Here was clear evidence that inoculated smallpox was much safer than natural smallpox. The risk of dying was reduced from 16 percent to 2 percent.

Chapter 15

BOYLSTON'S BOOK

One new problem appeared. There had been 29 attempted inoculations that had failed to have any effect. Did these matter? Jurin explored the reports and noticed that the likelihood of "no effect" increased with the age of the individual. Like Nettleton, he surmised that these were individuals who were immune to smallpox from previous very mild infections with natural smallpox that had gone unnoticed. Occasionally very young children had only one or two pocks and a mild fever so that it was not clear what disease they had. Other children had the infection at such a young age that they did not remember it and their parents were dead and had not told them of their infection. He also pointed out that there were numerous examples in medicine where a particular treatment did not work at one particular time for no apparent reason. However, these cases did not distort his conclusions since removing these 29 individuals from his analysis left the death rate unchanged.

His question, "did inoculation always grant protection?" would take many years of continuous observation to answer. However, several inoculators had performed experiments similar to the deliberate exposure of Elizabeth Harrison to natural disease and no failures had been reported so far. Perrot Williams took his inoculated teenage sons with him on his rounds to visit afflicted families and they had remained safe. Similar reports from Turkey and New England *"strongly favoured the affirmative side"*. Jurin promised to lay any cases of alleged inoculation failure that came to his attention before the public. He would also investigate them in minute detail because he recognised that even a few failures would be enough to sink inoculation. It was only worthwhile if it was both less likely to be fatal than the natural disease and provided the same lifelong immunity.

Jurin noted that no one, not even the most ardent opponent, had been able to find even one death from inoculation that he had not already reported. He published a long diatribe from a Mr. De Grave, whose daughter had become a celebrated case. Wagstaffe had claimed that she had contracted natural smallpox after having the inoculated form.[1] Now an apothecary, Francis Howgrave, had stated that she had suffered a withered arm, was unhealthy, and had a continuously draining sinus in her arm.[2] Her father, himself a surgeon, was livid. He had previously published a denial of Wagstaffe's claims, appended to Arbuthnot's defence of Maitland. Hundreds had come to inspect his daughter and all agreed she was fit, her arms were strong, and there was no sinus. Intimating that she was ill despite her father's testimony to the contrary meant that Howgrave was suggesting that De Grave could not be trusted, an insult to his honour. Jurin published the father's fierce rebuttal and pointed out that there were still no proven examples of second infection.

Jurin's journal for 1726 was almost entirely devoted to disproving false claims of second infection with smallpox.[3] A doctor named Clinch had published that he knew of three cases of second bouts of small pox in patients who had been inoculated.[4] If true his story would destroy confidence in inoculation. One of Clinch's cases was particularly complex. It involved a claim by a supposed surgeon, David Jones, of Oswestry, that he had inoculated his daughter, who had had a typical mild eruption of the smallpox followed by a second unequivocal crop of pocks a few weeks later. Jurin wrote to Mr. Parry, the local vicar, seeking to know whether the story was true, and was assured that Mr. Jones had indeed confirmed the story, and that the vicar believed him. However, it emerged that Mr. Jones seemed to have given somewhat different versions of events to two different commentators, and Jurin was suspicious. He enlisted the help of Amyand in writing to a surgical friend in Oswestry whose reply indicated that something was very fishy about the affair because he believed that Jones had never inoculated anyone. Jurin burrowed deeper. He wrote to Parry again and asked him to put several direct questions to Jones including exactly how he had performed the operation and where he had learned the technique. Jones stuck to his story but refused to answer any of the questions unless he was given a large reward to come up to London to answer Jurin directly. Eventually the pressure told and Jones sent a letter through Rev Parry confessing that the entire story was made up. He had been trying to dissuade his son from having his daughter inoculated. He could not give any details of his inoculation procedure because he had never performed the operation and even admitted that he did not know what inoculation was. Jones revealed that he had no medical training; he turned out to be a weaver.

Clinch's other two other cases were also challenging. One was an example of a long delay between inoculation and the pocks appearing or perhaps an example of failure of the inoculation to "take". This child had only one bout of smallpox, but it occurred a month after inoculation. There was confusion over whether a rash noticed a few days after inoculation was smallpox, but eventually most medical observers agreed that it was not. When the boy developed proper, distinct smallpox a month later it seemed likely that he had caught it from his sister and that the original rash was not due to inoculation at all. Occasionally inoculation failed to produce an infection possibly because of poor technique by the operator.

The third child, The Hon. George Percival, had developed a second crop of pocks about a month after a typical inoculation reaction. Lady Percival gave Jurin permission to publish her journal for the relevant period. George had been inoculated by Amyand and his mother had kept a detailed record of the appearance of typical mild distinct smallpox which occurred at the usual time after the operation. Apart from a boil in his armpit the child had done well, was hardly sick at all, and recovered fully. However, about three weeks later another eruption appeared, and Clinch claimed that this was also smallpox. Lady Percival reported that the doctors who saw George were convinced that this second rash was chickenpox, and, confirming their opinion, one of his friends developed chickenpox at the same time.

Among the letters that arrived in 1726, one told the story of an audacious teenager, the 15 year old daughter of Walter Newberry, a merchant of the City of London.[5] She asked her father to pay for her inoculation which he refused, perhaps because of the cost. However, the child, like all young women, was concerned for her looks, and when her sister came down with natural smallpox she took the opportunity to do it herself. First she gave herself a vomit just in case things went badly. Then she persuaded her sister's nurse to go down to supper, promising to look after her sister. She took the bedclothes off the child to find the largest pock and found one on her sister's foot that seemed about right. She opened the pus-filled pock with a needle, dipped her finger tips into the sticky fluid, and then rubbed it into a scratch she had made of her forearm two inches below her elbow. She confessed when her mild smallpox appeared – the eruption at the inoculation site gave the game away, but her father forgave her and she recovered without incident.

Jurin could now speculate on the value of inoculation. There were only 13 deaths among the 624 patients inoculated instead of 100 that he calculated would have died if they had caught smallpox naturally, the difference between a death rate of one in six and one in fifty. But he also calculated that almost 2500 lives would have been saved among the 12,848 smallpox victims reported to him if only they had been treated. Jurin's project had come close to satisfying his original intentions. One further significant body of evidence would be enough to prove the case.

Between 1721 and 1723, Cotton Mather sent several accounts of the Boston trial of inoculation to London, always giving Zabdiel Boylston full credit for his resourcefulness and courage.[6,7]

However, Mather's accounts were contradicted by some of Douglass's claims and the true results of the Boston experiment were in question. Boylston had inoculated more than three times as many patients as any European doctor, and the outcome of the Boston epidemic had been exceptionally well defined by the selectmen. If anyone could confirm the probable benefit of inoculation it was the Boylston. Jurin needed his knowledge.

Exactly how Boylston was persuaded to leave Boston is unknown. Neither he, nor his father, had ever left Massachusetts. Sir Hans Sloane probably provided the most persuasive invitation, but there is a hint that Princess Caroline also added her encouragement, because Boylston acknowledged the urging of "*a very significant person*".[8] Trans-Atlantic travel required careful planning. In July 1724 Boylston invited anyone with a financial claim on him to come forward, and at the same time asked all who owed him money to settle their accounts.[9] He also sought a large supply of bear's grease, a common remedy for a wide range of aches and pains. Once his affairs were in order, he sailed from Boston in December 1724, braving the midwinter North Atlantic storms.

Almost no records of Boylston's activities in London have survived. There are unconfirmed suggestions that he spoke before the Royal College of Physicians, and an unverified claim that the King awarded him the huge sum of £1000 for his work. The Royal Society Journal Book says that he had come to London to study the "*new method of cutting for the stone*" with the leading lithotomist, Cheselden.[10] There is no hint of what this colonial doctor thought of the mother country, or what the sophisticates of London thought of him.

Sixty years later, during the American Revolution, Zabdiel's great nephew, Ward Nicholas Boylston, met Benjamin Franklin at his home outside Paris. Franklin was minister for the Continental Congress; Ward Boylston was a Tory who supported King George III. Despite this, Franklin greeted Boylston warmly:"*I shall always revere the name Boylston. Sir are you of the family of Zabdiel Boylston?*" When Ward replied that Zabdiel was his great uncle Franklin responded "*I owe everything I am to him. When*

Dr Boylston was in London in 1726, I was there and reduced to great distress, a youth without money, friends or counsel. I applied in my extreme distress to him who supplied me with twenty guineas, and relying on his judgement, I visited him as opportunities offered, and by his faithful counsels and encouragements I was saved from the abyss of destruction which awaited me, and my future fortune was based on his timely assistance."[11] If true, this shows Boylston as genuinely magnanimous, as Franklin had helped his brother to produce the "New England Courant" and had probably written some of its defamatory attacks on the inoculator.

The only certain sight we have of Boylston in London begins on May 19, 1726, when he was a guest at the Royal Society. He had written a book reporting all his cases of inoculation and describing the simple method he used to perform the operation, which was presented to the Society along with a brief summary by one of the members. Sir Hans Sloane was presiding when the doctor was proposed for fellowship of the Society. At the next weekly meeting a Dr. Campbell gave the Society an extended account of the contents of Boylston's book, and praised the value of his outstanding contribution to humanity. On July 7, after the Council of the Society had agreed his election, Boylston signed the book accepting the rules of the Royal Society. A week later he sailed for home.

Zabdiel Boylston dedicated his book to the Princess of Wales indicating her knowledge, support, and consent. His title is a typical eighteenth century table of contents:

An Historical Account of the smallpox inoculated in New England upon all sorts of persons, whites, blacks, and of all ages and constitutions. With some account of the nature of the infection in the natural and inoculated way, and their different effects on human bodies.

With some short directions to the inexperienced of this method of practice.

His title was also a reply to many of the criticisms of William Wagstaffe and other opponents of inoculation. His patients were of varying ages and races whereas most of the English patients were children from the upper classes.

Boylston explained that he began inoculating after only a little reflection because he was concerned for the safety of his children *"whose lives were very dear to me"*. At the start of the epidemic he recognised that they were in great danger because he would be visiting smallpox patients every day. After the success of his first few inoculations *"I resolved to carry it on for the saving of lives, not regarding any or all the menaces and opposition that were made against it"*. He was adamant that his experiment left no room for doubt that *"Inoculating the smallpox is a certain means of moderating that distemper"*. Many who had been fierce opponents now agreed that the practice was beneficial; the only barrier to wide acceptance was the lack of eyewitness experience of the ease with which his patients passed through the infection. There were none of the severe symptoms following inoculation which occurred in confluent natural disease, nor were there parents left childless, children without parents, or both children and parents being carried off, and *"many families broken up by the destruction of the smallpox in the natural way."* All these calamities were preventable by inoculation.

Boylston apologised to his patients *"more especially the young ladies"* for giving their names and ages in his account. But he needed to use these particulars to convince any doubters of the *"truth and validity"* of his story. Those who doubted inoculation on religious grounds he forgave, and urged that they seek advice from their ministers. For Douglass and his clique he was forthright *"those who, out of private peaks, or views, have exclaimed and railed against it, and who have trumpt up the groundless ill consequences that would follow it: Such I leave to sweat it out with just reflection and due repentance!"* The opposing ministers he dismissed *"I know of no better way of judging between moral and immoral methods of medical practice, than from the good or ill success that does or may attend them"*.

Each of his 244 personal cases was listed with short notes on their course and outcome. The six deaths were presented in unsparing detail. Of Bethiah Scarborough he commented *"in short thro' my great hurry, she poorly doctored, and badly nursed, died before the pox came out"*.

He disarmingly recounted that he had been so busy that he had been unable to visit a Mr Tufts and his servant after their inoculations and only learnt that they had had very mild symptoms when Tufts came to pay his bill.

His careful observations suggested to him that the inoculated form of smallpox did not produce the encrusted nose and ulcerated throat and mouth characteristic of the natural, inhaled form. He pointed out that this distinction could be used to discriminate between those who had caught the disease naturally, and then been inoculated, and those who had true inoculation smallpox. He believed that at least two of his patients had probably been incubating the infection before he inoculated them and that this fact explained their severe reaction.

Boylston's descriptions are so accurate that it is possible to analyse from a modern viewpoint the six deaths that occurred. Mrs Dixwell gained lasting fame because Douglass used her death in his attempts to impeach inoculation in England. However, her case is not straightforward. *"Mrs Dixwell was a fat gentlewoman of a tender constitution, she came frightened into the practice, as most of the others had done; not only by living near the infected, but passing some days before the door wherein lay a corpse ready for the grave which died of confluent smallpox, the stench whereof greatly offended and surprised her with fear of being infected"* Uniquely for an inoculated subject, she developed a sore throat and had difficulty breathing, which are usually symptoms of natural smallpox. She appeared to be recovering and her scabs had begun to fall off when she suddenly developed "hysteric fits", a fever, and died three days later, more than three weeks after she had been inoculated.

Boylston's second fatal case is also open to debate. John White was such a weak, infirm man that Boylston had advised him to leave Boston to avoid the epidemic, but White got bored with country life and returned asking to be inoculated. Initially all went smoothly except that *"whereas the first days he took little nourishment, now he would take none"*. He refused to be comforted or to take the doctors advice and *"he complained of neither pain nor sickness. He lay there languishing like a plant without moisture"* and died three weeks after his inoculation. In Mather's commentary he explained that White had been wasting away for some time before he underwent treatment. Mrs. Wells was John White's sister and her death is also debatably due to smallpox. She recovered from her inoculation eruptions, but died from diarrhoea which had developed three days before she died six weeks after inoculation. Probably only three of Boylston's patients actually died of inoculated infection.

Jurin's accounts of those who died in England also reveal several cases where inoculated smallpox might not have been the cause of death. In both Boston and England, about half of the fatalities following the operation were probably not due to inoculated smallpox, and the true mortality of inoculation was probably nearer one percent than two.

Boylston speculated on why inoculated smallpox was so much less deadly than the natural infection. In a world where any concept of immunity was absent, his best guess was that the inoculated agent entered into the blood stream through cut blood vessels, where it caused less reaction than when it was inhaled into the throat, mouth and lungs. He pointed out that current medical opinion concerning the origin of smallpox was based on an apparent contradiction. If smallpox was due to some corruption in trapped menstrual blood transmitted from mother to child, how could a mother who had already had smallpox, and therefore expelled the noxious agent from her body, transmit the seed of the disease to her offspring? Although he was not given much credit for his insight, this was one of the critical factors that led to the rejection of the innate seed hypothesis of the origin of smallpox and its replacement by the idea that the agent of smallpox came from outside the body.

Boylston's most important contribution to the evolving debate over inoculation was to add his information to the growing body of data accumulated by Jurin. Six of 282 individuals inoculated had died; 844 of 5759 with the natural disease in Boston had died. The data were unquestionable; the mortality of natural smallpox was one in six, despite random fluctuations in particular small outbreaks, the large numbers collected from two continents produced the same result. Further, the mortality from inoculation was one in fifty when all the information, from both sides of the Atlantic, was tallied. The conclusion, which Jurin had tentatively reached with his English figures and which had now been confirmed by adding Boylston's, was that inoculation was very beneficial. The Secretary had accidentally conducted his study in a very modern way. By comparing results from several different sites, and by collecting large amounts of data, he had overcome some of the possible objections to his conclusions. It was virtually certain that the death rate after inoculation was no more than 2 percent and that the case fatality rate from the natural disease was about 16 percent, because several determinations gave similar results. The figures from Boston and England were almost identical.[12] At the time there was no valid explanation for the variations in death rates which were found in the different English towns that featured in Jurin's studies, and it was thought that there were some innate differences in strains of the infectious agent, so that a gentle form occurred in some outbreaks, but a particularly malignant form in others. Eighteenth century medical theory argued that the differences were the result of differences in the atmosphere, and were the result of particularly "epidemical" conditions, although the exact nature of these conditions was never specified. It wasn't until the twentieth century that it was finally settled that the virus was the same in all outbreaks, and that the variations in death rates were related to the age and health of the population attacked and to random variations. Jurin had managed to escape from the snare these swings set by combining the outcomes of many epidemics.

Boylston's book is a monument. Taken in isolation it appears to be the first report of a clinical trial. Similar studies are regularly published today, albeit with much more sophisticated statistical analysis and tortured considerations of the ethics of the study. But Boylston himself maintained that he was no writer and not comfortable with the written word. His book must be seen as the result of collaboration between himself, Sir Hans Sloane, and James Jurin. Boylston did all the clinical work and recorded the case notes, but only when he came under the influence of, and received moral support from, Jurin was he moved to publish his findings. Jurin had already given details of those who died after inoculation in England, and Thomas Nettleton, at Jurin's request, had given details of some of his inoculated patients. In form and content Boylston's book is one of the first recognisable clinical papers, where all the clinical details of the patients and an analysis of the failures are presented and it reflects the combined contributions of colonial individual enterprise and the scientific environment of the Royal Society. Boylston would never have published his book without the advice and encouragement that he found in London.

In 1727 Isaac Newton died and Sir Hans Sloane was elected President of the Royal Society. Jurin had supported Sloane's opponent for the post and disagreed with Sloane's "naturalist" as opposed to Newton's and Jurin's "mathematical" approach to studying the natural world, so he resigned as the Secretary to the Society.[13] Sloane asked his young protégé John Gasper Scheuchzer to carry on where Jurin had left off. In 1729 Scheuchzer produced what would turn out to be the final volume of the inoculation project.[14] There were now reports of 897 inoculations in Great Britain among whom 17 had died; there were also reports of 329 individuals, including Boylston's 280 cases, inoculated in other countries with nine deaths. In their separate publications Jurin, Boylston, and Scheuchzer gave clinical details for most of the deaths allowing any fair minded reader to draw his own conclusions about which deaths were really due to inoculated smallpox. No one had been able to identify a death following inoculation that had not already been reported by them.

Three thousand and eight deaths had occurred among eighteen thousand two hundred and twenty nine cases of natural smallpox. The relative risks of the two forms of smallpox had hardly changed between 1721 and 1729. It would remain the same for two centuries. The mortality during the last smallpox epidemic in Boston, in 1901, was about twenty percent among patients who had not been vaccinated.[15] One in five or six died of natural smallpox, one in forty seven of inoculation. If inoculation had been universally adopted over 16,000 of the 18,000 lives lost to smallpox between 1721 and 1729 could have been saved. Furthermore, no one had yet produced a genuine case of a second attack of smallpox in someone successfully inoculated.

Although only a long period of time could guarantee that immunity was life long, several inoculators had performed informal experiments exposing their own inoculated children to the disease and they had all resisted the infection. When Scheuchzer died of tuberculosis in 1729 no one took on the challenge of continuing to collect inoculation information for the Royal Society.

What had been achieved? The sheer volume of cases reported was strong evidence that inoculation really was less dangerous than natural smallpox. It had all the characteristics of the disease but in a much milder form. Since inoculated smallpox closely resembled the natural form it seemed logical, and highly probable, that it would be as effective in the long term as a mild case of the natural infection.

Thomas Nettleton, Zabdiel Boylston, and James Jurin deserve to be recognised among the initiators of modern clinical medicine and of the medical enlightenment. They were the first to use numbers to prove that a treatment was effective, and demonstrated that man could gain control of one of his most feared diseases, replacing fate or Providence with rational choice. Boylston had the support of Cotton Mather in Boston and the help of Sloane and Jurin in London. Jurin had the resources of the Royal Society and his series of papers is widely quoted. Thomas Nettleton is remembered for suggesting the project to Jurin, his role is actually greater than usually believed. To have the information that he sent to Jurin in his letter of June 16th, 1722 he must had thought about the problem and begun collecting the data at least several weeks earlier, about the time that the Princesses were inoculated. Without prompting or advice from anyone else, Nettleton identified the need to show that inoculation was actually safer than natural smallpox, which meant that he needed to know the risk of dying from natural smallpox. He then collected the information from the surrounding towns. Within six months he had a much larger sample which he relayed to London. Jurin included Nettleton's figures in *"A Letter to the Learned Dr.Dr Caleb Cotesworth."* his first account of inoculation. Jurin is deservedly famous for collecting and publishing the results of inoculation between 1723 and 1727 which established that inoculated smallpox was unequivocally safer than the natural form of the disease. However, in *"A Letter"* three quarters of the patients with natural smallpox and their mortality were provided by Thomas Nettleton and his letter was known to Jurin for a month before he produced his own first paper. The structure of this paper makes it clear that Jurin was pursuing the same line as Arbuthnot using indirect mortality data, when he switched to Nettleton's direct approach. In the modern world *"A Letter"* would have been published as a collaboration between Nettleton and Jurin with both named as authors. The singularity of Nettleton's enterprise can be judged by comparing his approach to understanding smallpox with that adopted by two mathematically astute Fellows of the Royal Society, John Arbuthnot and James Jurin, who relied on dubious manipulations of the London Bills of Mortality to try to deduce the chances of dying from smallpox.

Nettleton should be recognised as the first to use evidence to determine best practice and for being the first to use numbers to prove a case . Why he chose to collect exact figures is not known. Perhaps it was a response to the strong opposition to inoculation from his neighbours. Showing that inoculation was indeed safer than normal smallpox would have strengthened his justification for using it. One of the few things known about Nettleton is that *"he and Mr. West ... were the first who instructed Professor Sanderson in the principles of mathematics"* (Sanderson went on to be appointed Lucasian Professor of mathematics at Cambridge.) Perhaps Nettleton, like Jurin, was a mathematician at heart. Or perhaps he had plenty of time to reflect as he rode across the moors above Halifax. Families sent for the doctor who came on his horse in all weathers to give advice and treatment. On one of these winter rides he might have speculated on how to prove to his critics that inoculation was the better idea. His idea clearly started Jurin on his now famous path. We will never know whether Jurin might have chosen this way to determine whether inoculation was beneficial or not without Nettleton, but we can be certain that Nettleton's ingenuity laid the foundation for the eradication of smallpox. The true origins of evidence based medicine, the 20th century's most powerful tool for identifying best practice, lies with the inoculators in the early 18th century, not in 19th century Paris as is usually claimed.[16]

Remarkably, all the handwritten letters reporting the results of inoculation in England still exist in the archives of the Royal Society. They came from the Royal Surgeon as well as ordinary doctors all over the country. Anyone interested in the origins of evidence based medicine is free to examine them.

Chapter 16

SLAVES, PEASANTS, AND THE SONS OF RICH MEN

Did Jurin's work make any difference? Many historians interpreted the end of his series of articles as evidence that inoculation had been rejected and was considered useless until it was revived about 1750. However, Genevieve Miller has shown that the practice continued and was highly thought of, if only occasionally written about, during the 1730s and 1740s.[1] When reports were no longer collected by the Royal Society there was no way of tracking how often the operation was performed. Members of the English upper classes did not want their actions exposed to possible criticism and kept their inoculations out of sight. John Ranby, Sergeant Surgeon to King George II, performed about fifty inoculations a year among people of the "first rank".[2] Most of his patients, like those of his predecessor Claude Amyand, would have been the children of nobility and high government officials. Other fashionable surgeons, such as Sergeant Hawkins, another of the King's doctors, and Mr. Middleton, surgeon to the army, were also active in the highest social circles. Remarkably Ranby carried out over 1000 inoculations between 1727 and 1750 without a single death.

A second factor, seen in the earliest reports to Jurin, makes it impossible to guess exactly how many inoculations were performed. Inoculation was so simple that anyone who really wanted to could operate on themselves, their children, or, for a fee, their neighbours. Mrs. Ringe, the woman in Leicester, and Miss Newberry all testify to the ease with which untrained operators could inoculate.[3] At some point inoculation even became available at country fairs, although exactly when and how often it was performed is unknown.[4] Yet despite the continuing use of inoculation there remained deep seated opposition to the practice.

A debate between two Cambridge graduates in early 1733 reveals the level of disagreement among contemporary medical professionals. David Hartley was 28 years old with an unusual and unorthodox medical education.[5] He had studied for the ministry while at Cambridge but had learned enough medicine that he was able to establish himself in practice in the market town of Bury St. Edmunds. When, in 1732, smallpox appeared in the town and threatened to develop into an epidemic, Hartley argued for the introduction of inoculation.[6] He gave a series of reasons. Firstly there were so many people at risk, he guessed about 3000, that the epidemic would last about two years before it had run its course. During this time markets would be disrupted, the regular local court sessions would move elsewhere, and the fairs and local meetings that underpinned the commercial life of a market town would be destroyed. He thought that inoculation would eliminate the disease in about six months saving valuable trade. Secondly he drew on probability derived from the Jurin publications showing that the mortality following inoculation was only one in fifty while the mortality following natural smallpox was one in six. About 500 people would probably die if the epidemic was allowed to continue but only 60 or so would die if inoculation was adopted.

Thirdly he thought that smallpox spread in a like-for-like manner; mild cases produced mild disease and confluent cases tended to produce severe infections. So even if inoculation spread smallpox it would be less severe than the full blown disease spread in the usual ways. Finally, saving so many lives would act towards the general good of mankind.

Hartley then attempted to deal with the objections commonly raised to inoculation. Chief among these was the uncertainty of lifelong protection. However, he argued that there had been no failures in the 12 years since the practice began and that logic indicated that mild inoculated disease was as good as mild natural disease and no one doubted that very mild smallpox produced life long immunity. A second claim by opponents was that there were sometimes unpleasant consequences following inoculation such as the boils and abscesses described by Jurin. Yet Hartley replied that these occurred in natural smallpox as well and would almost certainly be less severe since the severity of the complications should mirror the severity of the infection. Hartley had consulted Nettleton and Jurin and found that they both still supported the practice and that Jurin had just inoculated one of his children. A further objection was that inoculation might transmit another disease or even worse the personality of the donor. Hartley argued that experience showed that inoculation only transmitted smallpox and no other diseases had appeared as a result of the operation. It was highly unlikely that another disease could be transmitted by the operation, after all, nurses did not transmit their personalities or diseases to the infants that they nursed.

Finally, the young doctor raised the issue of morality. He followed the line of reasoning first suggested by Cotton Mather; that your duty to protect your health required you to take the safer option, especially when there was a high chance of being exposed to the infection. Many clergymen opposed the inoculation because they believed that it did not promote human lives, health, or happiness; but Hartley said he had written his pamphlet to demonstrate that the practice did indeed lead to the greater good. Not only would lives be spared, but trade and commerce would also benefit.

Hartley's adversary was Martin Warren a conventionally trained Cambridge physician with an established practice in Bury St. Edmunds. He was opposed to *"this barbarous invention"* imported from Turkey which at first pleased *"but soon grew out of control and made great havoc and slaughter"* so that inoculation was now hardly practised.[7] He claimed that Hartley was attempting to distract the opinion formers of Bury by associating himself with famous men such as Jurin and Nettleton and by using his *"mathematical skill and through an acquaintance with the doctrine of chances"* to resurrect this discredited practice. Warren maintained that Jurin was an honest man but had been misled by his correspondents, who had covered up many unfavourable cases. He claimed he knew of families where inoculation had proved disastrous and said that he would name them when the right time arrived. Jurin had also been misinformed about the mortality of natural smallpox. In Bury there had been only 124 deaths so far among 1683 smallpox cases and half of these could be explained by lack of care, absence of clothing or bedding, or because they were people so ill from other diseases that no inoculator would have touched them. Incidentally not one in seventy of his own patients had died due to his wise advice to prepare for the disease before it arrived. Having disposed of Jurin's accounts he felt that he had undermined Hartley's reasons to his own satisfaction.

Warren suggested that the inoculators were premature when they held that inoculation provided the same security as natural infection. Although those exposed to infected individuals had escaped the disease the first time they were tested, that was no guarantee that they would always escape. There were many people who escaped smallpox during one epidemic only to come down with it the next time it appeared and inoculators were similarly overconfident that other diseases were not communicated along with inoculated smallpox. Some believed that nurses transmitted their personal characteristics along with breast milk and, if so, inoculators would need to take great care choosing their donors lest *"he may imprudently bring an honest man to the gallows, and make a modest virgin a brazen prostitute"* *"Every man of sense will observe a communication of diseases by inoculation POSSIBLE, PROBABLE, and CERTAIN. And every affectionate fond Mother and tender virgin may from this doleful instance see the mercies of inoculation are cruel, and dread a practice of an influence so malignant as may render the lives of them and theirs miserable and bodies a hospital of putrid sore, and incurable distempers."* Under the circumstances it was unwise to try to persuade individuals to take inoculation with promises of benefit and equally wrong to threaten them with dire consequences if they did not. Many would choose to trust in Providence rather than subject themselves to the attentions of an inexpert inoculator.

Throughout his piece Warren plays on Hartley's dubious claim to medical expertise. Phrases such as "unacquainted with men of our profession, "lack of skill", "inexpert practitioner" echo the attacks of William Douglass on Zabdiel Boylston. Warren was telling the town to ignore Hartley, this jumped up, untrained and untried "doctor"; better to rely on Providence and his own expensive doctoring. Hartley's appeal failed. He inoculated only four people at Bury.

Hartley's desire to inoculate in the face of an impending smallpox epidemic seems typical of the times. A major factor in the relative infrequency of inoculations in the 1730s and 40s was the absence of pandemics of smallpox such as those that had occurred in the 1720s.[8] Inoculation was most likely to find favour when there was a local outbreak of smallpox, a relationship first suggested by Rev. David Neal in his commentary on the Boston inoculation experiment.[9] When the disease was present, the relative risk of inoculation compared to the natural disease would recommend the operation, but when there was no smallpox in the area the small danger from inoculation would outweigh the minimal chances of catching the natural infection. Mothers,(it was usually the mother who made the decision as to whether to inoculate or not), were faced with a difficult dilemma: if you inoculated your child and it died you would never forgive yourself; but if it caught smallpox and died you would feel just as guilty for not protecting its life.

Inoculation was also used sporadically to combat epidemics of smallpox in the Americas. In late 1729 a few cases of smallpox appeared in Boston and then began to spread. The selectmen tried to get around their rule that inoculation could be used after twenty families were afflicted by raising the number to thirty; but the epidemic grew out of control and the operation reappeared. Boylston issued a Boston edition of his book to encourage the population to request the operation from their physicians. Perhaps because there was a fee attached, Douglass now found himself able to perform the operation and wrote a dissertation giving his version of the history of the procedure.[10] He now regarded the dead Mather as just a credulous fool, but he remained adamant that Boylston was a rash, illiterate, charlatan who had killed many patients and lied about his success. As usual, he could not cite a single specific example and relied on innuendo and rumour to support his opinion. He refused to recognise Boylston's book as it was *"jejune, lame, suspected and only in the nature of a Quack Bill"*. Douglass claimed that Boylston had gone to London seeking to make a fortune from his operation but had been ignored and gained no patients at all.

Boylston was furious and struck back in the Weekly Newsletter:[11] *"I think I am in Duty, Honour, and Justice to myself and the Practice, bound to Certify the Publick, That I never, directly or indirectly, Inoculated the Small pox upon any one Person more that died, than the six I mention"*. He had left two successful cases out of his original London version because he had forgotten to record them in his daybook. *"I have given a true Account of mine, which still stands firm and unshaken. And I defy Douglass with all his Malice, or any other, to prove the contrary. And now Gentlemen, the Practitioners in Physick and Surgery, forgetting what has past, let us all agree and unite as one, in our utmost Endeavours, either in this Method, or by other means… to help our Patients through their difficulties and save their lives"*. This time about 400 Bostonians were inoculated with favourable results.

Reports of inoculations in Philadelphia[12] and South Carolina[13] appeared in the English press, as did an account of a planter on the island of St. Christopher in the West Indies who inoculated 300 slaves to preserve his capital during an epidemic.[14] After an outbreak of smallpox had killed a third of the slaves during one transatlantic crossing, Sir Hans Sloane tried to introduce inoculation into the slave trade through the Africa Company base at Wydah on the Gold Coast.[15] Although not all slave ship captains adopted the practice it was recognized as a valuable way to preserve, even enhance, the value of their cargoes. In 1729, a Carmelite missionary many miles up the Amazon used inoculation to protect his natives after half of them had died from smallpox. He obtained his only knowledge of the practice from a European newspaper.[16]

In 1737 an anonymous author made a strong case for general inoculation as a means to prevent lingering outbreaks of the sort that were then present in several middle sized market towns along the Thames Valley.[17] In Gentleman's Magazine he argued that if everyone had been immunized, only the youngest children would be at risk, and the disease would not be able to gain a foothold. To this writer, smallpox was terrible because it caused much anxiety among those who had not had it, and it limited their ability to go about their normal business. No one knew when it would strike. A traveler might find himself in dangerous circumstances and greatly regret not having been inoculated. Smallpox *"seizes the Beauty, the pregnant, the young, the Adult, and the Aged"* and it hindered near and dear friends from providing assistance if they had not already been through the infection. Until they suffered the infection many could not take up positions as servants because their employers would not take risk of allowing a potential source of contagion into the family. The correspondent maintained that doubts arising as a result of the fact that inoculation sometimes miscarried were not valid since any human undertaking, even marriage, could sometimes result in disaster. All human activity could be seen as a kind of inoculation with risks and rewards, which were not criminal if undertaken in the expectation of a good result. Soon inoculation would have the same fate as *"other Notables at their first Entrance: as the Use of Hops, Tobacco, the Bark, Wiggs, Shaving the Beard etc. For once upon a Time each of these was criminal, and many a little argument muster'd against them 'till a better Acquaintance and Experience at last prevailed over Scruples, which in time vanished"*. Eventually the operation would become a mundane part of the everyday world he argued.

These articles imply that inoculation was available and in use throughout the 1730's. Both are arguing for the extended use of the operation to terminate established epidemics. If inoculation had been stopped, or gone out of favour, there would be no point in arguing for its general use as a public health measure. In particular, Warren does not cite the disappearance of the practice as supporting his claims that it was a dangerous procedure based on flawed evidence. If the operation had been abandoned he would have had been able to say that practice and experience supported him.

With so much evidence that inoculation was beneficial why was it not more widely adopted?

Several factors combined to limit its availability and acceptability. One particularly powerful inhibitor was opposition on moral grounds. The religious objections raised during inoculation's first use never fully disappeared. In the small communities that made up most of England in the early 18th century the minister was the intellectual leader of the parish. If he opposed inoculation his influence would usually be sufficient to block any attempt to introduce it locally. Coupled with moral scruples was the fear that the practice actually spread smallpox, so that in most places inoculation was strongly opposed by the man in the street. If there was no smallpox in the vicinity it seemed madness to introduce it.

Doctors themselves also contributed to making inoculation less acceptable. All three of the first inoculators, Zabdiel Boylston, Charles Maitland, and Thomas Nettleton abandoned the technique used in Turkey which was described clearly in both the Timonius and Pylarinius papers. Instead of a few punctures or scratches with a needle they opted to make an incision through the skin.[18] Possibly the Turkish technique produced such a very mild eruption that it was difficult to be sure that the operation had actually worked and that the recipient would be immune. A larger and deeper cut produced a more marked eruption with more pustules, so that it was clear that true, mild smallpox had been produced. In a world without any concept of bacteria or wound cleansing these cuts became infected and ran a mixture of pus and plasma, which increased in volume as the pustule at the incision grew in size. Nettleton thought that he had observed that the more "matter" that ran from the incision the milder the resulting smallpox.[19] Since most medical opinion held that the pustules of smallpox were an attempt by the body to throw out the corrupt poison responsible for the disease, this was a rational idea. If more came out through the inoculation site there was less to be got rid of through the pustules. Encouraging drainage from the incision also made sure that the poison was removed rather than remaining within the body where it was thought to produce death if it reached the internal organs. Inoculators thought that one reason why inoculation worked was that it removed some of the fuel driving the illness. But the result of this medical theorizing was that the patient had a painful, often infected wound or wounds, because many inoculators made incisions on one arm and one leg, which drained pus for weeks after the operation. Claude Amyand noted that the incisions ran for upwards of six weeks in some of his patients.

Medical theory also contributed a second obstacle to the early acceptance of inoculation. Most 18th century doctors subscribed to the humoral theories put forward by Galen in the 4th century AD. Health was defined as a balance between four humors and disease resulted when one humor was too strong or too weak. If the humors were out of balance then medicines or diets were a possible means to restore it. Bleeding, induced vomits, strong laxatives used judiciously were all considered to be means to restore balance. For example, a fever such as that induced by smallpox, was thought to be exacerbated by red meat and alcohol, so one way to diminish the fever of smallpox was to maintain a meat and alcohol free diet. In addition vomits and purges might remove corrupt matter from the stomach and bowels so that there was less material to produce the smallpox poison. However, the physician would usually not be able to begin treatment until the patient was so ill that he consulted a doctor, or until the doctor had been able to establish the diagnosis, and that might be too late. One advantage of inoculation was that the doctor was involved from the start. Not only could a favourable time be chosen, but the correct treatments were administered beginning early when they were likely to be the most effective.

It was a short step from this explanation of the benefits of inoculation to the logical conclusion that the treatments should be started before the operation to get the body into the most favourable state to cope with the disease. "Preparation" became a routine part of the inoculation process. Individual doctors developed their own protocols allowing them to claim distinct secret formulae that worked better than anyone else's. Some advocated abstaining from meat and strong drink but allowed vegetables and eggs. Others felt a more extreme regime was preferable and placed their patients on a bread and water diet. Then there were differences in the length of time required. At least two weeks was thought to be necessary by some physicians, but others argued that longer preparation was safer. The number and spacing of vomits or purges also varied between practitioners. Extreme preparation was actually harmful. Young Edward Jenner nearly died from his.

Yet all this preparation actually flew in the face of the evidence of the early inoculators. Boylston and Nettleton had not "prepared" most of their patients yet they had had excellent results. Charles Maitland revealed some of the reasoning behind preparation in his discussion of the Heath boy who was fat and glutinous and did less well than his brother.[20] Maitland felt that perhaps he should have used a period of preparation to smooth his course. An inoculator who did not prepare his patients was open to criticism if they did badly or died, whereas if he did follow a preparative regime he would not be accused of negligence when things went wrong.

There was another motive behind all this medical intervention: money. A doctor charged for each visit, each dose of medicine, and for designing the preparation. Bills for inoculation could easily reach £20, a sum sufficient to keep a family of four in London for six months. Faced with inoculating four children, a father might find that the bill added up to half his annual income. Lady Mary Montague noticed this tendency to over-elaborate medical intervention and wrote to a newspaper attacking the medical profession for abandoning the simple practices of Turkey for financial gain.[21]

Medical theory managed to make inoculation painful, dangerous, unpleasant, and expensive. It also took a long time. With at least two weeks of preparation and four or five weeks for the disease to run its course, the patient needed to commit six weeks or more to the procedure, far beyond the reach of the typical tradesman or labourer. Only the well off, or someone investing in a future, could afford to be inoculated. Many wealthy families would only hire servants who were immune to smallpox to reduce the risk to their children. Even if the children had been inoculated, a susceptible servant was a potential financial burden since the employer might have to pay for their care if they fell ill, and they would lose their services for a prolonged period. Inoculation offered the ambitious young country lad or lass a means of answering "yes" when asked if they had had the smallpox, thereby increasing their chances of finding a place in the city. Inoculation became one part of improving one's station in life.

Chapter 17

GRADUAL ACCEPTANCE

Although there were many obstacles to the growth of inoculation it progressed slowly and gradually became more widely available. One solution to some of the problems associated with inoculation was pioneered by Thomas Frewen, a surgeon practicing on the south coast of England. He opened a very early example of the "inoculation house".[1] The concept was simple and probably derived from the "pest house" that many parishes maintained as a place to send people suffering from dangerous contagious diseases. Frewin bought a house where his inoculated patients could live while they were prepared, received the infection, and lived while the disease ran its course. Several patients could be accommodated at one time and it was easy to supervise them and provide immediate medical support if anything began to go wrong. However, the presence of an inoculation house in a town or city was not popular and he was forced to close down and move into the countryside. Even there his enterprise was so hated that travelers would cut across the neighbouring fields rather than pass by the house along the road. His neighbours sued for the damage to their fields and he was forced to move to an even more remote location. Frewen persisted and eventually wrote a book analyzing his experience which he subsequently published in a Latin translation, which he submitted for an M.D. degree.[2] The inoculation house became a standard model for providing inoculation to an adult population that remained in use for the rest of the 18th century. One, dating from the 1760's, still exists in Kent.

Attempts to extend inoculation in London beyond the highest social circles began after 1740 when two hospitals became centres of the new practice and provided some access for the poorest citizens. Thomas Coram's *Hospital for the Maintenance and Education of Exposed and Deserted Children,* soon known universally as the Foundling Hospital, provided a home and education for a few of London's hundreds of unwanted children. Captain Thomas Coram was the archetypal British sea dog. Sent to sea at 14, he had crisscrossed the Atlantic before settling in Boston where he made a fortune from trade and shipbuilding. Returning home in 1719 he started on a twenty year campaign to provide for the abandoned children of London. Impoverished working women could not afford the time and cost of caring for an infant in their hand to mouth lives. Even worse off were the housemaids and serving girls who "fell pregnant" without a husband to provide for them, and with the certain knowledge that they would lose their places if they kept the baby. Many newborn babies were simply abandoned; many women took the only available expedient and murdered their children. Every morning a new scattering of infant corpses littered the ditches, dunghills, and roadways of the city. England's poor laws made a child the responsibility of the mother's parish, a system that was widely abused as poor pregnant women were expelled from one parish to another so that they would count as residents of some other place when the baby was born. If a child was presented to the trustees of the parish they paid "nurses" to look after the foundlings. The surest way for the nurse to profit from this arrangement was to starve the child. After 1722 abandoned infants were consigned to the poor house. Almost none left. Ninety nine percent of infants delivered into the care of the parish were dead before they were two years old.[3]

Coram devoted his time and much of his money to promoting a hospital to provide shelter and training for London's unwanted children. Eventually he succeeded, and in 1741 the Foundling Hospital received its first charges. Hundreds of women turned up to present their babies on an anonymous, no shame basis, but there was accommodation for only thirty. The hospital flourished from the first. Hogarth was a trustee and painted a famous portrait of Captain Coram; Handel conducted his Messiah for the hospital and presented it with the manuscript.

The governors embarked on an enlightened programme for their new dependants. Infants were sent to country families until they were five, when they returned to London to start their education. Most were apprenticed into a range of trades when they reached their 12th birthday. Some were prepared for the army or navy; many girls were trained for domestic service or taught to be seamstresses or milliners. Great emphasis was placed on the fact that children were not trained above their station in life so that they presented no threat to the hospital's wealthy benefactors. Although about a third died, this was similar to the death rate of all children in London.

When the children returned from the countryside they faced the threat of London's endemic smallpox because in the barracks-like hospital the conditions were ideal for an epidemic. To protect their charges the governors ordered that all children who had not had smallpox should be inoculated, and the Foundling Hospital became one of the few places in the world where regular inoculation was carried out, and where it could be studied over a long period of time. Between 1759 and 1769 1296 children were inoculated and only 5 died. Support by the governors of the hospital showed that inoculation was considered a respectable and valuable procedure among the upper and middle levels of London society who were represented on the board. Richard Meade and Sir Hans Sloane, probably the two most prominent physicians in London were members, as was William Hogarth, the painter, along with other leading merchants and nobility. While there was still considerable resistance to inoculation among the masses, the upper strata of society had mostly accepted it.

The other new London institution was the *Middlesex County Hospital for Smallpox and Inoculation,* which opened on Windmill

Street, in what is now central London, in 1746. Its charter, which was also an appeal for benefactors, justified its existence. *"Smallpox is the most contagious and fatal distemper destroying above ten to one of most other diseases"*.[4] No other hospital would admit smallpox cases. And smallpox patients required urgent treatment since the outcome of the infection was determined within the first few days after the eruption appeared.

The charter paints a portrait of the plight of families afflicted by smallpox in mid 18th century London. *"The Smallpox as it is the most contagious and dangerous of all Distempers is therefore most liable to produce more Disquietude, Dread, and Uneasiness in Families than any other; and hence it frequently happens that when this Distemper comes into a Family, either the Object afflicted there with is obliged to be immediately removed to some distant Place, or those in the Family, not yet having had the Distemper, are necessitated to abscond the house and retire elsewhere for safety. This is the case of Persons of superior Fortune, whose Affluence can suffice to defray Expenses of more than ordinary Nature: But as to Servants, how unhappily and miserably straitned are these poor Creatures ofentimes by this Complaint! Who being therewith seized, are generally no longer suffer'd to continue in the place of their servitude but are presently obliged to quit their habitation and be removed elsewhere. The Doors of all Public Hospitals are shut against them"* The poor servant had to find the cost of his lodging until he recovered; without any medical care, that was unlikely. Then he was faced with a huge debt incurred while he was sick. This *"happens almost everyday in one place or another of this great City"*. Even poor industrious families faced calamity if the breadwinner was stricken, but if he could be removed to a place of safety, the rest of the family could return to work and be spared the disaster of finding themselves with debts that they could not pay.

The Smallpox hospital was intended to offer more than just care for those struck down with casual smallpox; it was the first institution devoted to inoculation. *"How much would Parents pay to ensure their children mild passage through the disease, what adult wouldn't give half his fortune to have it behind him safely and be rid of the fear and anxiety"*? Smallpox was likened to *"a thorny hedge through which all must pass, and some die, to reach a field of safety"* or a *"storm or tempest which may lead to shipwreck, especially as it may occur when they are least prepared for it"*.

"And what is Life if encompassed about with Fear?" The great anxiety of waiting for smallpox was a disease in itself, and therefore inducing a mild disease to cure it was justified. The hospital's charter was also a plea to "please give generously".

Although founded from the most idealistic motives, cynics viewed the Smallpox Hospital as a private nursing home devoted to the care of the servants of its benefactors. Admission criteria were defined in the Charter and specified that patients were usually admitted on the recommendation of a patron. First preference was given to those introduced by Peers or Noblemen, next the greatest contributors, then patrons who had not introduced a patient for the preceding six months, and finally to casual patients if space was available, and only then was preference given to those in the most deplorable state.

The Smallpox Hospital got off to a slow start. In its first year only 17 patients were inoculated, in 1750 twenty nine, in 1751 eighty five, but the numbers rose in a stepwise fashion thereafter as the number of beds increased. Initially the hospital consisted of three small houses, one for patients undergoing preparation, one for those who had been inoculated, and one for smallpox cases. Preparation lasted four weeks, and it usually took three weeks for the disease to complete its course, followed by a week of cleaning and airing the premises, meaning that that new batches of patients were only admitted every eight weeks. Within four years of opening its doors the hospital was inoculating about 100 individuals every year and there was a waiting list of about one hundred and twenty, which continued to grow. The existence of the hospital and its financial support by the upper levels of society was further evidence that inoculation was viewed favourably even if it made almost no contribution to public health.

Despite the obvious need and the demonstrable demand for its services the Inoculation Hospital was despised by its immediate neighbours. The overseers of the poor and church wardens of the parish where it was located applied to the courts to have it shut. But the Lord Chancellor ruled *"that the hospital was of great public utility, and had not been proved a nuisance"* and refused the indictment. Hostility to the patients ran high. They were often abused and insulted in the streets around the hospital when they were well enough to leave so they were advised to go home after dark.

The benefactors of the hospital met annually to conduct business and to hear a sermon from a leading minister of the day. In 1752 the speaker was the Rev. Isaac Maddox, Bishop of Worcester, who was probably the most knowledgeable contemporary layman on the subject of smallpox. His brief was to encourage the benefactors to continue their good work and show them the value of their efforts. Smallpox *"was an instrument of Death which slays without distinction! Youth and Beauty, Dignity and Power, Wealth and Affluence, are no Protection: the Palace and the Cottage stand in this respect upon a level and the Rich and Poor meet and fall together."*[5]

He conjured up the image of the destitute labourers who came into London at harvest time and found themselves afflicted with smallpox without food, without medicine, without a bed to lie on, or house to cover their diseased bodies from the coldest blasts of the open air. He gave an example of a recent patient who was found with severe disease lying beside his dead wife, surrounded by four children all with the eruption on them, whose only relief was to be admitted to the Smallpox Hospital, which also cared for his children. Many suffered from those *"two most woeful and tormenting companions- Poverty and Sickness"*. But the hospital was full. *"Brethren we hope better things of you."* More money was needed to buy larger premises.

Maddox also expounded on the advantages of inoculation which he said *"always protects, never involves the lungs or produces difficulty breathing"* and had a mortality of less than one in 150 in experienced hands. Although the process was not perfect, Maddox reasoned that God had intended it to have complications and occasional disasters to stop man believing that he was in complete control. Divine guidance and prayer were still essential for success. The operation gave *"a safe passage through this distemper, like the emancipation of slaves,[and] is a deliverance to vast numbers of people, kept as it were in bondage; who before they had undergone this abhorrent disease are excluded from many offices of life and prevented from pursuing their business"*. The Bishop preached *"if man be a useful Creature, and Life a valuable Thing what greater Argument can be drawn in Favour of Inoculation"* than that *"thereby so many precious Lives may be preserved from Death"*.

Gradually the Hospital expanded and within a few years was providing inoculation to about 1,000 people a year. To be admitted one needed a recommendation from one of the subscribers, denying access to the poorest Londoners. As the first, indeed the only, institution specializing in inoculation, the Middlesex Hospital became a magnet for foreign physicians anxious to learn the technique and the correct management of patients after the operation.

Outside London inoculation was available from a wide range of operators and was paid for in an equally wide spectrum of ways. Near Guildford, in Surrey, an anonymous nobleman gave the local surgeon 40 shillings for every poor person he inoculated, which prompted the doctor to carry a supply of inoculum at all times. He soon found many customers *"Country people came every market day to have the operation performed, then went home, kept themselves warm, drank whine whey, and in eight days took the distemper: and so much success attended the practice, that it was answer to their acquaintance, of 3 or 4 hurrying along the town together, that they were going to be oculated".*[6]

Many district inoculators were probably locally trained country apothecaries, or even amateurs, who had learned the simple technique by observing country surgeons. It is the nature of such unqualified operators that they leave no records and their illiterate clients never recorded their experiences. The evidence that they were active stems from the complaints of the medical profession, who disputed their right to compete for business. Kirkpatrick's discussion of the state of inoculation published in 1754 records his disdain: *"we have certain Accounts that the Populace, who were at first strongly prepossessed against this Practice, and who so rarely stop for the Golden Mean, are rushing into the contrary Extreme, and go promiscuously from different Distances into little Market Towns, where, without any medical advice, and very little Consideration, they procure*

Inoculation from some Operator, too often as crude and thoughtless as themselves,: congratulating each other after it over strong Liquor, and returning immediately to their ordinary Labour and Way of living".[7]

Inoculation finally gained public approval from the fellows of the Royal College of Physicians in December 1755 who unanimously agreed *"The College being informed that the Success of inoculating the smallpox and it's reputation in this Country, have been lately Misrepresented among Foreigners, came to the following Resolution.*

That in their Opinion the Objections made at first to it have been refuted by experience and that it is at present more generally esteemed and Practised in England than ever, and that they Judge it to be a Practice of the utmost benefit to Mankind."[8]

The statement was triggered by a pamphlet circulating in France, where inoculation had not been adopted, suggesting that inoculation was a failure and had been abandoned in England. Many of the old arguments long given up in England had been resurrected by French opponents of inoculation when several doctors suggested that it should now be acceptable.

At about this time attitudes towards preparation changed. Adam Thomson, a Scot living in Maryland was struck by the work of the famous Dutch professor, Herman Boerhaave, who had pioneered the idea of chemical treatments for diseases. Boerhaave imitated Hippocrates by presenting his teachings in the form of aphorisms. In aphorism number 1392 he suggested that a mixture of antimony and mercury was an antidote for the "variolous poison" and could be used as a treatment for smallpox. Thomson reasoned that a valuable treatment would be even more beneficial if applied before the poison began to act.[9] He believed that smallpox resulted when an external trigger ignited pre-existing "variolous fuel" within the body. Pretreatment with inhibitors of the fuel should lessen the severity of the disease. Not only did he use his compound for patients preparing for inoculation, he also supplied it to families who intended to contract the infection naturally. Thomson's method acquired wide renown and was soon accepted throughout the colonies. At the same time there was a trend towards shallow cuts or even scratches for inoculation, rather than the deeper cuts used by the early inoculators, which led to a decrease in the mortality associated with the operation from one in fifty to one in three or four hundred. Naturally Thomson's remedy was credited with causing the improvement.

Thomson moved to Philadelphia, then the largest city in North America. In 1750 he delivered a long discourse on his method and its applications which Benjamin Franklin published. Like many other European-trained physicians, Thomson considered his American colleagues so poorly educated as to be medically illiterate. He deliberately gave only a general outline of his therapy on the grounds that any "judicious physician" would easily see how to proceed, while quacks and impostors would remain in the dark. He excluded *"all those who by the courtesy of America are stiled doctors, because it is well known that surgeons, apothecaries, chymists, and druggists, or even mere smatterers in any of these, are all called by that title, as well as real physicians"*. But his attempt to disguise his recipe was soon foiled by a Mr. Barnard of New Jersey. Thomson characterized him as *"a man of little or no education in physic, or indeed in anything else,"* and a *"Jersey secret monger"* who had paid a legitimate physician to reveal the method to him and then sold the secret to other charlatans. Barnard had apparently performed over one thousand inoculations, and, despite his lack of formal qualifications, only two or three of his patients died.

Thomson's innovation spread to England. Gradually the combination of antimony and mercury became accepted as the standard preparation for inoculation and were often continued following the operation. John Adams, who became the second President of the United States, wrote an account of his inoculation in 1764 in letters to his fiancé, Abigail, which reveal what a typical mid-century inoculation under Thomson's method was like.[10] First he and his brother, who was inoculated with him, began preparing themselves for the operation by taking ipecac to produce vomiting. John and his brother laughed at each other as the drug took effect but fell silent when they both vomited at the same time. They were limited to a bland diet of porridge without salt, spices, or butter and took antimony pills that their doctor had prescribed.

After a week of "preparation" John and his brother went up to Boston to lodge with a Captain Cunningham who kept an inoculation house and who seems to have been Adams' uncle. As they travelled north from Quincy towards Boston they would have passed through the village of Muddy River passing the house of John Adams' 88 year old maternal uncle, Zabdiel Boylston. Once they were settled at the Cunninghams' their doctors arrived and *"they took their lancets and with their points divided the skin for about a quarter of an inch and just suffering the blood to appear, buried a thread about a quarter of an inch long in the channel"* then dressed their wounds and let them put their coats back on. They were given red and black pills with instructions to take them night and morning and left to their own devices. While the brothers had abundant milk, pudding, rice and other starchy foods, the five people who shared the room with them were under the care of a doctor who kept his patients on half milk, half water and gave them medicines which made them both sick and weak. As their housemates developed their pustules John hoped that he would be next; his companions were faring so well that he felt that there was nothing to worry about.

Finally the pustules appeared and John could write that *"None of the race of Adam, ever passed the small pox with fewer pains, aches, qualms… than I have done. I had no pain in my back, none in my side, none in my head, none in my bones or limbs, no reching or vomiting or sickness."* He thought that he had only about eight or ten pustules, he had not had time to count them yet, but only two were on his face. His brother was just as well, but had had a little more sickness and headache, but three of Adams' companions had had high fevers, severe pains, and many more pustules. Adams summed up the most disagreeable part of the experience as *"long and total abstinence from every thing in nature that has any taste, two heavy vomits, one heavy cathartick (laxative), four and twenty mercurial and antimony pills and three weeks close confinement to an house"* saying nothing about the actual illness. Throughout his letters Adams's main concern was that they should not infect Abigail with smallpox. He smoked each one (probably with burning sulfur, thought to be a disinfectant) and insisted that his father's servant Tom also smoked them before allowing her to read them.

Some idea of the status of inoculation in rural England at the same time can be found in the the diary of William Pulsford , a country surgeon-apothecary based in Wells, in Somerset, which outlines a rural doctor's daily practice, and his fees.[11] He performed inoculation at two prices; 4 guineas (84 shillings) if treating a single patient, and 1 guinea (21 shillings) if the patient was part of a general inoculation. This is still expensive, but clearly shows that general inoculation was part of a regular medical practice. His receipts for eleven months in 1757, all that survives of his records, show that he performed inoculation on nine patients.

There is no reason to think that Pulsford was special, apart from the fact that part of his practice ledger survives. There were about 6000 doctors like Pulsford practising medicine in England. Ninety percent of the population lived outside towns, and half still lived in villages of 500 or fewer. Most of the professional medical care they received was provided by men like Pulsford who rode about on horseback carrying saddlebags full of ointments, herbs, bandages, and surgical instruments. Their work mostly involved treating injuries, draining abscesses, dressing ulcers, in short, all the minor, but essential, treatments for the medical problems that afflicted their patients. Even if only one in ten country doctors practiced inoculation as often as Pulsford, there would have been thousands of inoculations every year. This was good for the inoculated, but made little impact on public health. Inoculation was still something usually undertaken on an individual basis for an individual's own motives. Some, like John Adams, were inoculated during an epidemic as preparation for a forthcoming marriage. Some would have the operation to improve their chances of employment and others to prevent the terrible anxiety of falling victim to smallpox while abroad.

Chapter 18

DISCOVERIES ARE
SOMETIMES MADE BY
MEN OF CONFINED ABILITIES

W hile inoculation was still expensive, it was now widely
known and used by many who could afford it. Then one
family changed inoculation from an expensive, painful,
inconvenient, and sometimes dangerous operation into a mild
and almost completely safe experience. Robert Sutton and his
second son Daniel produced a revolution which made inoculation
almost painless and lowered the price so that it became available
to all levels of society.

Robert Sutton was an obscure country surgeon practising
in the town of Kenton in Suffolk, who would have remained
obscure, but for his own curiosity and the public relations talents
of Daniel.[1] In 1731, at the age of twenty three, Robert began his
surgical career. That year his first son, also Robert, was baptized
and the growing family settled into country medical practice
and anonymity. Twenty three years later Robert Jr. finished his
apprenticeship and was ready to join his father's practice, but he
had not had smallpox and the certainty that he would soon be

exposed to the disease made it sensible for him to be inoculated. Ironically Robert Sr., who would change inoculation, was not himself an inoculator, so Robert was inoculated by John Rodbard, a colleague and near neighbour of the Suttons. The operation went wrong and Robert Jr nearly died. Robert Sr, began to speculate on how and why inoculation worked, why it was sometimes so frighteningly dangerous, and whether he could find a way to make it reliably safe. After mulling over many possible solutions, he settled on a simple change in the way inoculation was carried out. He abandoned the incision and resorted to a simple tiny jab with the sharp end of his lancet. He dipped it in smallpox matter, held the knife at an angle to the skin, and pushed it in only about a millimeter or so, just enough to penetrate the skin and draw the tiniest amount of blood. When the first patient he tried this on had a very easy time, he decided that he had found a method that would make inoculation much safer. In 1757 Robert Sr. was ready to unveil his innovation to the public. He advertised in the Ipswich Journal, the nearest newspaper to Kenton, *"for the Reception of Persons who are disposed to be INOCULATED by him for the SMALL-POX, on the following terms, viz Gentlemen and Ladies will be prepared, inoculated, boarded and nursed, and allowed Tea, Wine, Fish, and Fowl, at Seven Guineas each, for one Month; Farmers at Five pounds, to be allowed Tea, Veal, Mutton, Lamb, &etc.: And for the Benefit of the meaner Sort, he will take them at Three Guineas for a Month, if they are not fit to be discharged sooner: and those who can board and nurse themselves, he will inoculate them for Half a Guinea each. N.B He has for his constant Nurse the well known Mrs. ELIZ. ALEXANDER, Widow, of Framlingham."*[2] He was the first to advertise inoculation services in the area.

Within six months he had opened another inoculation house and had added a third within a year. He now advertised that he would attend for inoculation in four nearby towns on market days. By October 1760 he had agents in 16 towns scattered over a circular area roughly 20 miles in diameter centered on Kenton, all of whom would give advice on the treatment that he offered.

When another inoculator began to advertise in the Ipswich Journal, Sutton reduced his fee to five guineas and opened another house "for the benefit of the lower class of people" where he charged even less. He continued to experiment with various combinations and doses of medicines until in December 1761 he believed that he had hit upon a perfect recipe which guaranteed that his patients would not develop more than 100 pustules. In September 1762 he advertised inoculation, *"being done without incision, the most curious Eye cannot discern where the Operation is performed for the first forty-eight Hours; and with this advantage, that he is always certain whether the Patient receives the Infection or not. He has inoculated since December last, three hundred and sixty five; several of whom were drinkers for many years, and not one has been confined in Bed two Days"*[3]. He used his new plan on both patients with natural infection as well as inoculated smallpox with great success.

Robert Sutton Sr. involved his sons in his practice. One, probably Daniel, could look after patients in his inoculation houses while Robert Sr. could ride out to inoculate and stay with families as much as fifty miles from Kenton. He serviced the wealthy country gentry who would not be seen near one of his inoculation houses and who wished to keep their affairs secret. By November 1762 he could boast that he had managed 453 patients with his new method and was now morally certain of success if his methods and instructions were strictly adhered to.

Left in charge of the inoculation houses, Daniel began to try out some ideas of his own. He followed his father's inoculation technique and used the same drugs, but he began to cut the preparation time down eight or ten days from the month that his father required. He also began to require his patients to walk about outdoors or even continue with their employment while waiting for the symptoms to begin. Only the very few patients who had severe symptoms as the disease began were allowed to stay in bed, the rest continued with his outdoor regimen. The shortened program was cheaper and more convenient and the exposure to the outdoors was considerably better than being cooped up inside for two weeks. Patients began to prefer to be treated exclusively by Daniel Sutton.

However, Robert Sutton Sr. believed that his system had reached perfection. He would not stand for any innovation and condemned Daniel's approach as "not only rash but extremely dangerous". Clearly the father and son could not continue to work together so, in late 1763, Daniel moved about fifty miles south to a village called Ingatestone, in Essex. Here he could take advantage of the traffic along the main road between London and the important port city of Norwich, the third largest city in England. Merchants from the continent heading for London which was well known for its dangers of endemic smallpox, might be persuaded to stop and undergo inoculation which was not widely available in Europe. Equally, London traders could be protected from the horrors of succumbing to smallpox while in a foreign country. Ingatestone was also more than seven miles from the City of London and so outside the control of the Royal College of Physicians and the Corporation of Surgeons who controlled medical practice in the capital. Daniel Sutton did not have the medical qualification that he needed to allow him to practice within their territory.

The citizens of Ingatestone did not welcome their new doctor. Their town was free from smallpox and inoculation could only spread the disease, inhibit trade, and give the place a bad reputation with travelers. He would be a "detriment to the public, and … a nuisance", a "perpetual pest fixed among them ". For three months Daniel did not have a single customer and considered giving up. Eventually he persuaded a few poor families to accept inoculation for free. When they did well, a few more came forward. When they were successfully treated a few paying customers began to appear and his business expanded through word of mouth and advertising. By the end of his first year in independent practice he had inoculated 1629 people and made the large sum of about 2000 guineas. Sutton boasted that his patients had *"not more than twenty Pustules each"* which he felt would appeal to his female customers because it meant that the face was almost never scarred. Most of his clients were ready to resume their normal lives within three weeks *"a Circumstance which particularly affects the working hand"*. He charged four guineas on the day of inoculation and provided everything needed except tea and sugar.

Ingatestone's town officers were concerned that the large numbers coming into the village for treatment had overflowed Sutton's inoculation house and begun to take lodgings in the local inns. This practice could only inhibit others from using the facilities and was banned. However, they could find no examples of Sutton's patients infecting any of the local inhabitants, despite considerable exposure, so they began believed that inoculation was much less contagious than natural smallpox. Although the town's doctors and innkeepers would do their best to protect the public, they could only give assurances *"as it is not in our power, either through Defect in the Laws or Remissness in the Magistrates to execute them to remove the Evil to a greater Distance.* Also, several innkeepers seem to have profited from the overwhelming demand for Daniel's services. Public denials usually meant that the practice went on surreptitiously.

Despite the reluctance of his neighbours to have him in the village, Sutton's business mushroomed. He inoculated 943 patients in the first five months of 1765, 4,347 for the whole year, and earned £6,300; more than the income of the Archbishop of Canterbury and the Chancellor of England. Only a handful of noble families and the enormously fashionable Richard Meade earned more. Sutton could afford improvements *"MR. SUTTON being on a new Plan this Season, is determined to remove every Objection that can possibly be alleged against the Accommodation of his Patients, as far as it is consistent with his singular Method of treating the Small-Pox which has hitherto given universal Satisfaction, having inoculated near Four Thousand Persons, many of whom were upwards of Seventy Years old, others not more than Three Months, and of various bad Constitutions, without the loss of a single Patient. Agreeable to his present Scheme he has fitted up three very convenient Houses, classed out for Six, Four, and Three Guineas Patients; by which method one Class of Patients will not be subject to the Interruptions of another."*[4] Apparently his reasonable fees had attracted rowdy undesirables who offended the wealthier patients who had paid more for his attentions. The lowest rate was for customers who were prepared to share their rooms and even their beds.

Daniel employed a vicar, John Houlton, at Ingatestone, who had two functions: he visited and ministered to those undergoing the operation, but his more important role was to preach the enormous advantages of the Suttonian system. Who could doubt a minister of religion? And he could also publish his sermons extolling the "Sutton Method" without fear of having them labelled "quack bills" by jealous physicians. While his glowing references to the Suttons in his sermons must be treated cautiously, his statistics have never been challenged. Houlton claimed that the Suttons and their assistants had inoculated 55,000 people by 1767, with only six deaths. Their method had revolutionised the practice: *"it is natural to suppose that the great success attending, and emoluments arising from the Suttonian art, may induce many to become imitators of their method of inoculation. And in fact this is so much the case, that in every county In England you meet with these pretenders and itinerants … some of them advertise…that they inoculate according to the new method: others according to the Suttonian method; while others have the modesty to deck their imposition with the style of "the Suttonian Art Improved".*[5]

Daniel Sutton's staggering number of inoculations resulted from his success in setting up partnerships with local surgeons, in effect adopting his father's business model. As soon as trade from any one town became too heavy to handle at one of his houses, he licensed a local partner to carry out the work. Each assistant could carry out two thousand or so operations a year, a business that was extremely lucrative for both parties. Also, partners were not competitors and could be relied upon not to undermine the established fee structure. Daniel Sutton reckoned that he had personally inoculated 20,000 patients between 1764 and 1766 and only two or three had died. But one of these deaths was really due to his own negligence he confessed; he had *"been drunk several times during their eruption"*, and the other two were individuals suffering from other severe life threatening disease that would have killed them anyway.

Daniel's rapid rise to fame almost collapsed in the summer of 1766, just as his web of partnerships was forming. A serious outbreak of smallpox occurred in Chelmsford, a large town just a few miles north of Ingatestone on the main road. Townspeople blamed Sutton and had him indicted to appear before the summer assize. Houlton gives a detailed account of the event: *"This was a fine opportunity for Mr. Sutton's enemies (many of whom live in that quarter) to surmise invent, and propagate what calumnies they please: especially that he sometimes comes on market days to treat with people, who are inclined to be inoculated. If any person chanced to accompany him in his carriage, it was always industriously reported that such person was a patient brought to inoculate from. Others could see small pocks out in full bloom (as they expressed it) notwithstanding the companion was frequently an acquaintance; and it was diametrically contrary to Mr. Sutton's practice to inoculate from such kind of patients. But we shall prove that such... were no more no less than gross lies.*

Every Apothecary in the town was an Inoculator , and had long practised around the neighbourhood: nay some of them had absolutely inoculated persons of the town at their own houses. Mr Sutton must be the man (responsible) notwithstanding Chelmsford lies in the great road from London to Colchester, Ipswich, Norwich, Harwich etc where many stagecoaches stop and ...frequently bring passengers just come from infected houses and many doubtless that are just recovered from the Small-Pox with their infectious bundles of linen. Scandalous accusation! Base partiality!"[6] The grand jury accepted Sutton's defence and observed to the judge "that not one single article alleged against him in the inditement was proved;" Any of Chelmsford's inoculating apothecaries could have started the epidemic.

Although the publicity generated by the trial must have damaged Sutton's reputation, he retrieved some of his public credit by performing a mass inoculation at Maldon, a coastal town about eight miles from Ingatestone. In one day he treated 487 people, 417 poor who were sponsored by parish funds and 71 gentlemen or tradesmen who paid for themselves, bringing a smallpox epidemic to a halt. Many of those he treated were able to continue with their usual occupations while undergoing inoculation because they had very mild symptoms. Trade was restored and the good news was widely distributed by the town to encourage further business. A few weeks later he inoculated a large number of poor patients at Maidstone, thirty miles south, and south the Thames for no charge, further enhancing his reputation for working in the public interest. A shrewd business sense and an appreciation of human psychology underlay the offer to treat the poor gratis. When there were many people with smallpox, even if it was the inoculated form, those who could pay were frightened into taking up the operation. General inoculations meant that there was also a flood of private, fee-paying patients.

Daniel was reconciled with his father and brothers who seem to have accepted that his methods had proved so popular that they should adopt them as well. They went into partnership and developed a network of franchises, marketing a kind of MacSmallpox. Anyone could buy a license to practice the Suttonian system for a flat fee of 100 pounds or a share of the profits. By 1768 there were at least sixty partners scattered over the whole of England, parts of Ireland, the West Indies, and the colony of Virginia.[7] There was even a franchise holder attached to the Royal Regiment at Quebec who advertised his services to the civilian population. The Sutton brothers dispersed to promote their trade. Robert Jr. went to Paris, William joined his brother in London, Joseph was in Oxford, Thomas on the Isle of Wight, James had a base in Wakefield, in Yorkshire, one son-in-law(of Robert Sr.) took up residence in the Hague, and another in Birmingham. The brothers acted as a focal point for attracting new partners and a source of guidance to any doctor in the vicinity who wished to take up the Suttonian method. It was good advertising, and good business practice, to be able to claim that a member of the renowned Sutton family was directly involved. Daniel Sutton went for the most prestigious position. He moved to London and set up an inoculation house called "Sutton House" in Kensington Gore, then a country road about 2 miles from Westminster Abbey and far enough from the city of London to leave him outside the grasp of the Royal College of Physicians.

Suttonian inoculation was now the preferred method for many patients. Huge numbers were recorded for parts of their network; Daniel and his appointed partners in the counties of Essex, Suffok, and Norfolk inoculated 55,000 people. Unfortunately no one kept accurate records of the number inoculated by their franchise network. One clue to their widespread success lies in the reactions of establishment inoculators. Men such as Sir George Baker F.R.S, physician to the royal household, soon to be physician to King George III, Thomas Dimsdale, a well connected, socially acceptable inoculator with a practice in Hertford, and other members of the "Faculty," Fellows of the Royal College of Physicians, took notice of the Sutton's spreading fame. They quickly established that whatever it was that the Suttons were doing, it was a genuine improvement on previous methods. Dimsdale, who will feature in the next chapter, was a wealthy Quaker who had been a specialist inoculator since about 1747. In 1764 he began to write a textbook giving the details of his approach and examples of difficult cases that he had managed. Although he had only lost one patient in his practice he noted that sometimes the results were not as gentle as he hoped. *"in this situation I first heard, and with the utmost satisfaction, that in some parts of the nation, a new and more successful method of inoculating was discovered…The relators gave incredible accounts of the success, which was more marvelous, as the operators…could lay little claim to medical erudition.*

Knowing that improvements which would do honour to the most elevated human understandings, are sometimes stumbled upon by men of more confined abilities…"[8] Dimsdale revealed the ambivalent attitude to the Suttons among the established, socially acceptable tier of medicine. On the one hand they had done something amazing, but on the other they were ignorant "mechanicks" who had no understanding of why they succeeded.

Dimsdale sought to find out what the Suttons were doing *"to expose patients, even in inoculated smallpox to all weather, was a thing unheard of."* He marvelled that patients went about their usual business and that there had been no immediate or long term bad consequences. He began to force his patients to walk about in cold air even if they preferred to remain in bed, and complained that his biggest problem was to prevent them going into public places where they might spread the disease. In some patients the inoculation produced only a single pustule at the inoculation site and these he allowed to return to their work, a great advantage to poor labourers, as long as they took precautions not to expose anyone who had not had smallpox. A further benefit of the new method was that abscesses in the lymph glands in the armpit, a particular problem in children, had disappeared. Only one of his 1500 patients had experienced this problem. Dimsdale speculated that there were two parts of the Suttonian method that made the difference. One was the exposure to cold air and the other the use of fresh fluid material to inoculate rather that the pocky thread that many inoculators used. He concluded *"If these conjectures should be true, perhaps we shall be found to have improved but little on the judicious Sydenham's cool method of treating the disease, and the old Greek Woman's method of inoculating with fluid matter"*.[9]

Sir George Baker, a physician to the royal family, tried to find out what the Suttons did by interviewing some of their patients. He concluded that there were four parts to their programme: exposure to cold air, the very slight puncture, fluid matter for inoculation, and their special nostrum. The Suttons had their own recipe of powders and pills which they gave in a secret pattern to their patients. He could guess that at least one of these ingredients was mercury, since the symptoms produced were similar to mercury poisoning.[10]

Other physicians thought that the nostrum was the crucial component and suggested that the government should offer to buy the recipe from the Suttons to make it widely available. However, a London physician, Thomas Rushton, obtained samples of the "secret" medicines and subjected them to chemical analysis revealing mercury, as expected, and antimony. In other words the special mixture contained the same ingredients used by most inoculators.[11]

Word of the remarkable improvements reached foreign courts. In 1766 the first surgeon to the King of Poland visited Daniel and was surprised at the slight effects of the operation. In 1767 enquiries from Brussels and from the ambassador of the Hapsburg court were referred to the royal physicians and surgeons for an opinion of the new method who begged *"..leave to observe that no report whatsoever in respect to the general success of Inoculation in this country can greatly exceed the truth; that for many years past, scarce one in a thousand has failed under the inoculated Small-pox, even before the time of the Suttons".*[12] The Suttons had added the use of open cold air and "the *inoculators in England in general have adopted this method, and experience the success of it daily.*

That they are of the opinion, that the great success of Messrs Suttons is to be attributed to the advantages arising from the exposition to colder air,... and not to any particular nostrum or specific remedy".

The royal doctors were sure that the method would succeed in Vienna so long as the rules were followed. It had been claimed that the number of pustules formed would rarely exceed one hundred. The doctors replied that this was usually so, but rarely 200 or more formed, although usually there were only about a dozen. Then they concluded "*the Suttons are undoubtedly in some respects improvers of the art of inoculation, but by applying their rules too generally, and by not making a proper allowance for the difference of the constitutions, have frequently done harm. All their improvements have been adopted by other inoculators and in the hands of these the art seems carried to very great perfection.*" They also doubted that the Suttons had inoculated 40,000 individuals without a single fatality. The medical establishment had reason to dislike the Suttons. As untrained, unqualified practitioners, almost beneath contempt as doctors, they had stumbled upon the greatest improvement in inoculation, and they had made a great deal of money from their discovery.

In 1796, Daniel Sutton published a collection of his observations and ideas concerning inoculated smallpox in his autobiography, "The Inoculator".[13] He intended it as an instruction manual for young practitioners and hoped that they would benefit from his years of experience. He warned his readers that many of his practices appeared trifles but:

"Despise not trifles, tho they small appear:
Sands rise to mountains, moments make the year;
and trifles life. Your time to trifles give,
or you may die before you learn to live."

Despite his lack of formal education, Daniel Sutton was an acute observer of the minute clinical details of his patients and an inveterate experimenter. While trying to understand why his father's simple puncture method was so successful, he explored the idea that the agent of smallpox required contact with the skin to infect a patient and he set up a series of experiments to test this idea.[14] In one study he made deep incisions down into the subcutaneous fat where he laid a thread impregnated with "pocky matter". He bound the wound, being careful that the infected thread did not touch the true skin, and left it for two days before removing the thread. There was never a local inoculation reaction, while the conventional operation, which he had performed on the other arm, always progressed as expected, confirming his view that the infectious agent had to make contact with the skin. He attempted to transmit the disease by having a subject breathe through a special contraption connected to the mouth of an inoculated patient. Nothing happened so he concluded that the disease was not transmitted by inhaling infected air. He collected blood from patients at various stages of natural smallpox and rubbed it into the skin of individuals that he was about to inoculate. Again nothing happened, confirming his belief that the state of the blood did not have anything to do with the infection. He took pus from suppurating lymph nodes and tried that. He collected material from early or late pocks and formed them into pills and gave them to his patients to swallow. He even took pocky matter, dissolved it in cold or hot water and gave it as enemas. Nothing happened. Smallpox was only transmitted when the "variolous poison" made contact with the skin.

Sutton challenged another tenet of the "Faculty", the Fellows of the Royal College of Physicians, who supported the idea that fatal smallpox involved the internal organs. One of the cardinal principles of treatment was to get the variolous poison to come to the skin to prevent it "going to the Heart". He obtained permission to perform an autopsy on a Negro who had died of confluent smallpox and showed that there were no pocks anywhere inside the corpse. The skin was the only part of the body affected.

In another experiment he observed that when he heated a patch of skin as the rash began to appear, more pocks formed there than on the rest of the body. Although he did not realize it, this was probably due to increased blood flow through the warm area at a time when the virus was present in the circulation. Greater blood flow led to a larger number of virus particles reaching the skin, offering an explanation for the face being the most severely affected part of the body, as it has the highest blood flow of any area of skin. Sutton concluded that Sydenham's cold method was beneficial in reducing the number of pocks that formed because it lowered the temperature of the skin. He also concluded that his practice of letting his patients have continuous exposure to fresh air probably worked for the same reason.

His experiments are probably without parallel for the time. Daniel Sutton, despite his lack of formal education, was a true clinician scientist. In modern terms we would say that he formulated a hypothesis and tested it in experiments that could have falsified that hypothesis. He had convinced himself that whatever caused smallpox, it was contact with the skin that triggered the disease.

Sutton's devoted clinical care led to surprising observations among his patients. One day he set out to inoculate all seven hundred inhabitants of a town and managed half before lunch and the rest after three-thirty in the afternoon. He was astounded when he noticed that those treated in the afternoon had about five times as many pocks as those treated in the morning. But when he consulted his notebooks he realized that this almost always occurred and modified his approach so that he only operated in the morning. By keeping copious meticulous notes he also showed show that inoculation never transmitted syphilis or scrofula as its opponents had claimed.

Sutton classified his patients into favourable, unfavourable, and untreatable. Among the eighty percent who were likely to do well were *"young children under two or three and in perfect health, placid but not timid, and especially who had not undergone prolonged preparation"* While those who were *"indolent, slothful, gross fleshy, corpulent adults in good health and who perspire on gentle exercise"* would also have an easy time. Such adults were probably free from other debilitating diseases such as tuberculosis and not malnourished. He advised special care for unfavourable children, those with nappy rash, worms, measles, or who were strongly opposed to inoculation and those *"with discoloured stools such as those children who milk to dram drinkers"*. He advised that great care should be taken to wet nurse infants from women whose breasts had been in milk for about the child's age because, if the breast was too old, *"costiveness (constipation), flatulence, and green griping stool"* were the result. Ominous signs in adults were *"wind, worms, gout, sailors, and those of thin delicate habit"*. He refused to treat anyone with *"jaundice, dropsy, hydrocephalous, hypochondriacs, hysterics, and pregnant women"*. Pregnancy was a notoriously dangerous time to catch smallpox; even in the most experienced hands inoculation might kill a pregnant woman.

Another of Sutton's observations was the discovery of a specific type of immune reaction known as the arthrus response or cutaneous hypersensitivity. He found that he could distinguish patients who had had smallpox before, however slightly, and were resistant to inoculation, by the response in their skin when the inoculum was introduced. In a susceptible individual the injection site was like a tiny red fleabite that only began to itch on the fourth day. However, if there was an immediate small swelling expanding to the size of a shilling piece within an hour or so accompanied by itching and a reddish ring around the site like an insect bite or sting, the recipient had already had smallpox. We now know that this was a reaction between the patient's antibodies and the smallpox virus in the injection site indicating prior immunity. Such local immune reactions became widely used in the twentieth century as markers of immunity to a range of infections.

By continuously monitoring the progress of the inoculation wound, Sutton could forecast the patient's course, and take prophylactic measures when indicated. His treatment included laxatives, calculated to produce four stools a day in a favourable patient; but, if there was any doubt about the likely outcome, the dose would be increased to produce six motions a day. The appearance of the pustule on the seventh day was critical. In patients destined to have a mild course there was a fully formed pustule with a domed top. If the pustule remained flat and failed to fill, then the patient was likely to develop convulsions and suffer from a high fever and severe back pain. Enemas were judged to be essential to head off the impending crisis.

Daniel Sutton's book is a remarkable account of a clinician scientist at work. His many detailed observations and experiments are probably unique in 18th century medicine. His investigation of the role of the skin in inoculation is one of the very first systematic studies of the pathogenesis of a disease process. Yet no one remembers him. Sutton made a serious mistake by publishing too late. He procrastinated. Every year some new little nuance persuaded him to delay until his system was perfect. If he had printed his book in the 1770s or 80s his ideas might have attracted attention and debate. Even those who disagreed with his conclusions might have been stimulated to perform experiments of their own. But in 1796 inoculation was no longer a focus of scientific interest. Edward Jenner and vaccination had altered the intellectual environment.

The Suttons were also victims of their own success. When numerous inoculators, many without any medical training at all, began to copy their methods, the price rapidly declined. So many inoculators were available that the advantage of being a Sutton soon wore off. Everyone could do it, and most got results that were just as good as the innovators'. Daniel Sutton lamented:

"Whether from an interested or other sinister motive, I neither know, nor wish to enquire, but I find it has been circulated , That I am not the person who introduced the new system of inoculation:... In short That some other person, having assumed my name has proceeded to the exorbitant length of declaring that for many years I had quitted my profession and was long since dead". His achievements were almost forgotten. The one thing that he valued above all his accolades and financial rewards, was the fact that the King had granted him a family crest. He had asked that this be made retroactive so that his father and brothers were allowed to claim the same distinction. This mark of gentlemanly status meant more to him than anything else that had happened during his career. It seems a small reward for a man whose efforts resulted in a discovery of world shattering importance, as we shall see later in this book. If

he had been a "member of the Faculty", not a mere "empirick", a knighthood or a financial reward from Parliament might have been forthcoming.

Daniel Sutton's impact on inoculation was recognised by his contemporaries. William Woodville, physician to the inoculation hospital, probably the leading authority on inoculation wrote, "*a new era in the history of inoculation had now taken place., by the introduction of the Suttonian practice…not a doubt ws entertained but that the Suttonian plan of inoculation was incomparably more successful than that of any other practitioner.*"[15] Gentleman's Magazine carried an obituary which concluded "*The Benefits which the world has derived from Mr. Sutton's practice have been duly appreciated, and will cause his name and memory ever to be recollected with respect and honourable distinction.*"[16]

But sadly he is now forgotten.

Chapter 19

A CLINICAL TRIAL

W
hat had the Suttons actually done? Huge public support
and the intense interest of their competitors showed
that their methods really were significantly better that
those of other operators, but which among their innovations was
responsible for their success?

In 1768 William Watson, a physician to the Foundling
Hospital, wrote *"An Account of a Series of Experiments Instituted
with a View of Ascertaining the Most Successful Method of Inoculating
the Smallpox."* which cast some light on the relative value of different parts of the "Suttonian system", as it had become known.[1]
Watson, born in 1715, had a varied career at the heart of the
English scientific establishment.[2] He began as an apothecary
with an interest in medicinal plants and soon established himself as a leading medical botanist. Sir Hans Sloane sponsored his
membership of the Royal Society in 1741 and made him a trustee
of the British Museum. In the 1740s Watson began experimenting with the new phenomenon of electricity and showed that
it seemed to consist of a single "fluid" with both positive and
negative states rather than being two different "fluids". He also
managed to transmit an electric charge through a wire two miles
long. For these experiments he was awarded the Copley medal

of the Royal Society, then, as now, its most prestigious award. In the 1750s Watson developed an interest in medicine. In 1757 he received a doctor of physic degree from Halle University, which allowed him to apply for a license from the Royal College of Physicians. In 1762 he was appointed to the staff of the Foundling Hospital.

Watson was responsible for the inoculation of many children every year as part of the Hospital's established practice of inoculating all children in their care who had not had smallpox by the time that they returned from the country. In London, where smallpox was endemic, it would soon sweep through the dormitories in which they were housed. From the beginning he noted that there were several different approaches to inoculation besides the Suttons' method. One doctor advocated a particular mixture of mercury and laxatives, another thought that the source of the "pocky matter" was crucial, yet another recommended bed rest and "sweating" until the eruption appeared. Watson had already compared exposing his charges to cool open air with his previous method of keeping them in bed, and found that the disease was less severe than before, confirming the value of the Suttons' practice. He was now *very desirous of knowing what it was, in the whole regime, that chiefly contributed to lessen the disease; particularly what share the kind of variolous matter had in the success, whether it depended upon its being taken from natural or inoculated small-pox, and then whether in its watery, or in its purulent state. It would be a desirable thing likewise, when the variolous matter inserted and every other circumstance was the same , to observe what effect mercurial purges had, when given as preparatory. Nothing hitherto had been done in a comparative view...An investigation of this sort therefore, which very few physicians are in a situation of making, I considered of no small importance. I resolved therefore, to put in practice several of the methods that have been used with success, together with some others which promised to be equally secure; to the end that if any one method was by experience found to answer better than others, it might be adopted....I determined to try what medicines of different kinds, under the same regimen, would produce: It was proper also to be informed of what nature unassisted, not to say undisturbed, would do for herself. This was not to be done, but where a number of persons of both sexes were inoculated at the same time and place, in the same manner, with the same variolous matter, and observing equally the same regimen. The only difference then was to consist in their medical treatment."*[3] Watson described, and now carried out, a controlled clinical trial with an added touch of genius. He would assess the severity of the smallpox in each case by counting the pocks that formed on each child. There was universal agreement that the number of pocks was a good indicator of disease severity so his approach was logical and also unique. There were no previous clinical studies where a quantitative variable was used to determine the success of a treatment. By introducing quantitation as a measure of differences in individual responses Watson may be considered to have invented clinical science or, more directly, scientific medicine.

He began on October 12, 1767 by inoculating thirty-one children aged six to twelve, twenty-one boys and ten girls. He split them into three groups, five boys and five girls took a laxative and mercury as preparation. A second group of five boys and five girls were given laxatives only; and a third group of eleven boys were not given any preparative medicines. When the nurses counted the pustules on each child it appeared that there was no difference between the children given mercury and those who got the laxative only. However, Watson fretted that since mercury had laxative properties combining it with another purge might have removed the drug before it had had time to act, so he repeated the experiment using material from an inoculated patient and giving the mercury compound alone. Again the results showed that there was no benefit from the mercury compound. For his final experiment Watson gave twenty children, ten boys and ten girls, no treatment and used the material from a "perfectly concocted" pustule described as "perfectly white and viscid as cream". This experiment was complicated because two children developed over one hundred pustules while most of the rest had less than twenty making the "medium" – what we call the average - over fifty each while not giving an accurate picture of the results.

Among the seventy-four children Watson inoculated, 12 had had only one pustule at the inoculation site. Inoculators always worried that this meant that they had done something wrong, but Watson reinoculated them and found that there was no reaction to the second puncture indicating that the children had become immune. The Suttons' method of inoculating with a very slight puncture had produced an advantage for the doctor as well as the patient. The puncture site disappeared within twenty-four hours so that an observer could watch the progress of the inoculation without interference from a discharging wound produced by an incision. A bright red circle at the puncture site appearing on the fourth day after the operation was the first sign of the developing infection. The operator could be sure that he had succeeded when it appeared, and normal skin indicated immunity.

The whole group had a total of two thousand three hundred and sixty-two pustules; a tiny number compared to the tens of thousands sometimes seen on bodies of patients with the confluent smallpox. But almost half these pustules had occurred on the five children with the greatest number, so that the average on the other 69 was only 18 each. Watson noted that even those with the greatest number had not been ill or stayed in bed for even an hour longer than usual. Comparing all the results of his different trials, the inoculator concluded that mercury compounds did not lessen the severity of inoculated smallpox, and that the best source of material to inoculate was "thin, watery, ichorous matter" taken from an early lesion. Because Watson had carefully treated all the children in a group in the same way he could draw a unique conclusion about his "outliers", the five children who had developed many more pocks than the others. Since they had shared the same air and food, and the same inoculum had been used for all the children in a group the differences between individuals must be due to some intrinsic property of the child. He argued that they differed in their "constitutions". Other explanations, such as a more malignant form of smallpox or some "variolous character of the air, which were commonly given to explain the differences in the severity of smallpox between individuals could not explain the differences between his subjects.

Now we would call it their genetic makeup and start scanning their genomes to find the causes.

Watson's general conclusion was of sweeping importance: *"I hold it as a truth, and I am not singular in my opinion, that inoculation, practiced by any person whatever, in any manner yet devised, and at any time, carries with it in general less danger to the patient than natural small-pox under the direction of the most able and experienced physician."*[4]

Watson's experimental design, emphasizing that all children got exactly the same treatment apart from one variable, and the inclusion of a control group who received no treatment, shows that he understood the principles of what would come to be called the "scientific method", the basis for experimental science. In the mid-eighteenth century almost no one had conducted such experiments with groups of humans and used the results to inform clinical practice. Watson's inoculation experiments deserve to be remembered alongside James Lind's very small trial of citrus fruits to prevent scurvy as the beginning of controlled clinical trials and the first examples of truly scientific medicine.

None of the sophisticated statistical methods developed in the twentieth century were available to help Watson analyze his results. When applied in the twenty-first century they reveal a fascinating result invisible to Watson. None of the treatments made any difference.[5] The results of each experiment are the same. In the end Watson's experiments showed that only two parts of the Suttons' method were responsible for their success, exposure to cold air and very slight punctures. As Thomas Dimsdale had guessed, they had returned to the methods of Sydenham and the old lady in Turkey.

Chapter 20

THE AGE OF INOCULATION

William Watson had reported that inoculation was often carried out by completely unqualified individuals but he, unlike Dimsdale, did not include the Suttons among the illegitimate operators. He referred to them as *"a certain family, who have practiced inoculation with great success. They have deserved well; not only on account of some real improvements they have made in this process, but also for the confidence they have excited in the public, from which vast numbers have been inoculated, who otherwise would not."*[1] Once the Suttons had made inoculation safe and popular it became a very competitive business. Another Mr. Watson (not William, above) and his partners in Sussex set out to attack the Suttons' business *"or else they will run away with all the cash in the County"*. He undercut their lowest price of 42 shillings (2 guineas) at their inoculation house nearby by offering to treat all 300 local inhabitants who needed the operation for 100 pounds (6 shillings 8 pence each, about one sixth of the Suttons' price). Watson achieved this low rate by dispensing with preparation altogether and only giving medicines if they were justified by severe symptoms. At the time, 1767, the Suttons were clearing 100 guineas a week from one house in Sussex, as well as inoculating large parties in the surrounding countryside. There were at least twenty doctors advertising inoculation in the local paper in Lewes, a small port on the Sussex coast. They all used the Suttonian method and were uniformly successful since *"if one should die, all the county would soon hear of it".*[2]

Sometimes competition between inoculators boiled over into arguments over who was the better operator. Dr John Smith, who wrote the first description of Stonehenge, obtained a house near Winchester and advertised in the Hampshire Chronicle: *"Dr Smith who had inoculated SMALLPOX between 30 and 40 years in Sussex, Kent, and Surrey and these last seven years in Hampshire and Wiltshire with the greatest success Is now at Southampton, where he attends daily several under inoculation."* Any who could not have the operation at home were advised *"They may, on the shortest notice, be Inoculated at Giles' Hill House on the most agreeable terms: Common Servants two Guineas, others agreeable to their Circumstances. He gives his advice to the poor gratis."*[3]

The next week, Nov 1, 1774, when the advertisement was repeated, it was accompanied by another signed by four other practitioners *"We, the undermentioned SURGEONS of the Town of Southampton, beg leave to assure our Friends and the Inhabitants in general, that we intend to inoculate the Smallpox during the Continuance in the Town."*[4]

Smith replied: *"Dr Smith informs his Friends, that, notwithstanding the quadruple Alliance entered into the Physical, Chirurgical, Pharmaceutical, and Obstetrical Operators of the Town, he continues his INOCULATION of the SMALLPOX with his usual Success"*... His son had now joined him in his practice after a period training with the Suttons and his piece concluded *"N.B. As they (we) follow no other Branch of the Business they have some Pretensions to believe themselves Superior to those who attempt to investigate every Branch of the Medical Art"*[5]

Thomas Jeans, one of the "quadruple alliance", retorted *"The Public are hereby acquainted that Mr. Jeans (a Member of the Corporation of Surgeons of London) inoculates the Smallpox according to the most improved and Successful Method of Practice...Mr. Jeans, with all due deference to Dr Smith's wonderful Abilities, presumes that there can be no Impropriety in his understanding to inoculate the* *smallpox as a Branch of the Art which he <u>legally</u> professes. The Doctor assumes an unnecessary Air of Consequence, in imagining that the Alliance of the Southampton Surgeons was established <u>merely</u> to oppose him; as no Part of their <u>innocent</u> Advertisement could justify his very acute Sneers; The Doctor's petulent Behaviour savours more strongly of that presumptive Principle which should characterise an itinerant Quack, rather than a Man of his <u>far extended</u> Reputation".*[6]

Their little spat revealed the intense competition between inoculators. It was a lucrative business which sometimes made up half a surgeon's annual income and was well worth fighting over.

The Smiths won this particular argument; Smith Jr. was given the contract to inoculate the poor of Southampton at 5shillings and 3pence a head. Following the precedent set at nearby Salisbury, local worthies, including the Bishop of Winchester, contributed to a charity to provide the operation to the poor during an epidemic. Everyone recognised that this was good for business as well as an act of kindness. The sooner the disease was eradicated, the sooner commerce resumed. Deserving paupers, but not domestic servants who were the responsibility of their employers, were given tickets directing them to attend Mr. Smith. With their inoculation chit, the objects of charity received a set of instructions admonishing them to avoid church, and forbidding them to visit markets, or attend any public gathering. They could gain the recognised benefit of fresh air by walking in the fields, or, if they lived in Southampton, walking on the beach.

The Smith's practice resembled the Suttons' in offering inoculation in a range of formats. Wealthy individuals could have their children inoculated at home. Those who were old enough to board out in an inoculation house could sign up for a range of accommodation and food and stay for up to a month. But these were expensive options, and the poor, who made up about two thirds of the population, did not have access to them. They were frequently provided with "general inoculation" when part or all of a local population were inoculated at one time. Funding for general inoculations came from a range of sources. In Southampton and Winchester a charitable fund was set up, and local worthies, again including the bishop of Winchester, contributed to pay the costs involved and doctors were invited to bid for a contract to provide the service. In the three general inoculations carried out in Southampton, in 1774, 1778, and 1783 the majority of those inoculated were children under the age of five, and about 30% were in the age range 11-30.[7] Very few were over thirty, suggesting that the common opinion that sooner or later everyone caught smallpox was probably correct.

Although funded by charitable contributions, such general inoculations were often undertaken for uncharitable reasons. Smallpox ruined business in a town like Southampton, and after a general inoculation the town authorities could publicise that the town was now free of the disease. In Southampton the magistrates advertised that they had eradicated smallpox and also banned any further inoculations. They would prosecute anyone inoculating strangers who had come into town for the operation and would also fine and imprison anyone found walking about in a public place with smallpox broken out upon them. Furthermore they blamed vagrants for spreading the disease and introducing it into the town in the first place. Anyone harbouring a vagrant, whether in their houses or barns, would be fined forty shillings and anyone apprehending a vagrant would be given ten shillings reward. The vagrant would be whipped and confined to jail. Vagrancy even applied to the army. When the militia was garrisoned in Southampton their wives and families were considered and treated as vagrants and banned from town.

Sometimes parish overseers and the guardians of the poor undertook general inoculations as part of their duty of care to their community. Again financial considerations were often compelling. In Brighton in 1786 the Town Fathers had to cope with the very high costs of caring for smallpox patients in the local pest houses, which averaged almost 6 pounds for each patient.[8] After a careful survey of the population they concluded that they could inoculate the 545 individuals who qualified as "paupers" for 151 pounds compared to the 140 pounds that they had already spent on only 25 infected individuals. The cost of inoculation was made up of 68 pounds at a fee of 2 shillings and 6 pence paid to the surgeons for each pauper treated, and a total of almost 83 pounds spent on providing food, fuel, and pocket money for the paupers while they were under inoculation and unable to work. A local census showed that there were 1733 people in Brighton who had already had smallpox and 1887 who had not. Since the parish was only paying for the "paupers" that meant that over 1300 other residents paid for their own inoculations. For these the surgeons charged 7 shillings and six pence and so they earned over 500 pounds for their services.

Brighton was an example of a "complete" general inoculation as defined by Thomas Dimsdale. His book, published in 1767, in which he subscribed to the Suttons' system of inoculation, had made him the leading authority on inoculation in England.[9] In 1768 he was approached by a Russian ambassador with a request that he travel to Russia to inoculate the empress Catherine the Great because Daniel Sutton, her first choice, had declined. Although he initially refused, he was eventually persuaded and travelled with his son to inoculate the empress and teach Russian doctors the appropriate techniques. Mindful of the potential dangers involved, Catherine arranged for a sleigh and team to be ready at the rear entrance to her palace so that Dimsdale could escape if the operation went wrong. Both Catherine and her son were successfully inoculated and Dimsdale returned to England with an enhanced reputation. Catherine made him a Baron of the Russian Empire, gave him 10,000 pounds and 500 pounds a year for life, as well as granting him the professional title of "First Physician and Actual Counsellor of State to her Imperial Majesty the Empress of all the Russias" - his F.R.S seemed almost insignificant by comparison.[10]

Dimsdale had already built himself an inoculation house and offered home inoculations to those who could afford his fees,as well as undertakimg a general inoculation of his home town, Hertford, bringing a smallpox epidemic to a halt.

As general inoculations became common, Dimsdale noticed that a potentially dangerous approach had appeared. In some communities the parish paid for the paupers but left the rest of the population to their own resources. Some were unable to pay and others were opposed to inoculation in principle; as a result the inoculated paupers spread smallpox into the rest of the community with disastrous results. Many doctors, like the Suttons, believed that inoculated smallpox was not contagious and that it was safe to perform such partial inoculations. Dimsdale disagreed and gave a few examples of catastrophes that had resulted from inoculation, especially when it was performed by unqualified operators. His own footman had left his service and set himself up as an inoculator on the basis that he had learned the technique from his master. Sadly he had killed a girl when his inoculation gave her confluent smallpox. Dimsdale also knew of a dangerous farmer who had inoculated another farmer who could only afford five shillings and three pence for his own operation. The inoculator sent him home, telling him inoculation was never contagious, but when he got home he infected his wife who died, leaving him with five children. This same inoculator had treated only the members of a nearby parish who could afford his fee and assured the others that they were safe. His patients spread the disease through the neighbourhood and several died. On another occasion Dimsdale was called to a house to treat a child with confluent smallpox only to discover that the boy's father, a schoolteacher, was using his home as an inoculation house without protecting his children. One died and another went blind as a result.

Of course Dimsdale was right. Inoculation could spread smallpox and those who caught it from inoculated individuals had the natural dangerous disease, as both Zabdiel Boylston and Charles Maitland had discovered. Whether inoculated smallpox was more or less contagious than the natural disease was irrelevant.

To counter the threat of inoculation spreading smallpox Dimsdale proposed a rigorous protocol for carrying out general inoculations to counter partial inoculations. His process began with a decision by the appropriate local body, whether magistrates or parish guardians, perhaps supplemented with some of the leading citizens, to inoculate the whole population. There would then be a door-to-door census to determine exactly who was susceptible and who was immune. Anyone who was considered a bad risk due to another illness, and anyone who refused on grounds of conscience would be ordered to leave the area. A contract would be given to a group of skilled inoculators to carry out the procedure and all would be inoculated on the same day. Everyone could return home and, if severely affected, the inoculators would provide the appropriate medicines. Since most of the inoculees would have very mild disease they could provide nursing care for any who required it saving the parish the extra expense. The whole process would take about three weeks, and most of those who wanted to could continue working, or at most lose one or two days wages, sparing the parish most of the cost of supporting paupers during their inoculations. Carried out to this detailed format, inoculation would immunise the entire population of the parish, effectively eradicating smallpox for several years. Dimsdale recognised that any child born afterwards would be susceptible and advocated regular general inoculations every five or six years. By following his own programme he almost eliminated smallpox from Hertford, his home. Between 1766 and 1776 there were only six deaths from smallpox compared to an average of about 20 a year before.

As we have seen, the improvement in inoculation results and acceptability was largely due to the Suttons' reintroduction of minimally traumatic operations and exposure to fresh air. However, not every inoculator used the same techniques. Some preferred a small incision into which they laid a thread impregnated with the smallpox matter which they then covered with a bandage for a few days. Others used a North African technique in which a small blister was raised on the skin and a smallpox soaked thread passed through the blister. Some even persisted with the original method of an incision through the full thickness of the skin into the underlying fat. Edward Jenner later recalled a colleague who "liked to see a bit of fat" and whose results were terrible.[11] In some cases these were individuals who were following techniques that they had learned years before, while others thought that their method, particularly incision, was essential to the success of the procedure. Since no one was keeping records, no one knew which method was safest. Certainly the Suttonian system was the most acceptable to the patients, but a persuasive operator could still insist on his favoured method. Also there was no agreement on exactly what or how much preparation was necessary, or if any treatment after the operation was essential. Despite these wide variations in procedure among inoculators, there was general agreement that the death rate was now about one in 500, and many inoculators had treated over a thousand patients without a single death.[12]

Some idea of the place that inoculation had reached by the 1770s is given in a book written by William Buchan M.D. He was a Scot who had trained in Edinburgh and then practised in the North of England for seven years before returning to Edinburgh. In 1769 he wrote "Domestic Medicine", a book intended for a general audience, which combined advice on how to stay healthy, coupled with a description of most of the major diseases and their treatments.[13] Probably the first such work in English aimed at the literate but non-medical reader, it was a fantastic success. The 5000 copies of the first edition soon sold out and a second edition, extensively expanded, was printed in 1772. Thereafter there was a new edition almost every year until the seventeenth edition in 1800. Domestic Medicine also had a huge following outside Britain. Editions appeared in Philadelphia and Dublin at regular intervals until 1871; overall 142 separate English language editions went on sale during the hundred years that the book was in print.[14] Buchan's views on inoculation must have been known to a great many people in the English-speaking world.

Buchan argued that one of the leading factors retarding the general spread of inoculation was the medical profession itself. "The fears, the jealousies, the prejudices, and the opposite interests of the Faculty, are, and ever will be, the most effectual obstacles to the progress of any salutary discovery."[15] It was only when men who were not physicians began inoculating that the practice became safe and more extensive. Men like the Stuttons taught the regular doctors that the greatest danger to the patient occurred when there was too much, not too little medical intervention.

He reserved some harsh remarks for many of his colleagues "They know very little of the matter, who impute the success of modern inoculators to any superior skill, either in preparing the patient or communicating the disease. Some of them indeed, from a sordid desire of ingrossing the whole practice to themselves, pretend to have extraordinary secrets of nostrums for preparing persons for inoculation , which never fail of success. But this is only a pretence to blind the ignorant and inattentive. Common sense and prudence alone are sufficient both in the choice of subject and management of the operation."[16]

Another factor retarding the growth of inoculation was the opposition of some of the clergy. Buchan wondered how they could oppose something that was so wholly beneficial to the public. Instead of opposing inoculation, or speaking in support of the practice, they should lead by having their own children inoculated. This would give the strongest possible support. How could they, as parents, deny their children the obvious benefits of getting smallpox out of the way in early childhood. If a daughter grew up without becoming immune to the disease she ran the risk of catching it while pregnant, when the chance of dying was very high, or of developing the disease while nursing her infant, when the child would have to be removed for its own safety and might well die without its mother's milk. Or she might continue to nurse the baby and they might both die of smallpox. How melancholy to lay a mother and her newborn in the same grave.

In some families the parents were divided about whether to inoculate their children or not. In one case Buchan helped a father who was desperate to inoculate his only surviving son after smallpox had killed his other children but whose wife would not give her consent. He instructed him to collect a little smallpox pox on a small cloth, take the boy into a private room, make a small scratch on his arm and rub the cloth over it, then cover the site with a plaster. Everything went well and no one suspected that the child had had anything other than very mild natural smallpox.

Buchan argued that the benefits of inoculation were so great that some method or means had to be found to make it universal.

If it became fashionable then everyone would do it and the reluctance of some would be overcome. Perhaps every parish should employ an inoculator; possibly the local clergy could provide the service. They often gave medical advice and were frequently the best educated members of their community. They could inoculate since it was no more difficult that bleeding which the clergy often undertook if no surgeon was available. Priests working with the wild Indians had inoculated their own flocks successfully. A planter in the West Indies had inoculated all his slaves without mishap. But if no one else would undertake the operation then people could always do it themselves and inoculate their own children. Buchan said that he knew of many families who had done this and that not one had had a bad result.

Buchan then revealed the simplest possible way to inoculate, one that he had used on his only son. *"I ordered the nurse to take a bit of thread which had been previously wet with fresh matter from a pock, and to lay it on his arm, covering it with a bit of sticking plaster. This staid six or seven days, til it was rubbed off by accident. At the usual time the small-pox made their appearance , and were exceedingly favourable."*[17] No skill was necessary and this method avoided any incision which many people found the most worrying part of inoculation.

Inoculation had become imbedded in English life. Many children were inoculated before they were ten. Families who could afford the fees would arrange their operations. Children who were wards of the parish were inoculated at parish expense because they could not be apprenticed or found work in service until they were immune to smallpox. In many small towns there were regular general inoculations. But one large group remained unable to take advantage of the benefits. The urban poor, especially in London and the rapidly industrialising cities of the north were largely excluded from access to inoculation.

Chapter 21

HOW TO SAVE LONDON?

W hy were London's children cut off from inoculation?
Several factors seem to have been at work. In many
cities, especially London, smallpox was a childhood illness and so much a part of regular life that people were not afraid
of it. Smallpox was just one of several diseases that killed half of
all children before they were five. Many families could not afford
the fees required to obtain medical help for any illness, let alone
smallpox. The parish social structure that supported inoculation
in many rural areas was much weaker in London and the parish
authorities did not see the benefits of the extra costs. Why bother
when most children were immune by the age of ten when they
became productive members of society? Finally, the religious
objections that retarded the adoption of inoculation were still
prevalent in poorer parishes.

When a group of London physicians led by John Coakley
Lettsome attempted to make inoculation available to poor families by founding a dispensary to provide inoculation for the
poor in their own homes an unholy row erupted. Although
inoculation was well known and trusted there was still scope for
extreme differences of opinion about how to proceed in urban
areas. Lettsome was a hyperactive, compulsive philanthropist.[1]

He once reckoned that he had only twenty minutes at home each week and had not taken a holiday for over twenty years. Born to a Quaker family in the Virgin Islands in 1744, he came to England to be educated at the age of six. When he was 17 he was apprenticed to a surgeon in Yorkshire and five years later went to London to train as a surgeon at St. Thomas's Hospital. When his father died he returned home to the Virgin Islands and promptly gave away the family plantation leaving him with no fortune and effectively destitute. He did not stay that way long. Within two years he had earned over £2000 from medical practice allowing him to return to London and resume his medical studies. By 1770 he had studied in Edinburgh, acquired an M.D. from Leiden, and a license to practice from the Royal College of Physicians. He became a prolific author beginning with a treatise on the tea tree and the way that tea drinking was poisoning British society.[2]

Once he had begun medical practice he joined with a group of like-minded physicians to establish the General Dispensary in Aldersgate, the first institution devoted to providing free medical care to poor Londoners. Applicants could receive medicines from an apothecary based at the dispensary and request visits by staff to their homes to see relatives too sick to move. Lettsome claimed to have visited over 6000 poor persons in their homes, giving him an unrivalled insight into how the poor lived. In 1775 he aided another group of physicians in establishing *a General Dispensary for Inoculating the Poor in Their Own Homes*.[3] Inoculation was now recognised as being of the greatest benefit, so why should it be denied to London's poor? Since the Inoculation Hospital would only take children over the age of seven and most London children had smallpox before they were five, there was no point sending them to the Smallpox Hospital. Why not inoculate them at home just as wealthy families had their children inoculated at home?

Baron Dimsdale was angered by the suggestion. He had spelled out a detailed plan of how to conduct general inoculations and the dangers of partial inoculations.[4] To him cities such as London were an insoluble problem. Far too large for a single inoculation on a single day to cover everyone, there was no way his programme could be followed. Even partial inoculations limited to a single parish were likely to fail. London's poor lived under such wretched circumstances in narrow lanes, blind alleys, often with several families in a single room that they could not take advantage of the fresh air that was thought to be the basis for the success of the Suttonian system. Such families lived a real hand-to-mouth existence and could not afford to have the parents take a few days off to nurse their sick children. Nor would the parish officers support the scheme, since they would see it as an increased expense if they were required to find the food and fuel required for their impoverished families. Worse, when families became aware that fresh air was necessary they would begin to wander through the city streets and parks, spreading smallpox as they went.

But anything less than a complete general inoculation would inevitably lead to the spread of smallpox. Children who were only mildly affected would go outside to play with their uninoculated friends, while anyone ill enough to be confined to bed would be visited by friends wishing to gossip. Furthermore, it would be unfair to expose those who opposed inoculation or who were too ill with other diseases to be inoculated without their consent. Dimsdale's solution to the problem was to call for Parliament to establish a network of hospitals, which he wanted to call inoculation houses to avoid the prejudice against hospitals among the poor. These could provide the best standards of care and keep their charges in isolation until the disease had passed and they had been thoroughly fumigated. While some parishes might be tempted to scrimp by employing unqualified inoculators he advised against this. One parish that he knew of had put inoculation out to tender and, although the local doctors offered a very low price, the village blacksmith undercut them with a bid of 18 pence. When the council were about to accept his offer, one member objected that the blacksmith's inexperience meant that some patients might die and the parish would have to bear the costs of the burials. To which the blacksmith replied *"give me half a crown a head (30 pence), and them that die I will carry to the church –yard without putting the parish to any further expense"*. The blacksmith won the contract. Dimsdale thought *"that to trifle with the lives of their indigent fellow creatures must be an indelible reproach to any people."*

There were only two problems. To inoculate the whole of London would require building enough hospitals to carry out over 20,000 inoculations a year. Not only was this impractical, but Parliament was not inclined to vote in favour of the huge sum required.

An unseemly squabble broke out between Lettsom and Dimsdale which developed into something reminiscent of the pamphlet wars of the 1720s. Dimsdale, among others, had noticed that the London Bills of Mortality showed that there had been 10,179 deaths from smallpox between 1772 and 1776 but only 8,642 in the four years before that.[5] He blamed the increase on the unregulated use of inoculation in London and insisted that the rise in mortality rate vindicated his view that inoculation outside his rigid protocols was dangerous. Since his scheme for hospital inoculations was clearly unworkable, this meant that inoculation should not be carried out in London unless patients were rich enough to be inoculated and isolated in their own homes, or if they went to one of the inoculation houses that surrounded the city such as that run by Daniel Sutton just outside the seven mile limit. In effect the poor were to be denied access to the procedure which Dimsdale acknowledged was actually very beneficial to anyone inoculated.

Dimsdale took exception to one of Lettsome's letters, which seemed to claim that they were on friendly terms. He went to great lengths to show that they were barely acquainted and so distance himself from any hint that he might actually have approved of the Dispensary. Also, Lettsome was a notorious social climber and Dimsdale seems to have felt that Lettsome was trying to associate himself with his betters. Lettsome replied, pointing out that he had dined with Dimsdale on more than one occasion and he was actually less well educated than himself, and that his vaunted title actually came from a Russian authoritarian ruler not the glorious British monarch.[6] Things got so petty that a Gentleman's Magazine critic advised the public not to bother reading Lettsome's last pamphlet.[7] It is hard to believe exactly how petty this childish argument became.

More intelligent arguments came from two of Lettsome's supporters. John Watkinson attacked two of Dimsdale's principles in a pamphlet giving the rationale for the Dispensary.[8] First he cited fourteen physicians from many of the leading cities of Europe who had observed that inoculation had taken place in their own towns without a subsequent increase in the number of smallpox cases. He referred to an incident where a group of soldiers suffering from smallpox had not spread the disease when billeted in a town without the disease. Here was evidence, as Daniel Sutton and many others had claimed, that inoculated smallpox did not spread the disease. He argued that smallpox required more than just "contagion" but some other "variolous condition" before it became epidemic. When the "variolous condition" was absent, the infection did not spread.

Watkinson also reworked the figures for the Bills of Mortality since it began in 1629. He showed that the mortality attributed to smallpox had been increasing since records were first kept many years before inoculation began. If anything, the deaths from smallpox per thousand total deaths had actually gone down since the widespread use of the operation after 1770. Claiming that inoculation was dangerous because it was responsible for spreading fatal smallpox was simply not a sustainable argument. Inoculation was actually saving lives, and it seemed "*to recommend it to the poor, without furnishing them with the power of adopting it, would be an insult to humanity.*"[9] That was exactly why he and his colleagues had founded the Dispensary.

Watkinson also pointed out some flaws in the plan for inoculation houses to inoculate the poor. Dimsdale had recommended following the model established by the Hospital for Smallpox and Inoculation which only took in patients over the age of seven. The majority of poor Londoners caught smallpox before they were seven. Either the model was useless, or, if younger children were taken in, then their mothers would have to go with them, since no mother, even in the poorest families, would hand over her infants to an impersonal nurse. She would insist on bringing all her other children with her since they could not be left home alone. The costs would be enormous.

Dimsdale was enraged.[10] Watkinson had tried to refute the dangers of partial inoculation without any experience of the disasters that might result. Watkinson's witnesses to its safety had been quoted in a mixture of foreign languages to give an aura of authority, but which made it difficult for the reader to assess exactly what they were saying. Dimsdale promised to be more direct. He presented cases involving a series of families that he had seen in which a child or children had been inoculated but not the family servants who then came down with dangerous smallpox, clear evidence of contagion following inoculation, he argued. Watkinson dismissed them as examples of smallpox caught from casual contacts in the notoriously dangerous streets of London.

Dimsdale contacted two of Watkinson's foreign experts inquiring about their views and experience. Both replied that they fully appreciated the dangers of inoculated smallpox and always took the greatest care to separate their own patients from the public. They were not impressed with the suggestion that contagion did not occur in the absence of some other "variolous state". An ingenious idea, but no one knew what that state was and therefore could not predict whether it existed at a particular time and presented a danger. If it was uncertain whether the condition existed it was probably safer to act as if it were always present. Watkinson had recalculated the deaths from smallpox in the Bills of Mortality to show that they had not been increasing as Dimsdale claimed; if anything they had gone down since the number of deaths was roughly the same as it had been before inoculation was introduced, and the population had grown hugely. Dimsdale attempted his own reanalysis of the figures but the only result was to leave the issue confused. It seemed a good example of being able to prove anything as long as you chose the right set of figures.

William Black, otherwise known only for his studies of English mortality figures, gave a comprehensive critique of the Dimsdale's arguments.[11] He began by quoting Dimsdale: "*The*

disease by general inoculation throughout London, spreads by visitors, strangers, servants, washer-women, doctors and inoculators, by means of Hackney Coaches, in which the sick are sent out to take the air, or by sound persons approaching them in the streets,

The poor in London are miserably lodged, their habitations are in close alleys, courts, lanes, and old dirty houses: they are often in want of necessaries, even of bedding. The air in their houses is impure: they have neither areas nor garden… as a result the community at large sustains a greater loss, the practice therefore is more detrimental than beneficial to society."[12]

Black pointed out that if this argument was correct, then it applied equally well to inoculations carried out in the private houses of the rich. So why did Baron Dimsdale *"labour all in his power to increase the dispersion of variolous infection, and to injure the community at large, by Inoculating all rich persons in London and its vicinity, who employ him?"* While he did not like to descend to personal abuse, the author felt compelled to point out the Baron was a hypocrite.

Black claimed that London's poor were only poor in relative terms. They were small tradesmen, artisans, and even the middle classes who had just enough money to live on but not enough to pay medical expenses. Real abject poverty was uncommon. Only 70 or so Londoners died of starvation every year. If Dimsdale really felt that they needed gardens and carriages before they could be inoculated, they would wait until judgment day. In such families inoculation would actually be a financial blessing. Where the Baron had argued that women would not be able to a take time away from work to nurse their children, Black replied that they had managed to have children. A newly delivered woman was kept in bed for three to four weeks; how could she manage to have a family if she faced penury every time she became pregnant? Natural smallpox would run slowly through the children of such a family, first one, then another about two weeks later, then a third perhaps a couple of weeks after that. A mother would be stuck at home nursing all these children for several weeks, but, if they were inoculated all at once then the disease would have run its course in a week, or two at the most, and she would be free to return to work.

As for spreading smallpox, the supporters of the Dispensary advocated that inoculation should be carried out at the time a child began teething. At this early age they were hardly likely to be able to run about in the streets and alleys. Even if inoculation were delayed for a few months, the chances of infecting anyone outdoors were minimal.

Everyone agreed that inoculated individuals had many fewer pustules than a patient suffering from the natural disease. Black argued that not only did this make an inoculated individual less infectious than a patient who had acquired the disease naturally, but the total amount of "variolous matter" present would decrease. Since these same poor were the principal source of smallpox in London, any reduction in their disease load would have public health benefits. The number of cases of "casual smallpox" would gradually decline and the city would become a healthier place if the poor were inoculated. As things stood there were about 15,000 cases of smallpox in the capital every year, and many more of a sufferer's friends and relatives would have been carrying infectious material on their clothes and bodies. If Dimsdale really wanted to prevent the spread of smallpox he must invent a scheme which barricaded infected individuals in their homes, hanged the old clothes men, (retailers of rags, and hawkers of woollen clothes that might be contaminated with smallpox), sent doctors and inoculators to the galleys, or at least made them wear a distinguishing badge so that they could be avoided. All travellers would be banned until given a clean bill of health, all goods quarantined until inspected. Clearly this was an unsupportable tyranny. The only alternative was inoculation.

But what really irked Black was Dimsdale's attitude "*If the Baron is serious in considering partial inoculation as injurious to the community, it is highly criminal in him to be one of the most active instruments in their destruction. In a matter of so great moment, in which the dearest concerns of mankind are linked, I feel myself warmed and provoked to stigmatize such double dealing with exemplary reprehension.*"[13] Perhaps Dimsdale should recant his views and give away the money that he had made from inoculating the rich in their own homes. It was simply unacceptable to allow the wealthy to make use of so a great a blessing while denying it to the industrious poor.

Lettsome reacted to Dimsdale with sarcasm: "*The Baron professes a tender regard for the poor; but it should be considered how far his practice corresponds to his profession. This tender regard is surely not evinced by endeavouring to deprive them of a benefit, which he himself is conferring every day on the rich. He surely will not assert, that the danger of communication is as the inverse of the price paid for the operation; that an inoculated pauper is a very hazardous object to the community; that when five guineas are given the hazard is diminished, that ten will reduce it still more, and that by fifty it will be totally annihilated*.[14] Some flavour of the degree of rancour felt by Lettsome towards Dimsdale is shown by his comment that the Baron seemed overly fond of his empty title which had been granted by "*the Autocratrix of all the Russias*" along with the titles Body Physician and actual Counsellor of State which he employed in all his publications and frequently dropped into his writings. Lettsome was saying that Dimsdale was cashing in on a meaningless claim to nobility.

But Thomas Dimsdale had an answer to his opponents. The rich could be relied upon to keep their inoculated children at home and under control, the poor could not. He went so far as to distribute a pamphlet outlining his views which he circulated by leaving free copies in pubs and coffee houses. Lettsome thought that this was ridiculous propagandising, but Dimsdale replied that everyone had a right to see his arguments and wide distribution was in everyone's interests. Even those who could not afford a shilling or two for a copy would be able to read and understand it.

The debate was well summarised and the case for general inoculation of the poor of London was put in an anonymous pamphlet. The poor, due to their terrible living conditions and diet, were more likely die of natural smallpox than individuals who were better off so inoculation was the safest option for them. Furthermore, smallpox was so widespread in London that a child who did not catch it today would certainly catch it tomorrow. In that case inoculation was also the safer option. And because the disease was already present throughout the capital there was little chance that inoculation would cause an epidemic since the disease was everywhere already. And children with inoculated smallpox were much less likely to spread it to their uninfected friends than children with natural smallpox so inoculation would actually promote public health.[15]

Dimsdale was the leading inoculator in England. He had instructed many of the most prominent physicians and surgeons in the techniques of the Suttons and he had gained great renown through his activities in Russia. Lettsome was just getting started. While in a few years he would be one of London's most successful and famous doctors, now he was just a social climbing upstart. The Dispensary for Inoculating the Poor in Their Own Homes never got off the ground. Dimsdale had choked off the contributions needed to support it.

It is hard to grasp exactly how tragic Dimsdale's victory proved. Numberless, probably thousands, of London poor children would die unnecessarily because of his childish argument with Lettsome. What makes the whole argument doubly tragic is that he was both right and wrong. Inoculated smallpox was contagious and could spread fatal disease, but the supporters of the general Dispensary were also right. In the special conditions that applied in London there was little danger beyond what already existed. In London partial inoculations would have been successful and not promoted an epidemic. Dimsdale's unbending insistence on his own plan doomed many poor children.

Chapter 22

A GRAND UNWORKABLE PLAN

Part of the debate over the dangers of partial inoculations revolved around whether smallpox was spread by contagion alone or whether there was some "epidemic" or "variolous" property of the atmosphere that was required before the disease could spread. Although most people recognized that contact with someone infected with smallpox was dangerous, many doctors argued that something else was required to spread the infection. The answer to this question had an important bearing on strategies to prevent smallpox. If only contagion was important then strict isolation of the patient was required, but if the character of the atmosphere also played a role, then steps to improve the environment, such as removing rotting rubbish, or simply moving to somewhere with better "air", was equally beneficial. Watkinson and Lettsom had argued that one of the reasons that inoculation did not spread smallpox was because most of the time the air was not "variolous" so the infection could not spread. Their opponents replied that no one could tell when the air was "variolous" and therefore there was always a risk of inoculation starting an epidemic.

John Haygarth, a physician in the northern city of Chester, set out to determine exactly how individuals caught and transmitted smallpox. To do this he carefully traced and followed every single case of smallpox in Chester, in effect inventing what we now know as contact tracing, a very powerful tool for mapping epidemics and finding individuals who require treatment. It is still the basis for studying the spread of HIV/AIDS and for controlling outbreaks of sexually transmitted diseases as well as many infectious diseases. When a new disease, such as SARS or Legionnaire's disease, appears, contact tracing can help to identify the source and the routes by which it spreads. By finding and following every contact of a smallpox patient, Haygarth hoped to discover how smallpox spread.

When he began his investigation he was surprised to find that many experienced and distinguished physicians believed that smallpox could spread through the air over long distances. One friend stated that he knew of cases where the disease had spread over thirty miles. If this were possible, then strategies such as isolating infected individuals to prevent smallpox spreading could not possibly work.

Haygarth confirmed the well-established observation that the fever following inoculation appeared about 8 or 9 days after the operation and that in natural cases it appeared after about 11 days. Within families, where he could be sure who was the first child infected, he showed that secondary cases involving other children in the family usually appeared between 11 and 18 days, but a few did not show up for more than three weeks. Using these findings he could analyze everything and everyone with whom a patient had come into contact at the likely time that they were infected. In the process he also discovered that smallpox was responsible for about one third of all childhood deaths in Chester.[1]

He also discovered smallpox was only transmitted from an infected individual to a susceptible individual by close personal contact or by contact with the clothes, scabs, or "serum"(by which he meant the invisible droplets coughed up during active disease). In every case he could identify the individual who was the source of the infection and the route through which the next case had become infected. He advised doctors not to sit down when they attended a smallpox case to minimize the chance that their clothes would become contaminated. Whatever the "variolous poison" was, he showed that it was spread through inhalation since he had uncovered examples of individuals who had caught smallpox after standing very close to someone with the disease, but who had not actually touched them. Only close contact was able to spread the disease. While investigating families where he could be sure of the exact dates when the disease began in each child he discovered that there was a period of about six days after a child became infected before it became infectious to others. Thus he could conclude that close contact with an individual with smallpox pustules was necessary to contract the disease. He knew of one family in which four children happened to pass by a baby which was covered in recent smallpox pustules. The eldest girl, who was clearly very bright, was able to report that they had all passed within about 18 inches of the child in a narrow passage beside the town walls. She and two of her brothers walked on, but one brother turned back to get a closer look at the sick baby. She was sure that he had not touched the child, but had got much closer than she and her other brothers. Ten days later he came down with smallpox, and then infected his siblings about two weeks later showing that they had all been susceptible to the infection. From this and similar examples Haygarth concluded that the "varioulous poison" was quickly diluted in air and that contact closer than about 18 inches was necessary to pass on the infection. The only exceptions were where there had been contact with clothes, household goods, or possibly, food which had been contaminated by a patient with the pustules or scabs still on them. Material collected for inoculation was a special case because it was kept in tightly stoppered vials and retained the capacity to infect for about a year.

Haygarth's theories about how smallpox spread were supported by the observations of physicians in nearby villages during a recent smallpox epidemic. They noticed that the disease spread very rapidly through poor families who were in and out of each other's houses and whose children played together with friends or siblings who had smallpox. But better off families, who remained within their own homes often escaped the disease even when they were near neighbours of infected families. No one caught the disease from just walking past an infected house.

He distilled his findings *"Mankind are not necessarily subject to the small-pox, it is always caught by infection from a patient in the distemper, or poisonous matter, or scabs, that come from a patient, and may be avoided by observing these*

RULES OF PREVENTION.

I. Suffer no person, who has not had the small-pox to come into the infectious house. No visitor, who has any communication with persons liable to the distemper, should touch or sit down on anything infectious.

II. No patient, after the pocks have appeared, must be suffered to go into the street, or other frequented place.

III. The Utmost attention to cleanliness is absolutely necessary: during and after the distemper, no person, clothes, food, furniture, cat, dog, money, medicines or any other thing that is known or suspected to be bedaubed with matter, spittle, or other infectious discharges of the patient should go out of the house until they have been washed... When a patient dies of smallpox , particular care should be taken that nothing infectious be taken out of the house so as to do mischief.

IV. The patient must not be allowed to approach any person liable to the distemper , till every scab is dropped off, till all the clothes, furniture, food, and all other things touched by the patient during the distemper, till the floor of the sick chamber, and till his face and hands, have been carefully washed..."[2]

If the patient was kept away from anyone who might catch the disease, if all those things that he came into contact with were washed and if he and his room were carefully cleaned then Haygarth believed that smallpox would not spread.

Only then was there no risk to others.

Finding that there were no cases that could be traced to susceptible individuals, merely passing by the home of a patient eliminated the idea that a "variolous atmosphere" determined when the disease would be contagious. And no cases could be traced to a physician spreading the disease from house to house on his rounds to visit the sick. Haygarth identified individuals who had been infected in the street by close exposure to someone with pustules, or to infected clothes sent out for washing; but only direct exposure to an active case or the patient's body fluids spread the infection. He wrote: "*The small-pox continues spreading as long as persons liable to the infection approach patients in the distemper or infectious matter, either in the same chamber or very nearly in the open air, and then ceases*"[3]

In 1778 Haygarth put his rules to the test during an epidemic of smallpox. Twenty families agreed to comply with his protocol, and a charitable society, which he and several friends had founded, offered a reward of 10 shillings if all the rules were observed. An inducement was necessary as parents would have to remain at home to nurse their children and would lose their livelihood until the disease was gone. Without it the physicians couldn't expect poor families to follow the rules when they faced starvation as a consequence. The Society even had a written contract and appointed an inspector whose role was to visit each infected house every day to determine whether the rules were being followed. Only when the disease had been extinguished and the inspector signed the necessary certificate was the reward paid.

Fourteen families complied in full; six transgressed for a variety of reasons. One family didn't realise that one of their children had smallpox until the pocks were fully developed before sending for the inspector; by then the child had exposed his playmates. In another family an infected child saw one his friends playing in the street outside his window and passed him the candy he was sucking. In one case the inspector turned up too late to verify that the conditions had been observed. What delighted Haygarth was his finding that there were no examples of infection spreading from one family to another from any of the households who stuck to his rules. In several cases he could show that a secondary infection had occurred when there had been a lapse. Twelve families received the reward, and two, who were too well off to need compensating, were thanked for their care.

Haygarth began to wonder whether his "Rules" could be used to prevent smallpox becoming an epidemic by choking off the source of the infection. He was encouraged to develop and extend his "rules of prevention" by Benjamin Waterhouse, a young American physician who visited him in 1778. Waterhouse had experience of the successful practice in Rhode Island where epidemics had been absent for many years. Inoculation was still illegal in most of New England but had become acceptable in New York and Pennsylvania. Many New Englanders passed through Rhode Island to reach Long Island, New York where they underwent the operation. Patients were kept in strict isolation while the disease was active and were required to leave behind any clothes that they had used during their stay. If a case of smallpox did appear in Rhode Island then the patient was removed to a special "pest island" until they had recovered. Originally the patient was transported in a large box which would accommodate a bed and had a lid with several holes to admit air. However *"this formidable apparatus did more mischief, especially to timorous minds, than the disease itself"*[4]. so it was dropped in favour of an enclosed sedan chair. If the patient couldn't or wouldn't be moved, the authorities boarded up the entire street and blocked all traffic until the disease had run its course. Although draconian, these measures had successfully prevented epidemics from developing in Rhode Island.

While Haygarth admired the result he felt that the procedures were unacceptably harsh for England. He demonstrated that his own rules were just as effective by calculating death rates when his rules were in place, and when they were suspended. Mortality was reduced by about 75 percent when his system was followed, and he showed that if it was fully observed at all times, the death rate would fall by ninety seven percent.

The only problem arose when there were so many cases in town that there was too much work for the inspector, and the regulations had to be suspended. The arrival of a new regiment in Chester without officers started one such epidemic. A passing physician noticed a young soldier covered in pocks and admonished him to take care not to spread the disease, to which the soldier replied "nobody takes care or me, and I will take care of nobody" and continued on his way. Without officers, there was no one to discipline the men to remain in camp. The resulting epidemic swamped the system.

Poor children in Chester, like poor children in London, bore the main burden of smallpox. To try to save their lives Haygarth established a charitable foundation called *"A Society for Promoting General Inoculation at Stated Periods and Preventing Natural Smallpox in Chester"* which attempted to persuade those too poor to participate in a general inoculation by paying a reward. After some debate, the society's donors agreed that the inducement should be 5 shillings for the first child, 3 shillings for the second, and 1 shilling for each succeeding child to compensate the parents for the time and trouble involved in looking after their inoculated children. An additional 5 shillings would be paid to the inoculator for his services, but the doctors of Chester united in refusing this fee and agreed to provide the operation for no charge. Haygarth pointed out that the reward for observing the "rules of prevention" could be omitted during a true general inoculation because when everyone was inoculated at the same time there was no risk of spreading the infection. Although Chester had an inoculation house, it was useless for most cases because endemic disease usually affected children under seven, the age at which they could be admitted to the hospital. If partial inoculation of the poor was attempted, it would be impossible to isolate cases because mothers would insist on accompanying their children to the pest house, and if the mother went, then the rest of the children would have to go with her. There would not be enough room or food to accommodate everyone. It was only practical to inoculate the poor at home and enforce strict quarantine.

Although Haygarth advocated a general inoculation every two years and wanted to encourage the well off to postpone their own treatment until then, the poor wouldn't co-operate. *"In Cross-gun entry in Forrest Street the inhabitants deliberately spread the disease"*[5] by exposing their children to an infected child. Families didn't take up the reward for following the rules for prevention for several reasons. Despite the good intentions of the Society, many remained ignorant of the existence of a financial benefit, or were put off by the fact that it was only paid after the disease had completely cleared, and it often took several weeks before the virus had run through a whole family. Also, the inspector wasn't particularly welcome or efficient. Often he turned up several days after the pocks appeared and by then it was too late for the family to observe the rules even if they wanted to. The only real success for Haygarth's inoculation scheme was to prevent smallpox spreading through the workhouse.

Ironically, although the "Rules of Prevention" were not entirely successful in Chester, they were adopted in other northern cities such as Leeds, Newcastle, and Carlisle. Where carefully observed, they reduced the death rate from smallpox by about fifty percent.[6]

General inoculation never proved popular in Chester. Groups of children were brought forward when an epidemic threatened, but it proved impossible to persuade all the poor families to accept the operation at the same time. By 1785 the Society found that it had paid out so many rewards for agreeing to isolate cases under the rules of prevention that it was in danger of going bust. The members voted to end the reward for inoculation on the grounds that it was unacceptable to bribe a family to accept a practice if they felt that it was wrong. Of course when the payment disappeared, the incentive for treatment went with it. Haygarth began to view inoculation as a double-edged sword. Whereas in the past wealthy benefactors and country squires accepted that it was their duty to inoculate those in their immediate community at the same time as they inoculated their own families, once they were fully protected they no longer had a motive to extend the practice to those who could not afford it. Financial support for general inoculation began to melt away, leaving the poor more vulnerable than before. By selfishly inoculating themselves without providing for others, the well-off had made the practice dangerous. Haygarth intimated that it would be a good thing if inoculation were banned unless it was part of a general scheme covering the entire population. Wealthy patrons would force the poor to accept inoculation as it was the only way they could obtain the benefits for themselves.

Haygarth's careful investigation of smallpox in Chester plus his extended correspondence with physicians in other large northern cities paints a striking picture of smallpox in the last quarter of the 18th century. It was largely a children's disease. Over half the children who died between the ages of 2 and ten were killed by it. Even about one in four of the children who died under the age of one had died of smallpox making all previous estimates of smallpox mortality invalid because they had excluded deaths under the age of two. When Haygarth compared the number of deaths from smallpox to the number of christenings in several places he came to the conclusion that about one in six of all children died of the disease. He also concluded that almost all the poor had had the disease before the age of seven and that most teenagers were therefore immune. In the Chester militia less than ten percent of new recruits were still susceptible to smallpox and most of those who were immune had suffered from the natural form of the disease. These recruits were then in their late teens so they showed that inoculation was scarcely practiced in northern towns in the 1760s when they were infants. While Haygarth's insights into smallpox were all gathered from northern towns such as Chester, Manchester, and Leeds, there is no reason to believe that similar conditions did not prevail among the poor of London.

Extensive experience in Chester and Leeds showed that if a family followed the rules of prevention exactly then there was no spread beyond the initial case. In Lyon, France, a Dr O'Ryan had performed a series of experiments that reflected Haygarth's theory that smallpox did not spread far through the atmosphere. He took groups of children who had not had smallpox and had them sit around a table on which there was placed a cotton ball soaked in smallpox pus. They sat about 18 inches from the infected cotton for an hour and then they were allowed to leave and carefully followed for several weeks. None of them ever came down with smallpox. O'Ryan appears to have come up with these experiments before he knew of Haygarth's suppositions and Haygarth found them welcome proof for his own ideas.

Encouraged by the success of his rules and by further evidence that smallpox did not spread through the air Haygarth came up with a grand plan. Almost two hundred years before the virus was finally extinguished by immunization, he had done enough to realise that it should be possible *"to establish regulations which would exterminate the Small Pox from Great Britain"*[7] He also recognised that eradication would require a firm and efficient system to halt the spread of the infection. He proposed a fully developed network of public health inspectors who, like his agents in Chester, would be responsible for inspecting a community for smallpox and for ensuring that his rules of prevention, effectively tight quarantine, were observed by any affected family. His inspectors would be entitled to receive information when the code was breached, and they could impose a fine of between £10 and £50 on the transgressors, half to go to the informant and half to the costs of running the scheme. There were to be 500 health districts, each with its own inspector, one physician supervisor for every ten districts, and the whole network would be controlled by five commissioners appointed by the King and based in London. In outline it was a general method for identifying and controlling any infectious disease. Eventually something like his scheme would become the basis for the Public Health Acts in the twentieth century.

Haygarth could not calculate the exact cost of his scheme, but he believed that it would be substantially less than the cost of smallpox. According to his reckoning there were 38,000 smallpox deaths each year and 190,000 cases, which cost the public £394,500 for charitable care in the pest house as well as the costs of maintaining the widows and dependent children of the deceased in the workhouse. This huge sum did not reflect the loss of *"innocence, reputation, and that sense of independence which is the surest principle of industry"* which resulted when children were raised in the care of the parish.[8] Even generous payments to the inspectors and overseers would not cost as much.

Only two things stood in the way of his grand plan. Despite his argument that the inspector should be seen as a tutor whose function was to educate the poor so that they did not poison their neighbours, the public felt that the system infringed their liberties and it amounted to being spied upon by the government. Also the plan could not be introduced without legislation and government finance, and neither was forthcoming. Haygarth's visionary plan to eradicate smallpox, which presaged the development of public health laws, was a non-starter.

Chapter 23

IF WE ESCAPE SMALLPOX IN THIS CAMP IT WILL BE A MIRACLE

On the day that the American revolution broke out the minutemen on Concord Common routed the British troops sent to remove their arms and the royal army found itself trapped in Boston. Colonial forces controlled the mainland end of the neck connecting Boston to the rest of Massachusetts. Without heavy cannon the Americans could not force the British out; without reinforcements the British could not disperse their captors. In June 1775 the rebels attempted to interdict Boston harbour by building a fort on Bunker Hill above Charlestown, which lay across 1200 yards of water from Boston's North Battery. Recently reinforced, the British realised that the strategic position was untenable if their shipping, the only means of communication with the mother country, was exposed to hostile bombardment. From the heights of Breed's and Bunker hills above Charlestown the colonials had a clear view of the port and the movements of troops in Boston. They could even recognise friends and read the expressions on their faces.

The ensuing battle on Bunker Hill was a tribute to the courage and discipline of both sides. Although lacking experience under fire, the colonial farmers were adept diggers and erected solid earthworks. From behind their fortifications they exercised their unrivalled marksmanship, finding the white belts that crossed the chests of the British officers a particularly inviting target. British troops formed into neat ranks and marched into the fire. Long serving soldiers reported that the intensity of this battle was greater than any they had experienced in Europe during the Seven Years' War. Despite losing half their officers the British re-formed and attacked a second and then a third time. When the rebels' ammunition ran out, their position became hopeless and they retreated leaving Charlestown in British hands.

In one afternoon the British commander had lost a sixth of his whole force and over a quarter of the troops he had actually sent to attack the rebels. General Howe, who had led the charge, had lost all of his personal officers. Now too weak to fortify any of the heights around Boston, and forever after reluctant to charge entrenched colonial farmers, the Royalists settled down to a siege.

As winter approached it became clear that the army would have to subsist on the supplies of food and wood already in Boston because few provisions could be moved through the colonial lines. To reduce the number of mouths he needed to feed General Howe began to expel some of the townspeople, particularly those who supported the revolution or who were too poor to provide for themselves. Smallpox also appeared in the town. About 2000 people were thought to be sick, but many of them had been inoculated, on orders, to preserve the army. Most British soldiers would have been immune from prior infection, whether natural or inoculated. General Howe recognised that the revolutionaries were terrified of the prospect that smallpox might break out in the colonial army. Most of Washington's troops were strangers to the disease and therefore highly susceptible to it. By spreading smallpox through Boston by inoculating civilians, Howe hoped to deter Washington from attacking the town for fear that his troops would catch the disease and his army would collapse in the ensuing epidemic. Howe also had another motive.

At the end of November Washington informed the Continental Congress

"General Howe has ordered three hundred inhabitants of Boston to Point Shirley in destitute condition. I have ordered provisions to them until they can be moved, but am under dreadful apprehensions of their communicating the smallpox as it is rife in Boston. I have forbade any of them coming to this place on that account".[1]

On December 3rd four deserters from the town brought worrying news

"By recent information from Boston, General Howe is going to send out a number of the inhabitants in order, it is thought, to make room for his reinforcements; there is one part of the information that I can hardly credit; a sailor says that a number of them coming out have been inoculated with the design of spreading the smallpox throughout the country and camp."[2]

Washington alerted the Massachusetts legislature to the threat

"…it will appear that some of the people who came out of Boston are infected with the Smallpox. As the disorder, should it spread, may prove very disastrous and fatal to our army and the country around it, I should hope that you will have such necessary steps taken as will prevent the infection being further communicated."[3]

On December 11th he reported confirmation of his suspicions to Congress

"The information I received that the enemy intended spreading smallpox among us I could not suppose them capable of. I must now give some credit to it as it made its appearance on several of those who last came out of Boston."[4]

Four days later Washington wrote to Congress again,

"About 150 more of the poor inhabitants are come out of Boston. The smallpox rages all over the town. Such of the militia as had it not before are now under inoculation and considered surety against any attempt of ours (to attack). If we escape the smallpox in this camp… it will be miraculous." [5]

Howe was following the example of his illustrious predecessor, Lord Jeffery Amherst, who, when faced with the Indian uprising known as Pontiac's rebellion, had written to his subordinate, Colonel Henry Bouquet,

"Could it not be contrived to send the smallpox among these disaffected tribes of Indians? We must on this occasion use every stratagem in our power to reduce them" Bouquet replied *"I will try to inoculate the Indians... with some blankets that may fall into their hands and take care not to get the disease myself".*[6]

Two Indian chiefs were given blankets and a handkerchief from the smallpox hospital.[7]

In March Washington finally received the heavy cannon captured at Ticonderoga the previous autumn. By placing these on the Dorchester heights overlooking Boston and the harbour he could bombard British shipping at will. Howe conceded that the town was now untenable and ordered a withdrawal after threatening to burn the city if attacked while pulling out. Washington prepared his army for the withdrawal

"As the enemy with a malicious assiduity has spread the infection of smallpox throughout all parts of the town, nothing but the utmost caution on our part can prevent that fatal disease from spreading through the army and camp to the infinite detriment of both. Therefore, no officer or soldier may go into Boston when the enemy evacuates the town"[8]

Washington had been warned that Howe hoped to leave enough infected townspeople behind to cause an epidemic in the Continental army. When the British finally left the Continental commander ordered

"1,000 men who had had the smallpox under command of General Putnam to take possession."[9]

The threat of smallpox remained throughout the following summer. Some units attempted inoculation, but were balked by local ordinances, which only permitted the practice in Boston.[10] It seems likely that surreptitious inoculation went on in many units, and those units actually in Boston were inoculated, along with all the remaining uninfected citizens. At one point there were so many soldiers under inoculation that there were barely enough healthy men to guard the hospital.

While Boston was under siege, the revolutionary council addressed a second strategic problem. Quebec and New York were at opposite ends of a chain of rivers and lakes, which form a watery highway that allows easy passage between the two towns.

If British troops were to march down from Quebec, they could capture Albany and New York City, cutting the thirteen colonies in two and preventing them supporting each other. To forestall this possibility Congress initiated an invasion of Canada.

Two small armies were sent North.[11] One, led by General Richard Montgomery, followed the Hudson River and Lake Champlain route to Montreal. The other, led by Benedict Arnold, set off to march overland through the Maine wilderness to reach Quebec. Arnold's experience is one of the great epic marches of all time. Hacking their way through thick forest, plunging down rocky streams, climbing granite hills, and wading through deceptive swamps which appeared solid from a distance, the little army took six weeks to travel about 200 miles. In the depths of the wilderness the rear quarter of the column rebelled and voted to return home. Since there was no food to be had on the return trip they took most of the available supplies with them. Arnold's depleted force continued into the wilderness. Their food ran out; they ate their shoes; finally they reached the St Lawrence River and took shelter in a French trading village.

Montgomery's force had an easier passage up the lakes and captured Montreal in November. After re-equipping for two weeks he sent troops forward to reinforce Arnold. On New Year's Eve the combined force attacked Quebec. It was a close thing. Virginia riflemen reached the top of the city wall, but were captured following a fierce British counter attack. Arnold himself was badly wounded trying to force the lower passage into the town, and Montgomery was killed. Repulsed, the colonial troops settled down to a siege. The St. Lawrence River was frozen, and it would be months before British reinforcements could arrive. There were only about 80 British regulars inside Quebec, and they received little support from the Indians or the French settlers. The odds were still with the revolutionary army and the stakes were high. If they captured Quebec they would control all of Canada.

But smallpox had arrived along with the troops from Montreal. Some of Montgomery's New York officers appear to have sought inoculation as a way to delay their departure north. Others underwent the operation for the perfectly sensible reason that it was safer to have the disease by operation rather than wait for the more dangerous natural version. When some of the inoculated soldiers were sent north to be court- martialed for daring to be inoculated, the practice went underground. It was the worst possible situation. Surreptitious inoculation guaranteed that the infection moved along with the army; those who recovered continued to wear their infected uniforms and remained infectious long after their own disease was gone.

Smallpox epidemics often start slowly, and this one took several months to reach its peak. By May, 900 of the 1,900 troops before Quebec were sick, mostly with smallpox. Rumours of British reinforcements panicked the army and they fled, leaving over 200 men who were too ill to travel behind. In their terror 150 men with smallpox *"broken out on their bodies"* joined the march back towards Montreal.

Congress learnt of the disaster and dispatched a commission, including the aged Ben Franklin, to investigate. In mid-May Arnold wrote to them

"I shall be glad to know your sentiment in regard to inoculation as early as possible. Will it not be best considering the impossibility of preventing the spread of smallpox, to inoculate 500 or 1,000 men immediately and send them to Montreal, and as many more every five days until the whole army receive: which will prevent our army being distressed thereafter: and I make no doubt we shall have more effective men in four weeks than by endeavouring to prevent the infection spreading".[12]

The Congressmen approved the suggestion, but before preparations were completed, a new commander appeared and took charge of the army. John Thomas was a physician soldier who had gained his command by his early and vigorous action to seize Roxbury so blocking the land exit from Boston. Despite his medical experience he was adamantly against inoculation and ordered anyone caught performing it shot. Within two weeks Thomas was dead of smallpox, but he had delayed inoculation long enough to seal the fate of the invasion.

The Congressional commission reported *"The army is in a distressed condition and is in want of the most necessary articles...three fourths of the army have not had the smallpox...We cannot find words strong enough to describe our miserable situation."*[13]

John Adams, one of the commissioners wrote to a friend *"Our misfortunes in Canada are enough to melt the heart of stone. The smallpox is ten times more terrible than the British, Canadians, and Indians together. This was the cause of our precipitate retreat from Quebec."*[14]

British troops appeared in the field and the demoralised rebels began a rapid retreat down Lake Champlaign. Covert inoculation continued despite the ban; individuals or small groups of officers underwent the operation, completely disregarding the safety of their comrades. The army reached Crown Point, on the southern end of the lake, in early July after a harrowing retreat.

"Our northern army has left Canada and retreated to Ticonderoga and Crown Point. The smallpox has made great havoc among them. Several regiments had not enough men to row all their sick over the Lake and men were drafted from other regiments to do that service. In short the army had melted away in a little time as if the destroying angel had been sent on purpose to demolish them."[15] John Adams pointed out the solution *"I hope that measures will be taken to cleanse the army at Crown Point from the smallpox and the measures will be taken in New England by tolerating and encouraging inoculation, to render that distemper less terrible*[16]

However, inoculation was still against the law in most colonies and wholesale inoculation of troops from different jurisdictions was politically difficult.

About the 4th of July, 1776, Connecticut Governor Jonathan Trumbull wrote two letters to the commanding general spelling out the situation from the civilian viewpoint.

"The retreat of the Northern army and the present situation has spread great alarm...The prevalence of smallpox among them is in every way unhappy; our people in general have not had that distemper. Fear of the infection operates strongly to prevent soldiers from engaging the service and the battalions ordered to be raised in the colony fill up slowly. Are there no measures to be taken to remove the impediment? May not the army soon be freed from that infection? Can the reinforcements be

kept separate from the infected? Or may not a detachment be made from the troops under your command and the militia raised in the several colonies be ordered to New York, sending such men as have had the smallpox to the Northern department. Could any expedient be fallen upon that would afford probable hopes that this infection may be avoided? The smallpox in our Northern army carries with it greater dread than our enemies. Our men dare face them but are not willing to go into a hospital."[17]

The Governor did everything but say "inoculate the Army"; he could not advocate the practice: it was a criminal offence in Connecticut.

Meanwhile, inoculation, both official and covert, was performed among the troops recovering at Crown Point. Although no general order for mass inoculation was given, many regimental doctors began to protect the troops under their care, and within a few weeks, by one route or another, the entire force was immune and smallpox disappeared from this army. On August 28, General Gates, who had earlier suggested criminal charges against any doctor found practising inoculation, reported to Washington *"the smallpox is now perfectly removed"*.

The colonial army, which had been camped around Boston, moved south to New York in August. Following defeats on Long Island, it retreated further south into New Jersey where it shielded Philadelphia, the colonial capital, from General Howe in New York. As the weather closed in, both sides went into winter quarters giving Washington time to reflect and to assess the state of his forces. The situation was pretty dismal. In all about 74,000 men had served the colonial cause, either as regular soldiers who had enlisted for one year, or as short-term militia. Of these, only 1,000 had died in action, 1,200 had been wounded, 6,000 captured, and 10,000 died of disease, mainly smallpox.[18] The one-year enlistments were running out and the men were reluctant to re-enlist. The calamity that had befallen the northern army was now widely known. Few would volunteer to suffer smallpox, so the supply of new recruits was also drying up. Washington said that his army and the revolution it protected was smouldering away like leaves on an autumn bonfire. Furthermore,

Philadelphia, which permitted inoculation, was the only town where smallpox was always present. It would not be long before it spread into the army.

The Commander realised that the only way to preserve his army was to remove the major threat to its continued existence. On January 6, 1777 he ordered Dr William Shippen of the medical service to prepare for a general inoculation of all the troops.

"Finding the smallpox to be spreading much, and fearing that no precaution can prevent it from running through the whole of our army, I have determined that the troops be inoculated... Necessity not only authorizes but seems to require this measure, for should the disorder infest the army in this natural way and rage with its usual virulence, we should have more to dread from it than from the sword of the enemy."[19]

Congress approved the plan, and Washington wrote to Patrick Henry, Governor of Virginia, the largest colony and source of many of his best riflemen

"I am induced to believe that the apprehensions of the smallpox and its calamitous consequences have greatly retarded enlistment. But may not those objections be easily done away with by introducing inoculation into the state?"[20]

He reminded Henry of the consequences if troops returning home from the army brought smallpox with them. It was far better to ensure the soldiers', and the colony's, safety. Henry was receptive to Washington's request. He had been inoculated himself in 1774 because Philadephia had a notorious reputation for smallpox and he would be at risk when when he attended the continental congress.

Washington's appeal succeeded and Virginia established inoculation points for her own recruits and those from further South. Inoculating a large force in the field and a continuous stream of recruits presented a considerable logistic problem. Inoculation now became a part of the enlistment ritual. New recruits were inoculated, fitted out with uniforms and weapons, and given a little basic training while they recovered, so little time was lost, and the growing army was freed from the infection. However, each soldier had only one set of clothes, and they remained potential sources of infection as they marched north.

Special precautions were taken to route such units away from towns and susceptible forces. [21]

Eventually a formal inoculation of the whole army took place in May at Morristown, New Jersey. Several hundred were treated by the Suttonian method without any fatalities. But a number of unlucky townspeople caught the disease from the soldiers, and about sixty died. New troops were inoculated throughout 1777 and during the dreadful winter encampment of 1777 to 1778 at Valley Forge. Thereafter the threat to the revolution from smallpox was over. Inoculation became as much a part of soldiering as a musket.

Smallpox played one final important role in the American Revolution. In 1779 France was allied to the continental cause and, as always, looking for ways to discomfit England. Most of Britain's army was abroad, and even the navy was reduced in numbers in home waters. France combined with her ally, Spain, to organise and mount an invasion of England. Their combined fleets, with the invasion force on board, reached Plymouth, but failed to attack the weakly defended coast, remaining in sight of the town for three days until a storm dispersed the ships. Smallpox had broken out in the fleet and over half the sailors were too sick to manoeuvre their craft. Helpless, this last threat to England dissipated because inoculation was not widely practised in the French and Spanish navies.[22]

Inoculation, or lack of it, shaped the outcome of the Revolutionary War. For the first time, commanders had the ability to prevent one of the most dangerous diseases that could strike an army. Americans would almost certainly have lost the revolution without it because most American colonists had had little previous exposure to the virus, and therefore had no immunity to it. When smallpox spread through susceptible soldiers, the force always disintegrated.

Canada remained British, and England remained free because inoculation was employed too late to affect the outcome of events.

Chapter 24

1796. THE HIGHWATER MARK OF INOCULATION

By 1796 inoculation has become an accepted part of life in many countries. In England most families who could afford the doctor's fee had their children inoculated at an early age. There were numerous amateur and semi-professional operators as well. Many of these claimed to have inoculated thousands of individuals. No one knows how many families took Buchan's advice and inoculated their own children.[1]

In the newly independent United States almost universal inoculation of soldiers in the revolutionary army made the practice both more widely known and acceptable. Individual states still had widely varying rules from the free use of the operation in Philadelphia to almost complete prohibition in Connecticut. In Boston, where it all began, inoculation hospitals had appeared. During the last epidemic of smallpox in the 18th century 221 people in Boston caught smallpox naturally while over 9,000 were inoculated - essentially everyone in town who had not had smallpox already.[2] After about 1760 inoculation combined with quarantine reduced the average annual mortality from smallpox by about one third.[3]

wSy

Inoculation was the first medical innovation that saved lives by preventing disease. It was more extensively employed than most medical histories allow, and was given by the whole range of medical practitioners, from the complete amateurs, with no formal education, to the grandest of Fellows of the College of Physicians. The great majority of operations were never recorded. The only way to estimate how many people were inoculated is to look for passing comments revealing the views of those living at the time, or to examine population records to find changes in survival which might be correlated with the practice. Both approaches suggest that inoculation was very common.

Many who lived in the 18th century believed that inoculation was responsible for the dramatic population growth that had occurred during the second half of the century. In the fifty years after 1701 the population of England and Wales grew by 12 %; in the next fifty it rose by 42%. One anonymous correspondent wrote to the Gentleman's magazine in 1803

"One very great cause of the increasing population may be ascribed to the success of inoculation for smallpox. One in four or five, or about 200 to 250 in a thousand usually died of this loathsome disorder in the natural way of infection... so this saving of lives alone would account for our increasing number without perplexing ourselves for any other causes."[4]

The Reverend John Howlett, an example of that peculiarly English phenomenon, the vicar with scientific interests, had a passion for demography, and the effects of disease on populations. He wrote thousands of letters to other clergymen asking for details of their parish registers, and any other related important information, including inoculations. Among the replies was one from a village in Kent where the number of deaths from smallpox had fallen from 100 between 1688 and 1708, to 5 between 1760 and 1780; the respondent was certain that inoculation was responsible. Similar declines in smallpox mortality were reported from many places around the whole country. In those parishes where the number of births and the causes of death were recorded it was possible to see the ratio of smallpox deaths to total births fall from about one in six to one in forty or fifty. While all such statistics are plagued by selective reporting, and the wide random variations in the annual smallpox incidence between epidemic years and those when the virus was absent, the consistent decline in many communities indicates that deaths from smallpox really were dropping. Howlett thought *"the diminished mortality of (smallpox) in provincial towns and villages... appears to be chiefly due to the salutary practice of inoculation ... where two or three hundred used to be carried to their graves in the course of a few months, there are now not above 20 or 30."* In his own town, Maidstone, the annual loss had fallen from about 20, to 4 by1780, and he reckoned that the mortality in the whole country had diminished by half since 1760.[5]

In the town of Calne, Wiltshire, a local surgeon recorded his experiences during two general inoculations: *"in September 1793 when the poor of the parish were inoculated... We inoculated six hundred and upwards...Besides the poor I inoculated about two hundred (paying) patients...Now in inoculating a whole parish, we had no choice of patients, all ages, and the sickly as well as the others, were inoculated: but these were mostly children, as I assisted in inoculating the whole parish about 12 or 13 years ago"*. The Calne parish register of deaths is fairly complete for the period after 1723, and it reveals that deaths from smallpox declined from 205 between 1723 and 1742, to only 8 between 1783 and 1802. In fact the last smallpox fatalities occur in 1793 and represent the little epidemic that triggered the general inoculation described above.[6]

Observers of the English economic scene also noticed that the population was increasing. A reporter to the Shropshire Board of Agriculture recorded *"that since the year 1782 ...the population of this parish has been increasing; most certainly the inoculation for the smallpox has been most essential"*.[7] Another wrote of the population in industrial towns *"One reason why persons in large manufacturies in Lancashire do not frequently die in great numbers ... is that they have been inoculated in their infancy...many gentlemen pay for the inoculation of the children of the poor in their own neighbourhood"*.[8] In 1781 an observer pointed out that the rural population available to work in agriculture had been rising despite the *"considerable drains of men have been made from almost every parish in the kingdom for the public service in that period, I should not have expected this result, and know nothing to which it could be owing, unless the prevalence of inoculation which certainly has been attended with very great success."[9]* Such comments were a regular feature of the contemporary Boards of Agriculture reports from several English counties.

Increasing population can be due to one of two causes: an increasing birth rate, or declining mortality. Curiously, inoculation may have contributed to population growth by both mechanisms. The birth rate among the British nobility fell from 5 per couple in the early 17th century, to 3.5 per couple in the first third of the 18th century, mirroring the increasing incidence of smallpox.[10] In the 20th century physicians established that smallpox virus damaged the testes causing sterility.[11] Although speculative, it seems reasonable to blame smallpox for some of the declining birth rate. In India, in the first half of the 20th century, smallpox was the commonest cause of male infertility.

After 1740 fertility among the British nobility rises until it returns to about 5 per couple in 1820, which also parallels the rise of inoculation. Inoculation was used among the upper classes in England from the very start, and the large numbers inoculated by sergeant Surgeon Ranby, and other surgeons with practices among the nobility show that it continued to be popular through the 1730s and 40s in this group l. James Kirkpatrick claimed to know of about 14,000 inoculations and most of these would have been among the nobility and wealthy elite. So it is possible that inoculation contributed to the growth in the fertility among the nobility.

But did it have much impact on the growth of the whole population of England? While it may have played a small part, it seems unlikely that it was as significant a cause of population growth as many thought at the time. In the first place the population of England began to grow after 1750 and inoculation did not really become widespread until the end of the 1760s and the 1770s, too late to have been a major factor. Furthermore, the major impact of inoculation was on childhood deaths from smallpox and there would necessarily have been a 20 to 30 year lag until those children reached reproductive age. Finally it is impossible to calculate how the overall mortality from all causes was affected by inoculation. Children spared smallpox would have been prey to many of the others diseases of childhood such as measles or tuberculosis. No one knows whether inoculation led to an increase in the number of children who reached reproductive age.

An alternative explanation for the growth of the English population is that the age at which women married dropped by about a year or two after 1750 to around 24 years of age.[12] This added to the number of children they bore. The most likely explanation is that both a lower death or infertility rate due to inoculation combined with an important increase in a woman's child bearing years drove the increased population after 1750.

The year 1796 was the high water mark of inoculation because of events taking place in the west of England.

Chapter 25

THE PRETTY MILKMAIDS

In 1796, seventy-five years after Lady Mary Wortley Montague and Charles Maitland introduced inoculation into England, Edward Jenner performed an experiment that would eventually lead to the eradication of smallpox and the end of inoculation. He inoculated a child with material from a cowpox pustule just as he would have done from a smallpox pustule. About six weeks later he performed a conventional inoculation on the same child using smallpox material. When there was no reaction to the inoculation Jenner believed that he had demonstrated that cowpox could produce immunity to smallpox just like the real smallpox virus. His experiment had worked. But how did Edward Jenner get to this point, where had the ideas come from, and what lay behind his seemingly audacious practice on a defenseless child?

History texts and children's stories all focus on the supposed role of milkmaids in guiding Jenner to cowpox. Even the most recent histories of smallpox eradication say that he learned of cowpox's benefits from a milkmaid. In many cases the milkmaid is beautiful because she cannot catch smallpox. In some versions of this story the fabled beauty of the unscarred milkmaids is widely known and gives Jenner his first clue. Occasionally other names pop up but are quickly dispatched as not really significant and home in on Jenner as the man who realized why the milkmaids were so beautiful. Sadly the milkmaid story is a lie invented by John Baron, Jenner's friend and first biographer.[1] Jenner himself never claimed to have discovered the value of cowpox, nor did he ever say, despite a huge volume of correspondence, how he first came across the idea. The myths of the milkmaids are just that, myths. To modern eyes, Jenner is revered for eradicating smallpox by using cowpox; in his lifetime, however, Edward Jenner faced severe criticism from jealous competitors and from many ordinary doctors who did not trust his method because, unlike inoculation, it did not give permanent immunity to smallpox. John Baron invented the milkmaid story to counteract these criticisms

What really happened is more prosaic although no less fascinating.

The Suttons' improved method of inoculating spread rapidly through England. By 1768 a country surgeon, John Fewster, and his colleague, Mr. Grove, had become partners with them. Years later, in response to the renowned chemist George Pearson's inquiries, he wrote [2] *"In the spring of the year 1768 I came to live at Thornbury, where I have resided ever since. In that very year, from the following occurrence, I became well acquainted with the disease called Cow Pox. The late Mr. Grove and myself formed a connection with Mr. Sutton, the celebrated inoculator; and to inoculate for the smallpox we took a house in Buckover. We found in this practice that a great number of patients could not be infected with Small Pox poison, not withstanding repeated exposure under most favourable circumstances for taking the disease. At length the cause of the failure was discovered from the case of a farmer who was inoculated several times ineffectually, yet he assured us that he had never suffered the Small Pox, but, says he, "I have had the Cow Pox lately to a violent degree, if that's any odds." We took the hint, and, on enquiry, found that those who were uninfectable had undergone the Cow Pox. I communicated this fact to a medical society of which I was then a member, and ever afterwards paid particular attention to determine the fact."*

Thornbury was a village near Bristol on the river Severn. About six miles north is the town of Berkeley, and about seven miles inland is the market town of Chipping Sodbury. The events which led to vaccination evolved over a thirty year span in the rough triangle formed by these three Gloucestershire towns.

In 1768 nineteen year old Edward Jenner was apprenticed to Daniel Ludlow, a surgeon, based in Chipping Sodbury.[3] Daniel and his apothecary brother Edward were members of a medical society which met at The Ship, an inn at Alveston near Thornbury.[4] This was Fewster's local medical society referred to in his letter. At one of their meetings Fewster reported his conversation with the old farmer and his subsequent inquiries so there is a potential direct connection between Fewster and Jenner through the Ludlow brothers. Fewster's information probably spread through the West Country by word of mouth. It is just the sort of lightbulb moment that changes human knowledge forever. Before, the fact that some individuals resisted all attempts to inoculate them was a mystery and a considerable problem for doctors, since they were obliged to reinoculate their patients who had not had a smallpox pustule in response to their inoculation. Now that they had heard of cowpox on the grapevine they knew to ask their patients about cowpox, and if they did not respond to the operation there was a good explanation. The effects of cowpox would also have been of great interest to dairy workers who would have spread the information among their colleagues at fairs and market days. Within a few years the news had spread around the West Country so that most doctors and many farm workers would have heard of the phenomenon.[5]

On one of the few occasions when Jenner discussed farmers' knowledge of cowpox he said[6],

"it appeared that it (cowpox) had been known from time immemorial, and that a vague opinion prevailed that it was a preventive of the smallpox. This opinion I found was, comparatively, new among them; for all the older farmers declared they had no such idea in their early days- a circumstance that seamed easily to be accounted for, from my knowing that the common people were very rarely inoculated for the smallpox, till that practice was rendered general by the improved method introduced by the Suttons: so that the working people in the dairies were seldom put to the test of the preventive powers of the cow-pox."

Here Jenner himself draws the link between inoculations with smallpox and the discovery of the effects of prior cowpox. Many years later a friend of his confirmed that Jenner once said that he first heard of cowpox in 1768.[7]

By 1769 Jenner was in London working as a house surgeon to the famed experimental surgeon John Hunter at St. George's Hospital. Since he discussed the cowpox effect with Hunter, Jenner must have known about the discovery before leaving Gloucestershire. But the Suttonian method only became widely available after 1766/67 so that the discovery could only have been made in a narrow window between 1767 and 1769. while Jenner was still apprenticed to Ludlow. Whether Jenner was actually present at the dinner where Fewster discussed his findings is not clear, apprentices were probably not invited, but it seems likely that he would have heard about Fewster's observations from his boss soon afterwards.

The advantages of cowpox could not have been discovered before general inoculation became a feature of country life, because only when large numbers of people were inoculated at the same time could the existence of several resistant individuals become apparent. Smallpox epidemics often smoldered rather than exploded and it could take months or years for the disease to leave a particular area. The few who escaped might have had previous mild smallpox and have been rendered immune by the undetected infection, something that was particularly likely to happen when the individual was an orphan because the parents, who might have remembered the early childhood infection, were dead; or they might just have been lucky and avoided exposure to the virus. John Haygarth had shown that direct contact with a smallpox patient or their possessions was necessary to contract the infection. A few individuals, thought to be about one in twenty, seemed to be naturally resistant to smallpox and never caught the disease. Inoculation itself was also not one hundred percent effective, individuals sometimes had no response to the operation and it was common practice to reinoculate them to test whether they were resistant, immune, or whether, for unknown reasons, the first procedure had failed but the second was effective. If an individual failed to respond to inoculation after several attempts, it was usually assumed that they had had smallpox before. There was no way to link cowpox infection, which might have occurred years before and been forgotten, with inoculation resistance. However, once a large number of farmers and dairymaids were identified who resisted attempts to inoculate them it became possible to question them closely until, as Fewster relates, one of them provided the crucial piece of information. Only cowpox infection shortly before inoculation could provide the clue required, and only when a large group of individuals were inoculated together would the necessary individual turn up. Cowpox itself was a sporadic illness found mostly in the south and west of England, so the chance of finding an individual with the right sequence of infections would only turn up if a large group of dairymen was inoculated at one time.

Edward Jenner left his country apprenticeship for London where he had the good fortune to be the first pupil of John Hunter who is widely credited with developing scientific surgery. Hunter had an obsessive interest in experimentation - his most famous aphorism, which Jenner would have heard frequently, was "why think, do the experiment". Master and student became close friends and remained in correspondence for the rest of Hunter's life. When Jenner returned home to Berkeley, he took the habits of observation and experimentation gained from his mentor with him. The country physician shared some of his ideas about cowpox with his former superior who was intensely interested in the concept since he was also an inoculator.

Back home in Berkeley, Edward Jenner settled into the routine of a country doctor. He joined two local medical societies; one of them the group that met at The Ship where Fewster and the Ludlows still participated in the discussions. Why didn't cowpox fascinate them in the way that it became an obsession for Jenner?

Fewster's lack of interest was based on his long experience of country medicine, which had convinced him that cowpox was actually a more serious disease than inoculated smallpox. The cowpox virus was transmitted by contact, and probably could only infect through cuts or scratches in the skin. If there was only a tiny scratch then there would only be a single "pock", but if there were numerous scratches all over the arms, or extensively chapped skin from continuous outdoor work, then there would be many more pustules and the patient would have a fever and pronounced systemic symptoms. Sometimes the infection even spread to the face, transferred by scratching or licking a sore finger. A few patients who had widespread skin problems might have cowpox over their whole body much like children with eczema following vaccination in the 20th century. Suttonian inoculation was actually milder than natural cowpox in most cases. Fewster wrote,

"I think that it (cowpox) is a much more severe disease in general than the inoculated smallpox. I do not see any great advantage from the inoculation for the Cow Pox. Inoculation of the Small Pox seems to be so well understood that there is little need of a substitute. It is curious, however, and may lead to other improvements."[8]

In experienced hands the death rate after inoculation was less than one in five hundred, and about twenty percent of patients had only a single pock at the inoculation site. Although there was the risk of starting an epidemic, by then doctors knew how to prevent one, either by isolation or general inoculation. In contrast to inoculated smallpox, a cowpox pustule often matured into an intensely painful ulcer on the hand or fingers which left the sufferer unable to work for several days. On balance inoculation was less troublesome for the patient than having cowpox.

There was a second, and more compelling, reason why country doctors were not impressed by cowpox. It did not always protect against smallpox. Many individuals who said that they had had the cowpox before, had perfectly normal inoculation smallpox. There were also cases of natural smallpox among individuals who had thought that they were immune from a previous infection caught from cows. While immunity always implied prior cowpox, previous cowpox did not always imply immunity. What would be the point of investigating the potential benefits of something that simply wasn't as effective as current practice? It is easy to see why Jenner's colleagues found him tedious, and even he acknowledged that the imperfect protection problem was a major setback.[9]

It took Edward Jenner twenty-five years to unravel the mess. The problem lay in the definition of "cowpox". There were at least three diseases that produced ulcers on the teats of cows and only one of these was caused by the cowpox virus. *"this for a while damped, but did not extinguish my ardour"*. Jenner's remarkable achievement is that he spent all that time untangling true cowpox from spurious cowpox and defining its unequivocal appearances. He learned how to recognise "milker's nodes" a painful bacterial infection on the fingers, which lacked the typical erosive ulcer of cowpox, and he could differentiate between cowpox and *staphylococcal* infections of the udder because the damage caused by *staphylococcal* bacteria spread beyond the teats. Eventually he learned how to recognise cases of true cowpox and could confirm that they really were resistant to inoculation. Jenner had also had a second insight that his colleagues had not appreciated. Inoculated cowpox would be much less severe than natural cowpox, just as inoculated smallpox was less dangerous than naturally acquired disease.

In May 1796 Jenner was asked to inoculate an eight-year-old pauper child named James Phipps. At the same time there was a local outbreak of cowpox, something that only occurred every few years. Sarah Nelmes, a dairymaid, was infected with cowpox from her employer's cows and had developed a large pustule where she had been scratched by a thorn. *"matter was taken from a sore on the hand of a dairymaid, …and it was inserted, on the 14th of May 1796, into the arm of the boy by means of two superficial incisions, barely penetrating the cutis, each about half and inch long.*

In order to ascertain whether the boy, after feeling so slight an affection of the system from the cow-pox virus was secure from the contagion of the smallpox, he was inoculated on July 1 following with variolous matter The appearances were observable on the arms as we commonly see when a patient has had variolous matter applied, after having either the cow-pox or smallpox. Several months afterwards he was again inoculated with variolous matter, but no sensible effect was produced."[10]

Had Jenner done something unethical? In medical circles it is fashionable to claim that his first experiment would never have been approved by a modern ethics committee. Some writers even claim that the boy was an unwilling victim of Jenner's ego and he would never have "volunteered" for the experiment. In reality Jenner was acting in a completely acceptable way and actually giving Phipps, son of a poor labourer, protection against a feared disease. A child who had not had smallpox was almost unemployable because no one would take on a boy who might bring smallpox into the household and whose care and burial expenses would be charged to his employer if he did come down with the disease. Even if he remained in the workhouse his care would be an unnecessary expense for the parish. Inoculation was the standard way to give the child immunity and protect him from the consequences of the infection. The parish overseers who asked Jenner to perform the operation were acting in Phipps' best interests. Although Jenner had never "vaccinated" anyone before he had good reason to believe that the procedure might work based on numerous patients of his who had proved resistant to inoculation after having cowpox. All he was doing was attempting to see whether artificial cowpox worked as well as natural cowpox, just as artificial inoculated smallpox protected against natural smallpox. After vaccinating Phipps he was be inoculated in the usual way. If cowpox had failed, he would just have a normal mild inoculation response; if it worked nothing would happen. Jenner was following up his experimental treatment with the "gold standard" method of protecting the child. Since inoculation was a well-established and largely safe procedure that was widely used in England, there was no ethical issue with that part of the experiment. Inoculation would have been viewed as a necessary part of growing up for a child receiving parish support. Since cowpox was never fatal and had few systemic effects, there were unlikely to be any unexpected complications apart from failure to immunize. Even in the hyper health-and-safety conscious twenty-first century this experiment would have been given ethical approval.

 Edward Jenner attempted to publish the Phipps experiment in a manuscript which was rejected by the Royal Society[11]. Why would this august body turn down what we now regard as one of the most important discoveries ever made? Actually, the manuscript was a mess. Although Jenner gave short details of ten patients who had resisted inoculation several years after having cowpox, Phipps was one the only patient he had immunized with cowpox. One example was not enough to support replacing inoculation with smallpox with cowpox. When John Haygarth heard of the experiment he thought that it was potentially interesting but that one case provided insufficient evidence; twenty or thirty would be more convincing. The rest of Jenner's paper consisted of speculations on the animal origin of cowpox; he thought that it was derived from a horse disease called "grease". And he gave a rambling hypothesis that many human diseases were derived from animals and a very confusing observation that immunity seemed to work in only one direction. Cowpox prevented smallpox, but smallpox did not prevent cowpox. By rejecting the paper the Royal Society spared Jenner the criticism and derision that would have followed his weak evidence and unsupported ideas. They actually saved his reputation.

Undeterred by rejection, Jenner attempted to expand his experiment. He recognised that there were one or two problems that he needed to overcome before his idea became a useful treatment. He had shown that whatever cowpox was, it could make someone immune to smallpox. But was this a stable property of the cowpox, or would it only work when transmitted from someone who had been directly infected by a cow? In a world that had no idea what germs were, there was no way to be certain that an infection always produced the same result. Jenner believed that cowpox was derived from "grease", an infection of horse's hooves, which acquired the properties of cowpox when it infected a different species, the cow. Perhaps cowpox would also change when it was passed from person to person.

However, he could not perform any more immunizations because there was no cowpox in the neighbourhood. He had to wait until the Spring of 1798 when cowpox reappeared. This time he conducted a complicated experiment, first inoculating William Summers with cowpox, then twelve days later, using fluid from his pustule to "inoculate" William Paed. Eight days later he transferred fluid from Paed to several children and adults and from one of them, Hannah Excell, he inoculated a further four children seven days after that. Finally he used fluid from one of them, Mary Paed, to inoculate a boy, J. Barge. Sometime later Jenner arranged for his nephew Henry to inoculate Summers and J. Barge with smallpox fluid which, as he expected, resulted in no reaction.

Jenner's complicated passage of fluid from one child to another was important because it satisfied him that whatever was responsible for immunizing the children was stable and could be passed from one person to another without losing its potency. He once stated that it was the only original contribution that he made to the establishment of cowpox as a better form of inoculation. Now he was ready to publish his experiments.

Edward Jenner's first publication about cowpox, "An Inquiry Into the Causes and Effects of the Variolae Vaccinae, or Cowpox", did not arrive on a completely unsuspecting world. Jenner had discussed his ideas with many of his friends, including George Pearson who had discussed the basic concepts with John Hunter as early as 1789. However, Jenner's paper was actually rather thin. He provided 16 cases histories of individuals who had proved to be immune to smallpox following cowpox and he had "cowpoxed" at least ten others, but he had only performed a smallpox challenge on three of his subjects. Although they were immune, it was weak evidence at best.

William Woodville, physician to the Hospital for Smallpox and Inoculation, managed to find a cowpox-struck cow in London and collected material to perform his own trial assisted by George Pearson. From the beginning it was a disaster. Many of their patients developed pustules on their bodies, not just the solitary pustule at the inoculation site as Jenner had claimed. One of their five hundred patients died, which was more than the one in six to eight hundred that Woodville expected from his many years at the inoculation hospital. Woodville concluded that there was little difference between inoculated cowpox and inoculated smallpox.[12]

Jenner refuted Woodville's claims at once. None of his patients had ever developed more than a single pustule. The problem lay in the Inoculation Hospital where the atmosphere, fixtures, and even Woodville himself, were so marinated in smallpox that he had accidentally contaminated his vaccine. When none of Woodville's private patients, who were vaccinated away from the hospital, developed any other sores he concluded that Jenner was correct.

Although Pearson had confirmed many of Jenner's claims about cowpox, relations between the two men soured, especially when Pearson founded a vaccination clinic in London and offered Jenner a subsidiary role in its management. The Vaccine Institute, Pearson's project, was intended to monopolise the vaccination trade in London and generate a large private practice in vaccination for its founder. Matters came to a head in 1802 when Jenner's friends petitioned Parliament to grant Jenner an honorarium of £10,000 to compensate him for the lost income he suffered while developing his innovation. But Jenner made a near fatal mistake. He opened his petition, claiming that he was the true discoverer of the benefits of cowpox.[13] Later in the document, his nephew George corrected this, claiming instead that the person to person transmission was the original discovery which had established vaccination. Jenner's misstatement opened the way for George Pearson. During the House of Commons investigation Pearson gave testimony that he had gathered a great deal of information implying that Jenner did not deserve the reward. His case was based on several features of Jenner's work. Firstly, Jenner had not "discovered" that cowpox prevented smallpox, this fact had been known for at least 30 years before Jenner's The Inquiry was published. Secondly, Jenner did not understand the basis of his "discovery" since he believed that "grease" was the source of cowpox and claimed that he had immunised with material taken from horses' hooves. Numerous attempts to confirm this observation had failed. A farmer named Jesty and at least one other doctor had inoculated with cowpox material years before Jenner so he did not deserve to claim priority. Finally, Pearson and Dr William Woodville, physician to the Smallpox and Inoculation hospital, had been the first to confirm Jenner's observations by initiating a large series of vaccinations, which were far superior in their value to the few cases Jenner had produced.

Most of Pearson's comments were fair; only the claims that he and Woodville had initiated trials confirming the findings were shown to be untrue. Another physician, Henry Cline, had begun before them. Indeed, Jenner had never claimed that he had discovered the value of cowpox, nor had he claimed that he was the first to vaccinate. His claim was based on his demonstration that the agent could be passed from person to person while retaining its protective properties. Parliament found in favour of Jenner and voted to give him £10,000.

Many medical innovations divide public opinion. Immunisation has been opposed by some parts of society from its very beginnings. Opponents of vaccination (cowpox inoculation) used Pearson's arguments to denigrate Jenner and deprecate his discovery. Pearson went so far as to invite farmer Jesty to London where he had his portrait painted. This was hung in the Vaccine Establishment as a reminder of the view that Jenner's reputation was inflated.

Much of the opposition to vaccination stemmed from the undoubted success of inoculation. Woodville admitted that the Smallpox Hospital had misled their patients into believing that they were being inoculated when they were being vaccinated because they would have refused "cowpoxing". Families all over Britain had been inoculated in the great expansion of the practice brought about by the Suttons. Now parents and grandparents wanted the same well known and well regarded treatment for their own children. Country doctors who had used inoculation with great success for the whole of their careers were reluctant to give up a practice that they trusted for a less well understood innovation.

Within a decade of Jenner's first publication it was clear that there was a major flaw in vaccination: it did not produce lifelong immunity to smallpox. Shortly after the new practice began to spread, cases of true smallpox in patients previously vaccinated appeared. At first Jenner tried to explain them away by claiming that the inoculator was an unskilled operator, or that he had used spurious cowpox to perform the operation. However, soon there were cases where there could be no explanation, other than a failure of vaccination to provide protection. Eventually even one of Jenner's patients developed severe confluent smallpox ten years after the master had performed his vaccination. Although none of these cases had been fatal, their existence raised the possibility of severe disease. Everyone knew that sometimes smallpox was discrete and other times confluent. Parents now faced the anxiety of what to do about their vaccinated children. Should they have them inoculated to be on the safe side? To many, such failures argued that Jenner had been wrong and that vaccination was a failed experiment that should be abandoned. Since the idea that "grease" was the forerunner of cowpox had been proven false, perhaps the value of cowpox was also an illusion. Jenner's concept of "spurious cowpox" was attacked. Nothing like spurious smallpox or spurious measles existed, so why believe in "spurious cowpox". If that idea was also false, then all of Jenner's arguments relying on it as the explanation for failed vaccinations were also false. Inoculators resorted to the timeless medical teaching "never abandon experience for experiment".

One of the first to notice that vaccination sometimes failed was Daniel Sutton. He replied to a Royal College of Physicians circular asking for information about the success of cowpox, giving a report of two patients that he had personally vaccinated with cowpox who had subsequently developed smallpox. He was livid when the College demanded that he attend in person and bring exact details of his cases. How dare they imply that he was lying? It would be Sutton's last public appearance where he defended what had become commonly known as "the Suttonian method" in contradistinction to cowpoxing. But his treatment was a symptom of another issue surrounding vaccination. Opponents of vaccination felt that the medical establishment had sold out to Jenner and were censoring all criticism. Eventually it would become clear that vaccination "wore off" after a few years and that it only provided complete protection for 3- 5 years in some individuals. But to some even this was a nuisance since inoculation provided lifelong protection.

Because vaccination would eventually prove such a huge success and lead to the eradication of smallpox it can be difficult for modern observers to realise exactly how controversial vaccination was in the early 19th century. Jenner's reputation was under attack from several aspects. It becomes easier to understand why John Baron, Jenner's biographer deliberately mislead posterity by publishing a truncated version of Fewster's letter, which only included his comments that he did not think cowpox was better than smallpox. For years Jenner's opponents had argued that Fewster, not Jenner, was the true discoverer of inoculation and Baron wanted to stamp on this claim. Fewster himself never claimed that he was the originator and remained friends with Jenner, even sending him occasional case reports to add to his collection. Yet Baron clearly took Fewster's letter seriously enough to misrepresent its contents and to belittle Fewster's subsequent lack of interest in cowpox when Jenner tried to raise the subject at their medical society meetings. He inadvertently confirms the likely accuracy of the account by trying to discredit it. Baron even suggests that the other members of the society threatened to banish Jenner if he did not stop his continual dialogue around cowpox. The effect of Baron's autobiography is to characterise Fewster and his colleagues as ignorant fools who were unable to appreciate the genius of Jenner. Whatever Fewster did, it was enough to upset John Baron. Yet, despite having ample opportunity for over twenty years, Edward Jenner never refuted Fewster's account of the discovery of the cowpox effect. Modern smallpox texts cite Fewster as an example of a discredited claim for priority and never publish the entire text of his letter. Further, some of them confuse the issue by stating that Fewster claimed to have reported his findings to a London medical society and that no published records of the event remained.

Quite where the various versions of Fewster's actions came from is difficult to track down. Certainly there could not have been a presentation to "The London Medical Society" in 1765 since that organization wasn't founded until 1776, and Fewster could not have made his discovery in 1765, as some accounts claim, because he only moved to Thornbury in 1768. These versions appear to be attempts to defuse the claims of the importance of Fewster's role by reducing them to unpublished observations that had no impact on the subsequent development of vaccination. Baron's creation of the milkmaid myth serves a similar purpose. In the absence of any statement from Jenner about what had really happened the Fewster letter gained credence. By planting the milkmaid story, and claiming that Jenner had told it to him more than once, Baron provided an alternative version, which he strengthened by claiming that Jenner had repeated it on his death bed.

Baron's milkmaid fiction soon took on a life of its own. Subsequent authors attempted to explain how a milkmaid could have known that cowpox protected her from smallpox by inventing a tradition that milkmaids had singularly beautiful faces because they were not scarred by smallpox. However, no one ever commented on this at the time (the 1760's or before) and there are good reasons to believe that it was not so. For one thing boys as well as girls milked cows in England, and no one ever suggested that cowboys had smooth complexions. Furthermore, both smallpox and cowpox occurred sporadically and there was no reason why a future milkmaid would get cowpox first. There should have been both scarred and smooth milkmaids and, again, no one noticed.

Smallpox was actually not very contagious so that during an outbreak at a farm or small farming village a few individuals would escape the infection by chance or because they were resistant to the virus. There would be no way to connect their escape to a previous attack of cowpox until artificial infection, ie inoculation, made the link obvious.

Chapter 26

AFTER JENNER

Once the accumulated myths and misreadings of two centuries have been scraped away it is clear that the fact that cowpox produced immunity to smallpox was discovered by a country surgeon who was in the right place at the right time. Fewster was performing one of the earliest group inoculations in the dairying country where there were enough farmers who had had cowpox for the facts to emerge. He had enough sense to tell his colleagues, they would want to know why their inoculations sometimes failed, but he did not appreciate the true value of cowpox. Even after Jenner had published his "Inquiry" Fewster thought that inoculation was the better choice for his patients. Jenner's genius lay is seeing that cowpox might provide a safe and easy substitute for inoculation. The potential lay in the fact that no one ever died of cowpox, and that for most individuals a local pustule on the hand was the only lesion that they developed. And, importantly, cowpox was not contagious; someone needed to make direct physical contact with the pustules on an infected cow's udder to catch the disease. If the fine details could be worked out then a form of inoculated cowpox might be developed which would never kill the patient and could not spread to others except by directly implanting it into a cut or scratch. Jenner had the tenacious curiosity to sort out the fine details. He alone introduced vaccination as a replacement for inoculation and deserves full credit for the success it became.

Equally, however, if inoculation had not become a widespread and trusted practice there would have been nothing for Jenner to unravel as there would have been no way to discover the benefits of cowpox. Inoculation not only led to Fewster's s observation, it was the means which allowed him to test the idea. Without inoculation there would have been no way to determine whether someone who said that they were immune to smallpox because they had had cowpox was right short of deliberately exposing them to the natural disease. Inoculation provided the test bed for the idea. When many inoculation-proof farmers said that they had had cowpox that strengthened the idea. When many patients who said that they had had cowpox could not be inoculated that completed the proof. Jenner then sorted out why sometimes, someone said that they had had cowpox but succumbed to smallpox.

If inoculation had not been available the cowpox effect could not have been discovered when it was. It might have taken many years for the right conjunction of a smallpox epidemic and a recent cowpox outbreak to provide a clue, and then there would have been no way to test the idea. Smallpox might have remained the greatest killer of humanity until well into the 19th, or even the twentieth century.

Inoculation had a second powerful role in the eventual success of vaccination. By 1800 everyone in England and North America would have heard of inoculation and knew what it did. Even on the continent, where inoculation was only slowly adopted, many of the educated classes knew of the procedure. The principle that immunity could be induced by producing an artificial infection which was both safe and reliable was accepted. Although religious objections to the practice never completely disappeared it seems that the great majority of the English population was comfortable with the idea of inoculation. Seventy five years of debate and experience had eventually overcome the original objections. But think back to the original debates of the 1720s when inoculation was *a sick cow or sick cows,*

fiercely attacked on both scientific and religious grounds. Imagine what would have happened if, by some chance, Jenner, or someone like him, had proposed infecting people with material derived from sick cow? He might have been laughed out of town, but more likely he would have been ostracised and have lost all his patients. At least one West Country doctor had tried to promote cowpox before Jenner, but his patients would not accept it.[1] Even with the long history of inoculation behind them, many English critics of Jenner simple could not accept that something derived from a brute animal could possibly work. Cartoons appeared showing children with cows growing out of their arms and a rumour that a child had developed a cow's face following vaccination circulated.

One argument that helped vaccination to become acceptable to some was that it was really exactly the same as inoculation: only the vaccinator knew whether his lancet had been dipped in cowpox matter or a smallpox pustule. The patient had no way of knowing for sure. When Jenner suggested that cowpox was really smallpox of the cow the idea circulated that cowpox was actually smallpox that had been slightly modified by passage through a cow and not an animal disease at all.[2] So vaccination involved using material from a human disease that behaved just like the old tried and trusted inoculation and was therefore acceptable.

While members of the social elite and Royal College of Physicians enthusiastically supported vaccination, many of the "lower orders" refused to believe that it was any use. Families all over Britain had been inoculated in the great expansion of the practice brought about by the Suttons. Now parents and grandparents wanted the same well-known and well regarded treatment for their children. Country doctors who had used inoculation with great success for the whole of their careers were reluctant to give up a practice that they trusted for a less well understood innovation. Also, good quality cowpox vaccine was not easy to come by, so many lay inoculators continued as they had always done, using smallpox material. In the great smallpox epidemic that swept over Britain between 1816 and 1819 many people found themselves with a difficult decision: would they have their children vaccinated or inoculated? In many areas the populace "voted" for the older practice and demanded inoculation from their doctors. Even doctors who supported vaccination and had refused to inoculate in the past found that the demands from parish overseers for inoculation could not be resisted and returned to their former practice. In Norwich some practitioners adopted a belt and braces approach and performed both operations at the same time. Ironically vaccination was less favoured in the country that had discovered it because inoculation was so firmly embedded in British life. What had made it possible to discover and introduce vaccination also became a barrier to its full acceptance.

Inoculation continued to be used in Britain until well into the 19th century. When a Bill to ban the practice was introduced in 1840 the evidence collected showed that many of the "ignorant poor" in rural areas were still strongly opposed to vaccination and preferred the advice of empiricks to that of their better educated neighbours or the clergy. Parliament paid inoculation a backhanded compliment by making it illegal showing just how strong was the sentiment in its favour. Lord Landsdowne even said that vaccination and cowpox were "perfectly identical" although with somewhat different symptoms.[2] Vaccination was the direct descendant of inoculation.

Once it became criminal to inoculate the practice largely disappeared in Britain. What level persisted was probably confined to small scale home inoculations by worried parents who would not advertise what they had done because it was illegal. In Europe and North America vaccination had essentially replaced inoculation much earlier. Ironically where inoculation was less practiced vaccination was readily accepted. So inoculation fades from sight in the western world, but not everywhere. When the WHO began its drive to eradicate smallpox it became apparent that there were frequent inoculations in Africa and parts of India and Pakistan. [3] In part this reflected a centuries old custom and it part it was due to poor or intermittent supplies of good quality vaccine.

When, in the 1960s and 70s, the WHO programme reached Afghanistan and western Pakistan it found that about a third of the cases of smallpox were actually inoculated smallpox.[4] Itinerant inoculators would move from village to village offering their services for a fee. Reluctant to give up what for many inoculators was a familial business passed from father to sons, they resisted attempts to try to convert them to vaccination. However, eventually providing free good quality vaccine made it possible for inoculators to give up their old ways for the safer modern approach.

A similar problem faced the WHO eradication teams in Ethiopia where their efforts were inhibited by the outbreak of guerrilla warfare in several parts of the country. Finally a last outbreak among nomads in the Ogaden desert was identified where nine of the sixteen cases were due to true smallpox inoculation (variolation).[5] The last person inoculated anywhere in the world was a three year old girl.

Because inoculation continued in Ethiopia and Afghanistan into the 1970s there are still people alive who were inoculated.

Because inoculation persisted into the 20th century it became a barrier to the complete eradication of smallpox. As seen above, in some parts of Asia inoculation actually accounted for a significant number of smallpox cases with the attendant risk of starting an epidemic. With reliable vaccination available and a concerted campaign to eradicate smallpox underway it was important to show that inoculation was dangerous and unacceptable. In the attack on inoculation, that began in the nineteenth century and continued until full eradication had been achieved, history lost sight of the important role inoculation played in the discovery and success of vaccination. Inoculation came to be considered a useless forerunner of vaccination, of little significance, and no lasting value. Also lost was knowledge of the origins of many modern medical advances among them immunization, clinical trials, contact tracing, clinical science, and evidence based medicine which are still the foundations for 21st century medical practice. The moral and scientific arguments that were developed to justify inoculation formed an important part of what is now called the Enlightenment. Far from being a medical desert, the 18th century was a fertile period which allowed humanity to gain an important measure of control over its most feared disease. What could be more "enlightened" than to defy providence and choose your own fate?

Appendix 1

ORIGINS OF INOCULATION

Variolation (known in the 18th century as inoculation) triggered a number of important developments in medicine among them the first examples of evidence based medicine, immunisation, and quantitative measures of disease severity. Arguably the discovery of the protective effects of cowpox against smallpox was only possible because of the widespread use of variolation, and the definitive experiments to establish that cowpox was indeed protective could only be performed by variolation following vaccination with cowpox. Ultimately vaccination led to the eradication of smallpox, one of the great achievements of medicine. Given the central role of variolation in these significant events, it is worth investigating where the practice originated.

Working backwards from the first variolations in Britain and colonial Massachusetts in 1721 it is possible to trace the practice in Africa, the Ottoman empire, and Wales to about 1600 AD. Variolation was introduced into Constantiople about 1670 by a Greek woman who was followed by a woman from Bosnia.[1,2] Early reports suggest that it was only used by Christians, because Muslims thought that it interfered with divine providence.

In Boston, Massachusetts, Cotton Mather's slave, Onesimus, recalled that he had been inoculated in Africa sometime before 1706 when he was bought by Mather's parishoners and that the practice was well known and had been used for many years.[3] Onesimus was a Guarmantee, from what is now southern Libya.

Further confirmation of the use of variolation in Northern Africa before 1700 is found in a letter from the ambassador from Tripoli dated about 1728 who recalled his own variolation many years before and said that it had been used for so long that no one remembered where it had come from. He also mentioned that it was used by the "wild Arabs" as well as the citizens of Tripoli, Tunis, and Algiers.[4]

The most surprising evidence for early variolation appeared when James Jurin, secretary to the Royal Society, solicited accounts of both variolated and natural smallpox. Two Welsh doctors, Perrot Williams and Richard Wright, wrote that the practice was well known and had been used by many individuals in and around the port of Haverford West for many years.[5] Wright knew a man aged about 90 who had been variolated as a child as had his mother before him, and she had told him that it was a common practice all her time. Since this letter was written in 1722 variolation was probably used in Wales since about 1600 and possibly before.[6] Wright said that many people in the region considered it an ancient practice among the common people. In many cases the operation was performed by buying a few scabs or pus from someone suffering from natural smallpox and then puncturing the skin with a needle contaminated with the smallpox matter, although some individuals just rubbed the scabs on their own skin, and in at least one case a school boy scraped the back of his hand with a penknife until it bled and then rubbed the scabs into the wound. All witnesses agreed that they had had mild smallpox and have never had the infection a second time. Furthermore, a reliable witness, a mid-wife, said that during the previous fifty years she had only heard of one person who died following the operation. A similar low mortality was reported from Constantinople where multiple shallow needle punctures were used to transmit the infection[7], but in North Africa, where an incision was used about two in one hundred children died.[8] Several other descriptions of a practice known as "buying the pocks" exist and record it in Scotland and Europe. While they all agree that a sum of money or goods was exchanged for the pocks, they do not agree on how the operation was carried out. In Scotland a smallpox soaked bit of wool was wrapped around the child's wrist. In other places the scabs were held in the child's hand for some time. Still others had the child wear smallpox infected clothes. Despite evidence that "buying the pocks" was widespread in Europe, it did not penetrate deeply into life in the 18th century before inoculation was introduced from Constantinople.

Inoculation was established in Africa and Wales since "time immemorial" and had reached Constantinople by about 1650. But where had it come from?

Two possible origins for variolation have been suggested: China or India. The earliest written discussion of variolation in China is found in a book first published in 1549.[9] Joseph Needham, who investigated the origins of inoculation in China, believed that the fact that the author commented on the possibility that variolation would induce menstruation suggests that the practice was already well known, if little written about. Several other slightly later Chinese authors complain that many inoculators would not reveal their secrets so that it was difficult to establish exactly what was happening and when it had begun. One of Needham's texts says that variolation was first practiced between 1567 and 1572 and that it had been invented by an "extraordinary man" based on alchemical principles. Thereafter several families became hereditary inoculators but refused to reveal their secrets for commercial reasons.

In the second half of the 17th century the Khang-hsi emperor boasted that he had inoculated his whole family, his army, and other groups and that they had all passed through mild smallpox. Also, at about this time manuals setting out the techniques of inoculation were published. Remarkably they all were based on insufflation, blowing smallpox material up the nose of the child being inoculated. Sometimes dry scabs were ground to powder, at other times the scabs were extracted into water, and yet another approach was to collect fluid from a pustule onto a cotton plug and place that up the nose.

Needham also describes an even older, but much less well documented, tradition of inoculation in China.[10] In this version it was invented by a Taoist or Buddhist monk, or possibly a nun, about 1000 AD and practiced by Taoists as a mixture of medicine, technique, magic, and spells which were transmitted orally and which were covered by a taboo so that they were never written down. Needham can give no firmer evidence for this version than the fact that it was a widely accepted tradition. An editorial commentator wonders whether it is realistic to believe that something with the importance of inoculation would have remained completely secret for over 500 years.[11] The only certainty is that there were written accounts of inoculation by the mid 1500s.

An alternative option for the origin of inoculation is in India. Two 18th century accounts by early English residents give descriptions of inoculations by itinerant Brahmins.[12],[13] Their technique involved dipping a sharp pointed iron needle into a smallpox pustule and then puncturing the skin repeatedly in a small circle usually on the upper arm. Writing in 1731 Oliver Coult says that the operation was "first performed by Dununtary, a physician of Champanagar" about 150 years before ie about 1580, and that he learned of the secret in a dream. However, Dominik Wujastyk has suggested that this account is suspect because Dununtary, the supposed inventor of inoculation, is a mythological figure similar to Asclepius in western medicine. Writing in 1768 J.Z Holwell, describes a similar technique but was of the opinion that the practice was centuries old. Thus there is no firm date for inoculation in India before 1731.

Many modern texts claim that inoculation in India was much older and had been practiced for thousands of years.[14] These accounts are based on claims that the practice is described in ancient Sanskrit texts. However, it has been conclusively shown that this ancient text does not exist and that the piece cited may be a "pious fraud" invented in the 19th century. Although there are detailed descriptions of smallpox and its treatment in ancient Indian texts, "there is no evidence for prophylaxis".[15]

In summary, there are two accounts of inoculation in the middle of the 16th century, one Chinese and one Indian, each gives a specific place and name to the initial inoculators. Whether it was in use before about 1550 is entirely speculative. So where did it come from? Unfortunately the historical record is not clear. However, on the grounds of technique used it would appear that India was the source of the method used in the West. Puncturing the skin and rubbing in a little smallpox pus is common to the Indian practice and that used in Turkey, North Africa, and Greece. Blowing material up the nose distinguishes Chinese practice from the others so India seems the likely origin because no change in method is required. In addition, the Chinese method relied on the operator keeping his inoculum at body temperature for at least a month before using it. During this time there would have been a sharp decline in the number of infectious virus particles. On occasion, when time was pressing, some other method such as heating the inoculum was employed. On the one occasion when the Chinese method was used with fresh smallpox material in the West the results were disturbing.[16]

It is difficult to see how insufflations, blowing smallpox up the nose could have evolved into scarification with a needle suggesting that inoculation was invented twice. The remarkable similarity of the methods used in India and across the Ottoman empire argues that they share a common origin. In addition inoculation was often referred to as "buying the smallpox" in these areas supporting the idea of a single origin.[17] Since the claims that inoculation originated in India are dubious at best, perhaps the traditions of the Ottoman Empire are correct:[18] it was invented by the Arabs at some unknown time before 1550 and then spread along trade routes through Africa and the Middle East to reach India. [19]

Appendix 2

WHY IT WORKED

S mallpox is probably the only disease which can be made safer by inoculation. William Woodville recorded that attempts had been made to inoculate other infections but, although he claimed that they were successful, they never caught on.

The outcome of a viral infection is the result of a race between the body's many defensive mechanisms and the rate of virus replication. When resistance is high the disease is usually mild; when weak the result is often catastrophic. Natural smallpox usually spread as a respiratory tract infection. The nose and upper throat became a large ulcerated surface which shed enormous quantities of the virus with every cough. Usually the virus was inhaled by a susceptible contact and the cycle continued. Even when the virus spread through contact with contaminated clothing or scabs, the route of infection was usually through the respiratory tract. The site of infection probably explains the difference between inoculated and natural smallpox because it favoured different types of immune response. The dose of virus received may also have been important.

A virus is not a living organism but only a protein bag containing nucleic acids, which are the genetic code required to produce more virus. The protein coat protects the genetic material from environmental damage and also determines which cells the virus particles can stick to and penetrate. Once it adheres to a cell it must enter and release viral genetic material before a cycle of replication can begin. The smallpox virus probably passes through the cells lining the respiratory tract and enters cells such as macrophages and monocytes which carry the virus to lymphoid tissues where it replicates. Eventually cells producing new virus burst and the particles are released into the blood stream. A few infected monocytes also circulate and may be particularly important in carrying the virus back to the respiratory tract. While this process is occurring the lymphoid tissues are also mounting an immune response which will eventually kill any cell which is synthesising new viral proteins and thereby end the infection.

There are two main types of immune response, so called T helper 1 and T helper 2, which result in strong killer cell reactions or strong antibody responses respectively. Although the usual response is a mixture of both types, some organisms exploit the fact that the two types inhibit each other to gain an advantage. The respiratory tract is particularly suited to skew the response towards the T helper 2 type. This normally results in good levels of IgA antibody, the type which coats the surface of the respiratory tract and helps neutralise viruses before they can penetrate the protective layer. Type 2 responses also favour production of IgE antibodies, which are useful for expelling inhaled noxious dusts and parasite eggs. However, type 2 responses partially inhibit the development of type 1 responses, which are the most effective means of killing virus infected cells. Therefore a natural smallpox infection may have gained a head start on the immune response by starting off in a type 2 environment.

Placing small amounts of virus in the superficial layers of the skin may have favoured an early type 1 response because the virus started to multiply locally in skin cells and entered the dendritic cells present in large numbers in and just below the surface. These cells have an important sentinel function and sample their environment continuously. When they receive a chemical signal from infected skin cells they leave the skin and migrate though the lymphatic vessels to lymph nodes where they are exceptionally potent initiators of immune responses. At this early stage dendritic cells make a protein called interferon gamma which drives a type 1 response. Some inoculated individuals would only have virus replicating in skin cells at the inoculation site where a large pustule surrounded by smaller satellites would form. When the virus spread infected cells were killed before enough virus to infect contiguous cells had grown. Even when virus did enter the blood stream there were only enough particles to form a few foci and the number of pocks was usually very small.

But some individuals are genetically programmed to make stronger type 2 responses than most of the population. When inoculated they would develop weaker type 1 responses and so have more pocks. Pregnancy shifted the response towards a type 2 response. The hormonal changes which help protect the developing foetus against rejection by the mother's type 1 response also disable her response to the virus. Up to fifty percent of pregnant women who caught smallpox died; most of the rest had abortions or still births. The immune response is a little like Canadian log rolling; as long as you keep your balance you're fine, but as soon as you slip you're in the soup.

Early Western inoculators actually performed the operation in ways that tended to counteract the benefits of placing the virus into the skin. They made bigger incisions into the tissues producing larger primary inoculation sites, which in turn generated more virus. They thought that this was a good thing to do because the larger wound seemed to drain more of the "morbific matter" from inside the body. Because more of the inoculum reached white blood cells rather than dendritic cells it got carried to lymphatic tissues in cells that favoured replication rather than immune responses, so even more virus was produced. There were many more pocks formed and more severe symptoms until Robert Sutton rediscovered the Turkish method. The cool method advocated by Daniel Sutton was beneficial because it tended to reduce blood flow to the skin because being outdoors lowered the surface temperature. Fewer viruses found their way into skin cells where they could replicate and more were destroyed within the body instead. Even the folk belief that inoculation was best practised in cold months can be explained by reduced skin blood flow.

Both inoculation and vaccination produce immunological memory, the capacity to mount a stronger protective immune response whenever the virus is encountered again. Most of the time this response was so efficient that the individual did not realise that he had been exposed to the virus again. Occasionally nurses or nannies who handled infected individuals developed a small crop of pustules in the skin where they had close physical contact with a patient. These disappeared quickly and there were no signs of a systemic infection. Sometimes these local infections were confused with second attacks of smallpox, but they were always clearly distinguishable from the real infection. A single inoculation, or natural smallpox infection gave life-long immunity from a second attack. Vaccination also produced immunological memory, but it tended to fade with time. While complete protection lasted for three to five years, second infections could occur and these became more severe the longer the interval since vaccination. Those of us with long memories will remember having our "smallpox boosters" especially when travelling to a region where natural smallpox was still in circulation. The tendency of vaccination protection to wane was well known to 19th century physicians and was one of the reasons why many opposed the process and preferred inoculation.

There is much that is unknown about how inoculation worked. Smallpox was eradicated before phenomena such as type 1 and type 2 responses were discovered. The only animal model of smallpox is mouse pox, but little work is done on this infection because it is unfashionable to study smallpox. Who cares about an extinct infection?

Appendix 3

HOW DANGEROUS WAS INOCULATION?

M any factors influenced the risk of dying after inoculation. The very best operators, such as the Suttons or William Woodville at the Inoculation Hospital had mortality rates of between one in 800 and one in seven thousand. However, less experienced operatives , or those who made larger deeper incisions probably had death rates of about one in one hundred. Edward Jenner estimated that the death rate overall was about one in two hundred.

Risk was related to age, with a much greater chance of death among the very young or the very old. Pregnancy was a particularly dangerous time to be inoculated just as it was a catastrophic time to catch natural smallpox. People inoculated during smallpox epidemics, the very time when they were most likely to accept the operation, were also at greater risk because some of them had already caught smallpox and it was the natural, not the inoculated form, that killed them.

What seems clear is that a healthy child or teenager was very unlikely to die due to inoculation.

Acknowledgements

Many individuals and institutions have helped over the ten years that it has taken to research and write *Defying Providence*. The medical librarians of the St. James Teaching Hospital Trust, the Brotherton Library of the University of Leeds and the British Library were all supportive. I would particularly like to thank the librarians and archivists of the Royal Society who regularly fetched material from the archives for me to examine. Professor Lisa Jardine and Robyn Adams of the Centre for Editing Lives and Letters at Queen Mary, University of London taught me how to use and interpret those archives and also read and helped me structure parts of several chapters. Their assistance was particularly valuable in helping me to understand the role of Thomas Nettleton.

Gill Rizzello, Duncan Banks, and Martin Toseland read the entire manuscript and made many valuable editorial contributions. Hal Robinson of Librios was a constant source of encouragement. Sir Iain Chalmers read the manuscript and made many helpful suggestions, especially how to increase the number of commas in the text. His encouragement and willingness to publish parts of several chapters on the James Lind Library web site (www.jameslindlibrary.org) helped keep me going during some sticky patches.

My sons, Tom and Nick, read some of the early versions and were correct in suggesting that there was a lot of work to be done. Finally my wife Anthea gave help and support from beginning to end. Her editorial skills getting the manuscript into its final shape were invaluable.

Cover photo: inoculation lancets: courtesy of Phisick.com

Author Biography

Arthur W (Art) Boylston graduated from Exeter, Yale College and Harvard Medical School, before training in Pathology and Immunology at the Peter Bent Brigham Hospital, the National Institutes of Health and St. Mary's Hospital, London. *Defying Providence* is the result of his curiosity about how people in the 18th century came to practice inoculation; that is to deliberately infect themselves and their children with smallpox. This largely forgotten practice led to the development of many modern scientific tools such as controlled clinical trials, outcomes research and evidence-based medicine. When he came across a complete transcript of the Fewster letter, he realised that the story of the milkmaid who inspired Edward Jenner to invent vaccination was a myth. This naturally led him to try and understand what really happened. The result will hopefully restore the reputation of inoculation and the inoculators as true pioneers of scientific medicine.

Art, a former elected officer and trustee of the British Society for Immunology, has retired from his Professorship of Pathology in the University of Leeds and now lives in Oxford with his wife Anthea.

NOTES

Chapter 1

1. Fenner, F, Henderson DA, Ariita, I, Jezek, Z, Ladnyi. ID, 1998, Smallpox and Its Eradication. WHO Geneva, pp 70-119.
2. Ibid, p 216.
3. Hopkins, DR, 1983, Princes and Peasants. University of Chicago Press, Chicago, p 104.
4. Fenner op cit, p 217.
5. Hopkins op cit, pp 139-142.
6. Dixon, CW, 1962, Smallpox. J & A Churchill, London, frontispiece and p 188.
7. Fenner op cit, pp 217-226.
8. Ibid, pp 235-237.
9. Bradford, W, 1900, Of Plymouth Plantation. Edited by Samuel Eliot Morrison. Wright Potter Printing Co, Boston, pp 201-271.
10. Parkman, F, 2003, The Jesuits in North America in the Seventeenth Century. Bridegroom Press, Plano, TX, p 105.
11. Hopkins, op cit p 52.
12. Guy, WA, 1882, Two Hundred and Fifty Years of Small Pox in London. Journal of the Royal Statistical Society, vol 45 pp 431-433.
13. Creighton, C, 1891, A History of Epidemics in Britain. Cambridge University Press, Cambridge, vol. 1 pp 463-465.
14. Miller, Genevieve, 1957, The Adoption of Inoculation for Smallpox in England and France. The University of Pennsylvania Press, Philadelphia, pp 34-35.

Chapter 2

1. Creighton, op cit. vol 1 pp 456-458.
2. Dixon, op cit pp 5-20.

3. Dixon, op cit p 187.
4. Landers, J, 1991, London's Mortality During "the Long Eighteenth Century": A Family Reconstitution Study. In Living and Dying in London. Bynum, WF and Porter, R eds. Medical History Supplement 11. Wellcome Institute for the History of Medicine pp 21-28.
5. Halliday, FE, 1955, Queen Elizabeth I and Dr Burcot. History Today, vol 5 pp 542-544.
6. Census of England, 1861, Report of the Registrar General, vol 3 p 43
7. Web site www.who.int/mediacenter, fact sheets/smallpox

Chapter 3

1. Stearns, RP and Pasti, G, 1950, Remarks on the Introduction of Inoculation for Smallpox in England. Bulletin of the History of Medicine, vol 24 pp 103-121.
2. Timonius Emanuel, 1714, An Account of History, of the Procuring the Small Pox by incision, or inoculation: as it has for some time been practised at Constantinople. Being the Extract of a Letter from Emanuel Timonius, Oxon and Patav. M.D. F.R.S dated at Constantinople, December 1713. Phil Trans vol. 29 pp 72-82.
3. Miller, Genevieve, 1957, The Adoption of Inoculation for Smallpox in England and France. University of Pennsylvania Press, Philadelphia p59.
4. Miller, ibid 59-63.
5. Pylarini, Jacobus, 1716, *Nova et tuta variolas excitandi per transplantationem emthodus; nuper inventa et in usum traacta: qua rite pereacta immunia in posterum praeservanter ab hujus- modi cntagio corpora* Phil Trans vol 29 pp 393-399
6. Stearns and Pasti, op cit p 109.
7. Miller, op cit pp 64-69.
8. Grundy, Isobel, 1999, Lady Mary Wortley Montague. Oxford University Press, Oxford pp 99-167.
9. Dixon, CW, 1962, Smallpox. J & A Churchill, London pp 219-22.

10. Maitland, Charles, 1722, Mr. Maitland's Account of Inoculating the Small Pox. Printed by J. Downing and sold by J. Roberts at the Oxford-Arms in Warwick Lane. pp 7-8.
11. Kittredge, GL, 1912, Lost Works of Cotton Mather. Massachusetts Historical Society. pp 418-423.

Chapter 4
1. Fitz, RH, 1911, Zabdiel Boylston, Inoculator, and the Epidemic of Smallpox in Boston in 1721. Bulletin of the Johns Hopkins Hospital, vol 22. And Boston Selectmen's minutes, 1701-1736. Box 12, vol 1 p4. May 8.
2. Colman, Benjamin. Rev. Some Observations on the New Method of Receiving the Smallpox by Ingrafting or Inoculation. B. Green, Boston p 2.
3. Silverman, Kenneth, 1984, The Life and Times of Cotton Mather. Harper and Row, New York. For details of Cotton Mather's life.
4. Kittredge, op. cit
5. Kittredge, ibid.

Chapter 5
1. Mager, GM, 1975, Zabdiel Boylston : Medical Pioneer of Colonial Boston. Unpublished PhD thesis, University of Illinois. Contains a detailed account of Boylston's early life and training
2. The Boston Newsletter, July 17-24, 1710.
3. The Boston Gazette, Nov. 21-28, 1720
4. Colman, op cit p 3.
5. Boylston, Zabdiel, 1726, An Historical Account of the Small-Pox Inoculated in New England Upon all Sorts of Persons, Whites, Blacks, and of All Ages and Constitutions. London, S. Chandler at the Cross Keys in the Poultry. pp2-3.
6. Boylston, ibid, preface ii.
7. ibid. p 6.
8. Boston Gazette 1721, July 10-17, no 85.

9. Diary of Cotton Mather 1709-1724. Massachusetts Historical Society Collections- seventh series, 1912, Boston, MHS vol 8 pp 631-632.

10. Boylston, op. cit pp 4-6, and pp 58-62. This is Boylston's account of the hearing including the testimony presented against inoculation. An unpublished letter in the Royal Society Archives by Dr. George Stewart, who was present, says that Boylston was challenged over the safety of the procedure and could only answer that all medical interventions were potentially dangerous. Stewart says that the selectmen, presented with the damning evidence of Dalhounde had no choice but to forbid inoculation.

11. Boylston, op cit p 62.

Chapter 6

1. Boston Newsletter, 1721, July 17-24 no. 912. The letter is signed "Philanthropus", but is easily recognised as written by William Douglass.

2. Kitteridge, op cit pp 423-425.

3. Boston Gazette, 1721, July 27-31 no 88.

4. The Boston Newsletter, 1721, July 24-31 no 913 p 2.

5. The New England Courant, 1721, August 7 no 1 p 1.

6. NewEngland Courant, 1721, August 7-14 no 2 p 1.

7. Boylston, ibid pp 8-9.

8. New England Courant, 1721 August 7-14. no 2.p.1.

9. Boston Gazette, 1721, August now lost.

10. New England Courant, 1721, August 14-21 no 3.

11. Diary of Cotton Mather, op cit p 639.

12. ibid pp 637-638 and Boylston op cit. p.9.

Chapter 7

1. New England Courant, 1721, August 21-28 no 4.

2. Some Account of what is said about Inoculating or Transplanting the Small Pox. By the Learned Dr Emanuel Timonius, and Jacob Pylarinus. With some remarks thereon. To which are added a few Quaeries in Answer to the Scruples of many about the Lawfulness of this Method.

Published by Dr Zabdiel Boylston. Boston, 1721. In Several Reasons Proving that Inoculating or Transplanting the Small Pox, is a Lawful Practice, and that it has been Blessed by GOD for the Saving of many a Life. Sentiments on the Small Pox Inoculated. Cotton Mather. 1721, 1-79. Expands his arguments.

3. Kittredge, op cit p 429 argues that that Boylston published this tract, but that Mather actually wrote most of it, hence the curious "published by" rather than "written by" on the title page.

4. An Account of the Method and Success of Inoculating the Small-Pox in Boston in New-England. In a letter by a Gentleman there to his friend in London. 1722. 1-26. Mather had this published anonymously. Kittredge p 444.

5. Thatcher, Peter, 1789, Massachusetts Magazine vol 1 pp 776-778.

6. Kittredge, GL, 1921, Several Reasons Proving the Inoculating or Transplanting the Small Pox is a Lawful Practice and that it has been Blessed by GOD for the Saving of Many a Life. By Increase Mather. And, Sentiments of the Small Pox Inoculated by Cotton Mather. Printed for Private Distribution. Cleveland. Kittredge discusses the issue of Mather's FRS and the meetings at Richard Hall's Coffee House in the Introduction pp 15-17.

Chapter 8

1. The estimate of one in four suffering from smallpox during mid October is derived from the number of deaths in that month – 412- multiplied by the mortality rate of one in six to give a figure of over 2400 cases. At the time the population of Boston was bout 11,000. Mather's diary records that the number of prayer requests for individuals suffering from smallpox peaked at 322 on October 15th and fell to 180 the next week. Mather Diary pp 652-653.

2. Boylston, op cit pp 10-11.

3. Douglass, William, 1722, Inoculation of the Small Pox as Practiced in Boston, Considered in a Letter to A.S.M.D. and F.R.S. in London. J. Franklin, Boston.
4. Boston Gazette, 1721 Oct. 30.
5. The "Dr. Thompson" who carried out inoculations with Boylston is identified here as Dr.Philip Thompson. His relationship to Mrs. Thomas Walter is revealed in the biography of Rev. Joseph Belcher, Harvard University class of 1690, in "Colonial Collegians", Project director Edick Wright, a CD ROM produced by the Massachusetts Historical Society. Belcher had a stroke in 1721 and went to stay with Thomas Walter so that he could be cared for by his "wife's brother, Philip Thompson". Joseph Belcher and Abigail Thompson were Rebecca Thompson Walter's parents. Abigail Thompson was Philips Thompson's sister.
6. Boylston, op cit p 26.
7. Greenwood, Isaac, 1722, A Friendly Debate; or a Dialog Between Academicus and Sawney and Mundungus, Two Eminent Physicians About Some of Their Late Performances. Boston.
8. New England Courant, 1722, May 21-28 no 42.

Chapter 9
1. Warden, GB, 1970, Boston 1689-1776. Little, Brown. Boston pp 15-27.
2. Hall, MG, 1988, The Last American Puritan: The Life of Increase Mather. Wesleyan University Press pp 207-302.
3. Levin, David, 1978, Cotton Mather, The Young life of the Lord's Remembrancer 1663-1703. Harvard University Press, p 232.
4. Warden, op cit pp 34-79.
5. Mather Diary, op cit p 607.
6. Mather Diary, ibid.
7. Warden, op cit pp 80-101.
8. Miller, Perry, 1953, The New England Mind: From Colony to Province. Harvard University Press, Cambridge, p 371.
9. The Boston Newsletter, 1721, no 912 July 17-24.

10. Weaver, GH, 921, Life and Writings of William Douglass M.D. (1691-1752) Bulletin of the Society of Medical History of Chicago vol 11, pp 229-259.
11. Letters of William Douglass to Cadwallader Colden. Massachusetts Historical Society Collections. 4th series vol. 2 pp 164-169.
12. Mager, GM, 1975, Zabdiel Boylston: Medical Pioneer of Colonial Boston. Unpublished PhD Thesis University of Illinois.
13. Loudon, Irving, 1986, Medical Care and the General Practitioner 1750-1850. Clarendon Press, Oxford, p 35. Also Mager, op cit, pp 39-41 and 61-62.
14. Letters of William Douglass, op cit
15. ibid
16. Miller, Perry, op cit pp 371-372.
17. Boylston, op cit p 20. Also Osburne, Capt. John, 1722, Phil Trans vol 32 pp 225-227.
18. Morgan, ES, 1966, The Puritan Family. Harper and Row, New York, p19.
19. Morgan, op cit pp 157-160.

Chapter 10

1. Maitland, Charles, 1722, Mr Maitland's Account of Inoculating Small Pox. London, pp 1-33.
2. Grundy, Isobel, 1999, Lady Mary Wortley Montague. Oxford University Press, Oxford, pp 211-212.
3. Sloane, Sir Hans, 1755-1756. An Account of Inoculation by Sir Hans Sloane, Bart, given to Mr. Ranby to be published anno 1736. Phil Trans, vol 49; p 517.
4. Miller, Genevieve, 1957, The Adoption of Inoculation for Smallpox in England and France. University of Pennsylvania Press, Philadelphia, pp 75-76.
5. Maitland, op cit pp 20-25. This gives Maitland's day by day account of the experiment.
6. theoldbaileyonline website has the details of the six Newgate prisoners, their trials, and subsequent pardons or reconvictions.

7. 10 London Journal, 1721, July 29.
8. Maitland, op cit p 20.
9. Miller, Genevieve, op cit pp 84-85.
10. Maitland, op cit p 25.
11. Ibid, p 26.
12. Ibid, p 27.
13. Sloane, op cit pp 517-518
14. Maitland, op cit. unnumbered page labelled advertisement.
15. Daily Journal, 1721, Nov. 16, issue 255.
16. Douglass, William, 1722, Inoculation of the Smallpox as Practised in Boston Consider'd in a Letter to A_S_M.D. & F.R.S. in London. J. Franklin, Boston. Read to the Royal Society Nov. 16, 1721. RS Journal Book, vol 12, p163.
17. Flying Post or Post Master, 1721, Nov. 30, issue 4507.
18. The Way of Proceeding in the Small Pox Inoculated in New England, 1722, Communicated by Henry Newman Esq. of The Middle Temple. Phil Trans, vol 32, Jan-Mar, no. 370, pp 33-35. Known to have been written by Cotton Mather.
19. Colman, Benjamin, 1721, Some Observations on the New Method of Receiving the Smallpox by Ingrafting or Inoculating. Boston.
20. Colman, Benjamin, 1722, A Narrative of the Method and Success of Inoculating the Small pox in New England. With a Reply to Objections Made Against it from Principles of Conscience In A Letter to a Minster at Boston(William Cooper) which is now prefixed an Historical Introduction by Daniel Neal. London.
21. Douglass, William, 1722, The Abuses and Scandals of Some Late Pamphlets in Favour of Inoculation of the Small Pox, Modestly Obviated & Inoculation further Considered in a Letter to A__S__M.D. & F.R.S. in London. J. Franklin, Boston.
22. Maitland, op cit, pp 29-32.
23. London Gazette, 1722, Mar. 6, issue 6040.
24. Daily Courant, 1722, London, March 26, 1722, issue 6373.

Chapter 11

1. Miller, op cit, p 92.
2. Nettleton, Thomas, 1722a, An Account of the Success of Inoculating the Smallpox in a Letter to William Whitakers. S Palmer, London.
3. ibid
4. Ibid, pp 7-9
5. Ibid, p 12
6. Nettleton, Thomas, 1722b, Further Progress in Inoculating the Small Pox. Phil Trans. Vol 32, no. 370, p 51.
7. Sloane, op cit p 518.
8. Ibid, p 519.
9. Royal Society Classified Papers vol 23, no 27. Persons inoculated by Mr. Maitland
10. Miller, op cit pp 97-99.
11. Royal Society Classified Papers, vol 23, op cit. 1, no 1. Persons Inoculated by Claude Amyand

Chapter 12

1. Sparham Legard, 1722, Reasons Against the Practice of Inoculating the Small-Pox. As Also A Brief Account of the Operation of this Poison, infused after this manner into a wound. Printed for J.Peele, at Locke's Head in Paternoster-Row. London.
2. Miller, Genevieve, 1957, The Adoption of Inoculation for Smallpox in England and France. University of Pennsylvania Press, Philadelphia, p 127.
3. Massey Edmund, 1722, A sermon against the dangerous and sinful Practice of Inoculation. Preached at St Andrew's Holborn on July 8th, 1722. Printed for William Meadows at the Angel in Cornhill.
4. Wagstaffe, William, 1722, Letter to Dr Friend; Shewing The Danger and Uncertainty of Inoculating the Small Pox. Printed for Samuel Butler next Bernard's Inn in Holborn. London.
5. Massey, Isaac, 1722, A Short and Plain Account of Inoculation with Some Remarks on the main Arguments

made use of to recommend that Practice by Mr Maitland and others. London. Printed for W. Meadows at the Angel in Cornhill, and sold by T. Payne in Pater Noster Row, pp 3-4.

6.   Massey, Isaac, 1727, Remarks on Dr Jurins Last Yearly Account of the Success of Inoculation. Printed for W. Meadows, at the Angel in Cornhill, London.

Chapter 13

1.   Crawford, J, 1722, The Case of Inoculating the Small-Pox Consider'd and its Advantages Asserted: In a Review of Dr Wagstaffe's Letter. Wherein Every Thing that Author has advanced against it, is fully Confuted and Inoculation proved Safe, Beneficial, and a Laudable Practice. Printed for T. Warner, at the Black Boy in Pater Noster-Row.

2.   Brady, Samuel, 1722, Some Remarks upon Dr Wagstaffe's Letter and Mr Massey's Sermon Against Inoculating the Small-Pox with An Account of the Inoculation of several Children and Some Reasons for the Safety and Security of that Practice in Three Letters to a Friend. Printed for John Clark, at the Bible and Crown in the Poultry, near Cheapside, London.

3.   Arbuthnot, J, 1722, Mr Maitland's Account of Inoculating the Smallpox Vindicated, From Dr Wagstaffe's Misrepresentations of the Practice; with some Remarks on Mr. Massey's Sermon. The Second Edition. To which is added, His First Account of Inoculating the Small pox. Printed and Sold by J. Peele, at Lock's Head in Paternoster-Row

4.   Douglass, William, 1721, Inoculation of the Smallpox as Practised in Boston Consider'd in a Letter to A__S__M.D. & F.R.S. in London. 1722, J. Franklin, Boston. Read to the Royal Society Nov 16, RS Journal Book, vol 12, p 163.

5.   Arbuthnot, op cit p 33.

6.   Ibid, pp 52-54.

7.   Ibid, p 49.

8. A Letter to the Reverend Mr. Massey Occasion's by his Late Wonderful Sermon a Against Inoculation, 1722, printed for J. Roberts near the Oxford Arms in Warwick Lane, London, p 7. This is catalogued as by Maitland in the British Library. The pamphlet itself does not give an author.

9. Wilson, Adrian, 1990, The Politics of Medical Improvement in Early Hanoverian London. In Cunningham, A and French, R. eds, The Medical Enlightenment of the Eighteenth Century. Cambridge University Press, Cambridge, pp 4-39.

10. See 3 above.

Chapter 14

1. Arbuthnot, J, 1722, Mr. Maitland's Account of Inoculating the Smallpox Vindicated from Dr Wagstaffe's Misrepresentations of that Practice; with some remarks on Mr. Massey's Sermon. Printed and Sold by J. Peele, at Lock's Head in Paternoster Row, London.

2. Mather Cotton, 1722, An Account of the Method and Success of Inoculating the Small-Pox in Boston in New-England. In a letter by a Gentleman there to his friend in London, pp 1-26.

3. Nettleton T, 1722b. A Letter from the same Learned and Ingenious Gentleman, concerning his further Progress in inoculating the Small Pox. Phil Trans, vol 32, no 370, pp 49-52.

4. Bernoulli, Jacob quoted in Bernstein, PL, 1996, Against the Gods. John Wiley and Sons, New York. p 119

5. Rusnock, A, 1996, The Correspondence of James Jurin (1684-1750) Physician and Secretary to the Royal Society. Editions Rodopi B.V, Amsterdam.

6. Nettleton, Thomas, 1722, An Account of the Success of Inoculating the Smallpox in a Letter to William Whitakers. S Palmer, London.

7. Nettleton, Thomas, 1722, Further Progress in Inoculating the Small Pox. Phil Trans, vol 32, no 370, p 51.

8. Nettleton, op cit
9. Nettleton, op cit
10. Wagstaffe W,1722, A Letter to Dr Friend Shewing the Danger and Uncertainty of Inoculating the Smallpox. London: Printed for Samuel Butler next Bernard's Inn in Holborn.
11. Arbuthnot, op cit
12. Arbuthnot, John, 1692, Of the Laws of Chance or a Method of Calculation of the Hazards of Game. London. Printed by Benj. Motte and sold by Randall Taylor.
13. Sackett, DL, Rosenberg, WM, Muir, Gray, J A, Haynes, RB, Richardson, WS, 1996, Evidence Based Medicine: What it is and What it isn't. Brit Med J, vol 312 (7023) pp 71-72.
14. Arbuthnot, Mr Maitland's Account, op cit
15. Miller, Genevieve, 1957, The adoption of Inoculation for Smallpox in England and France. University of Pennsylvania Press, Philadelphia.
16. Rusnock, A, 2002, Vital Accounts: Quantifying Health and Population in Eighteenth Century England and France. Cambridge University Press, Cambridge.
17. Maitland, Charles, 1722, Mr. Maitland's Account of Inoculating the Small Pox. London: Printed by J. Downing and sold by J. Roberts at the Oxford Arms in Warwick Lane.
18. Nettleton Thomas, 1722c, Part of a letter from Dr Nettleton, Physician at Halifax. To Dr Jurin R.S. Secr. Concerning the Inoculation of the Small Pox, and the Mortality of that Distemper in the Natural Way. Phil Trans, vol 32, pp 209-212.
19. Jurin J to Thomas Nettleton, letter dated 2, June 1722. Published in Rusnock, A, 1996, The Correspondence of James Jurin (1684-1750) Physician and Secretary to the Royal Society. Editions Rodopi B.V, Amsterdam, p 104.
20. Nettleton, 1722c, op cit
21. ibid
22. ibid

23. Jurin, James, 1723, A letter to the Learned Caleb Cotesworthy M.D. Containing a comparison between the mortality of the natural small pox and that given by inoculation. W and J Innys at the Prince's Arms at the West End of St. Paul's Churchyard, London.

24. ibid

25. ibid

26. Phil Trans, 1723, no 378 (July-August). It is bound at the back of this volume and is unnumbered. Strangely it is dated Dec 11, 1723.

27. Jurin James, 1724, An Account of the Success of Inoculating the Small Pox in Great Britain with a Comparison between the Miscarriages of that practice, and the Mortality of the Natural Small Pox. J. Peele at Locke's Head in Pater-Noster Row, London.

28. Royal Society Classified Papers, 1660-1740, vol 23, "Inoculation". Inoculations performed by Sergeant Amyand, pp 1-4.

29. Williams, Perrot, in Jurin 1724.

30. Wright, Richard, in Jurin 1724.

31. Jurin, James, 1725, An Account of the Success of Inoculating the Small Pox for the Year 1724. Printed for J. Peele, at Lock's Head, in Pater-noster-Row, London.

Chapter 15

1. Wagstaffe, op cit pp 41-44.

1. Howgrave, Francis, 1724, Reasons Against the Inoculation of the Small-Pox. In a Letter to Dr Jurin. Printed for John Clark at the Bible under the Royal Exchange, London.

2. Jurin, James, 1726, An Account of the Success of Inoculating the Small-Pox in Great Britain for the Year 1725. With Comparison between the Miscarriages in that Practice and the Mortality of the Natural Small-Pox. Printed for J. Peele, at Lock's Head Pater-noster-Row, London.

3. Clinch, William, 1725, An Historical Essay on the Rise and Progress of the Small-Pox to which is added a short appendix to r prove that inoculation is no security from

the natural smallpox. 2nd edition. Printed for A.R. sold by T. Warner, London.

4. Royal Society Classified Papers, vol 23 "Inoculation".

5. Mather, Cotton, 1722, The Way of Proceeding in the Small Pox Inoculated in New England Communicated by Henry Newman Esq; of the Middle Temple. Phil Trans, vol 32, no 370 pp 33-35.

6. Mather, Cotton, 1722, An Account of the Method and Success of Inoculating the Small-Pox in Boston, New England. In a Letter from a Gentleman There to His Friend in London. J. Peele, London.

7. Boylston, Zabdiel, 1726, An Historical Account of the Small-Pox Inoculated in New England, Upon all Sorts of Persons, Whites, Blacks, and of all Ages and Constitutions. With some Account of the Nature of the Infection in the Natural and Inoculated Way, and their different Effects on Human Bodies. With some short Directions to the Unexperienced in this Method of Practice. Printed for S. Chandler, at the Cross-Keys in the Poultry, London, p i.

8. Boston Gazette, 1723, no 193, July 29-August 5.

9. Royal Society Journal Book. XII pp 533-34, 656-60, 673-75. and XIII p 148.

10. Fitz, RH, 1911, Zabdiel Boylston, Inoculator, and the Epidemic of Smallpox in Boston, 1721. Bulletin of the Johns Hopkins Hospital, vol 22, no 247, p 325

11. Boylston, AW and Williams, AE, Zabdiel Boylston's Evaluation of Inoculation Against Smallpox. JLL Bulletin: Commentaries on the History of Treatment Evaluation. www.jameslindlibrary.org

12. Rusnock, Correspondence. op cit

13. Scheuzer, JG, 1729, An Account of the Success of Inoculating the Smallpox in Great Britain for the Years 1727 and 1728. London.

14. Albert, MR, Ostheimer, KG, Breman, JG, 2001, The Last Smallpox Epidemic in Boston and the Vaccination

Controversy 1901-1903. New England J Med, vol 344, pp 375-379.
15. Sackett et.al. 1966 op cit.

Chapter 16
1. Miller, Genevieve, op cit. pp. 134-146.
2. Kirkpatrick, J, 1754, The Analysis of Inoculation: Comprizing the History, Theory, and Practice of It: With an Occasional Consideration of the most Remarkable Appearances in the Small Pox. Printed for J. Millan near Charing Cross; J. Buckland in Pater-Noster-Row, and R. Griffiths in St Paul's Church Yard.
3. Jurin, James, 1724, An Account of the Success, op cit pp 9-11.
4. The Gentleman's Magazine, 1750, vol 20, p 532.
5. Webb, ME, 1989, The Early Medical Studies and Practice of Dr David Hartley. Bulletin of the History of Medicine, vol 63, pp 618-636.
6. Hartley, David, 1733, Reasons Why the Practice of Inoculation Ought to be Introduced into the Town of Bury at Present. Bury St. Edmunds.
7. Warren, Martin, 1733, I have perused a pamphlet entitled, Some Reasons why the Practice of Inoculation ought to be Introduced into the Town of Bury at Present. (This pamphlet has no title page or printer acknowledged. It is in the British Library Catalogue under the first sentence which I have given above and Martin Warren).
8. Miller, op cit pp 138-139
9. Colman, Benjamin, 1722, A Narrative of the Method and Success of Inoculating the Smallpox in New England. With a reply to the objections Made Against it from Principles of Conscience. In a Letter from a Minister at Boston. To Which is Now Prefixed an Historical Introduction by David Neal. George Grierson, Dublin.
10. Douglass, William, 1730, A Dissertation Concerning inoculation of the Small Pox. Giving Some Account of the Rise, Progress, Success, Advantages and Disadvantages of

Receiving the Smallpox by Incisions: illustrated with sundry cases of the Inoculated. D. Henchman, and T. Hancock, Boston.

11. Boylston, Zabdiel, 1730, The Weekly Newsletter, no 166. February 26 to March 5.

12. Gentleman's Magazine, 1738, vol 8, p 55.

13. Kirkpatrick, James (formerly Kilpatrick), 1743, An Essay on Inoculation Occasioned by the Small-pox being brought into South Carolina in the Year 1738. London

14. Woodville, William, 1796. The History of Inoculation of the Small-Pox in Great Britain, vol 1 printed and sold by James Phillips, George Yard, Lombard Street, London, p 221.

15. Stewart, Larry, 1985, The Edge of Utility: Slaves and Smallpox in the Early Eighteenth Century. Medical History, vol 29, pp 540-570.

16. Miller, op cit p 209.

17. Gentleman's Magazine, 1737, vol 7, p 561.

18. Miller, op cit p 162.

19. Nettleton, Thomas, 1722, An Account of the Success of Inoculating the Small-Pox; in a Letter to Dr. William Whitaker. Printed for S. Palmer, for J. Batley, at the Dove in Pater-Noster-Row.

20. Maitland, op cit

21. Grundy, Isobel, 1999, Lady Mary Worley Montague. Oxford University Press, Oxford, pp 217-218.

Chapter 17

1. Miller, op cit. p 163-166. At least one example still exists. See Steer, Francis W. A Relic of and Eighteenth Century Isolation Hospital. 1956. The Lancet; Jan 28. 1956 pp 200-201.

2. Frewen, Thomas, 1749, The Practice and Theory of Inoculation. With an Account of Its Success. In a Letter to a Friend. London.

3. Dorothy, GM, 1984, London Life in the Eighteenth Century. Academy Chicago Publishers, Chicago. pp.56-59.

4. Middlesex County Hospital for Smallpox and Inoculation, situated in Windmill Street, Tottenham Court Road, July 2 1746, reasons for instituting this Hospital and objections against it answered. London. 1748.

5. Maddox, Isaac, Bishop of Worcester, 1752, A Sermon Preached before His Grace John Duke of Marlborough , President, the Vice-Presidents and Governors of the Hospital for Small-Pox and Inoculation at the Parish Church of St Andrew's Holborn, on Thursday March 5, 1752. London.

6. Gentleman's Magazine, 1752, vol 22, p 532.

7. Kirkpatrick, op cit pp 267-268.

8. Royal College of Physicians, in Miller, Genevieve, op cit. p 170.

9. Smith, HL, 1909, Dr Adam Thomson, the Originator of the American Method of Inoculation for Smallpox. Johns Hopkins Hospital Bulletin, vol 20, pp 49-52.

10. Adams Family papers an electronic archive. Massachusetts Historical Society. www.masshist.org. Correspondence between John and Abigail(Smith) Adams. The inoculation references are the letters between 7 April 1764 and 7 May 1764.

11. Loudon, Irvine, 1985, The Nature of Provincial Medical Practice in Eighteenth Century England. Medical History, vol 29, pp 1-32.

Chapter 18

1. Smith, J.R, 1987, The Speckled Monster; Smallpox in England 1670-1970 with particular reference to Essex. 1987. Essex Record Office, Chelmsford. Smith has rescued the Suttons from oblivion and written the definitive account of their lives and activities. Unless otherwise stated, references to the Suttons refer to this book.

2. ibid p 68.

3. ibid p 69.

4. ibid pp 73-74.

5. Houlton, Robert, 1768, Indisputable Facts Relative to the Suttonian Art of Inoculation with Observations on its Discovery, Progress, Encouragement, Opposition, etc etc. Printed by W.G. Jones in Suffolk Street, Dublin, p. 16.

6. A Sermon Preached at Ingatestone, Essex, October 12, 1766. In Defence of Inoculation to which is added an Appendix on the Present State of Inoculation; with Observations, &c. 1767. Printed and Sold also by Lionel Hassal in Chelmsford, Essex and sold also by J. Wilkie, in St. Paul's Churchyard; J. Kingman, under the Royal Exchange, London, pp 56-60.

7. Houlton, Indisputable facts pp 13-16.

8. Dimsdale, Thomas, 1767, The Present Method of Inoculating for the Small-Pox. To which are added Some Experiments, Instituted with a view to discover the Effects of a Similar Treatment in the Natural Small-Pox. 1767. Printed for W. Owen in Fleet Street, London, p 5.

9. ibid p 83.

10. Baker, George, 766, An Inquiry into the Merits of a Method of Inoculating the Small-Pox, which is now Practised in Several Counties of England. 1766. Printed for J. Dodsley, in Pall-Mall, London. For those who have seen the film "The Madness of King George", Baker is the doctor who prescribes cupping for the King.

11. Rushton, Thomas, 1768, An Essay on Inoculation. 3rd edition.

12. Gentleman's Magazine, 1767, vol 38, p 75.

13. Sutton, Daniel. 1796, The Inoculator; or Suttonian System of Inoculation, Fully set Forth in a plain and familiar Manner. Printed for the author by T. Gillet, Bartholomew Close, London and sold by C. Dilley, in the Poultry, and J. Owen, Piccadilly.

14. Boylston, AW, 2011, Daniel Sutton, a Forgotten 18th Century Clinician Scientist. www.JamesLindLibrary.org. This gives a summary and overview of Sutton's experiments which was taken from a then unpublished draft of this chapter.

15. Woodville, William, 1796, The History of Inoculation of the Small-pox in Great Britain; Comprehending a review of all

the Publications on the Subject: with Experimental Inquiry into the relative Advantages of Every Measure Which has been Deemed Necessary in the Process of Inoculation, i, London.

16. Gentleman's Magazine,1819, vol 89, p 218.

Chapter 19

1. Watson, William, 1768, An Account of a Series of Experiments Instituted with a view to Ascertaining the Most Successful Method of Inoculating the Small-Pox. Printed for J. Nourse, London, Bookseller to His Majesty.
2. Biographical details from The Dictionary of National Biography online edition
3. Watson, op cit p. 4.
4. ibid p.37.
5. Boylston, AW, 2002, Clinical Investigation of Smallpox in 1767. New England Journal of Medicine vol 346, pp 1326-1328.

Chapter 20

1. Watson, William, op cit.
2. Razzell, Peter, 2003, The Conquest of Smallpox. The Impact of Inoculation on Smallpox Mortality. Caliban Books, pp 82-84.
3. Boorman, WH, 1986, The Mass Inoculation of the Poor in South Hampshire, 1773-1783. Southampton Medical Journal, vol 3, pp 93-100.
4. ibid p. 96.
5. ibid.
6. ibid.
7. ibid p 99.
8. Razzell, op. cit pp 119 122.
9. Dimsdale, Thomas, 1767, The Present Method of Inoculating for the Small-Pox to which are added some Experiments , instituted with a View to Discover the Effects of a similar Treatment in the Natural Small-Pox. Printed for W.Owen, in Fleeet Street, London.

10. Dimsdale, Baron Thomas, 1776, Thoughts on General and Partial Inoculation. Containing a Translation of two Treatises written when the Author was at Petersburg, and published there, by Command of her Imperial Majety, in the Russian Language. Also Outlines of Two Plans: one for the general inoculation of the Poor In small Towns and Villages. The other for the general Inoculation of the Poor in London, and other large and populous places. Printed by William Richardson; for W.Owen in Fleet Street; London, and T. Carnan and F. Newbery jun. no 65, in St Paul's Church-yard.

11. Jenner, Edward, 1798, An Inquiry Into the Causes and Effects of the Variolae Vaccinae, Discovered in some of the western Counties of England, Particularly Gloucestershire and Known by the Name of The Cow Pox. 1798. Sampson Low, No. 7 Berwick Street, Soho, London, and sold by Law, Ave Maria Lane: and Murray and Highley, Fleet Street, pp 28-29.

12. This was especially true of the Suttons and their partners.

13. Buchan, William, 1772, Domestic Medicine: or, a Treatise on the Prevention and Cure of Diseases by Regimen and Simple Medicines.2nd edition. Printed for W. Strahan, London, T. Cadell in the Strand; and A. Kincaid & W. Creech, and J. Balfour, at Edinburgh, p 294.

14. Buchan biographical details from the Dictionary of National Biography, online edition.

15. Buchan, op cit p 287.

16. ibid.

17. ibid p 298.

Chapter 21

1. Lettsom(e), John Coakley, biographical details in the DNB online edition. The name is spelt both with and without the terminal "e".

2. Lettsom, John Coakley, 1772, The Natural History of the Tea Tree, with Observations on the Medical Qualities of Tea, and the Effects of Tea Drinking. London.

3. Lettsom, John Coakley, 1778, A letter to Sir Robert Barker, knt, F.R.S. and George Stackpoole, esq.: Upon General Inoculation. London.

4. Dimsdale, "Thoughts on general..." op cit pp 35-45.

5. Dimsdale, Baron Thomas, 1779, A Review of Dr Lettsom's Observations on Baron Dimsdale's Remarks Respecting Dr Lettsom's Letter on General Inoculation. Printed by J Phillips, George Yard, Lombard Street, for W Owen, Fleet Street, and T Carnan and F. Newbery, jun St. Paul's Church-Yard.

6. Lettsom, John Coakley, 1779, An Answer to Baron Dimsdale's Review of Lettsom's Observations on the Baron's Remarks respecting inoculation. London.

7. Gentleman's Magazine, 1779, p 49:

8. Watkinson, John, 1777, An Examination of the Charge Brought Against Inoculation by De Haen, Rast, K Dimsdale, and other writers. Printed for J. Johnson, London, no. 72, St. Paul's Churchyard, and J. Sewell, in Cornhill.

9. ibid p. 45.

10. Dimsdale, Baron Thomas, 1778, Observations on the Introduction to the Plan of Dispensary for General Inoculation. London. Printed for William Richardson.

11. Black, William, 1781, Observations Medical and Political: on the Smallpox and Inoculation; and on the decrease of mankind. Printed for J. Johnson, London.

12. ibid pp. 52-54.

13. ibid p. 92.

14. Lettsom, John Coakley, 1779, An Answer to Baron Dimsdale's Review of Dr Lettsom's Observations on the Baron's Remarks Respecting a Letter on General Inoculation. London, p 33.

15. Anonymous, 1779, "Uninterested Spectator" A Letter to J.C.Lettsom M.D.F.R.S.S.A.S. &c occasioned by Baron Dimsdale's Remarks on Dr Lettsome's Letter to Sir Robert Baker. London.

Chapter 22

1. Haygarth, John, 1784, An Inquiry how to Prevent the Small-pox. And Proceedings of a Society for promoting General Inoculation at Stated Periods, and Preventing the natural Small-pox in Chester. Printed by J. Monk for J. Johnson, Chester, no. 72, St. Paul's Churchyard, London, and P.Broster, Chester.
2. ibid pp 117-120. Haygarth's rules were designed to prevent the spread of natural smallpox. They would also apply to inoculated smallpox, but their primary purpose was to prevent the spread of the natural infection.
3. ibid pp 114-115.
4. ibid p143.
5. ibid p. 198.
6. ibid p. 206-207.
7. Haygarth, John, 1793, A Sketch of a Plan to Exterminate the Casual Smallpox from Great Britain; and to Introduce General Inoculation: to which is added , a Correspondence on the Nature of Variolous Contagion. Printed for J. Johnson, London, No. 72, St Paul's Churchyard.
8. ibid pp. 148-154.

Chapter 23

1. George Washington to Congress 27 November 1775, as quoted in Gibson, JE, 1937, Dr Bodo Otto and the Medical Background to the American Revolution. Charles C Thomas, Springfield, Ill, p 88.
2. Washington to Congress, ibid p 89.
3. Washington to the Massachusetts legislature, 10 December 1775. ibid p 89
4. Washington to Congress, ibid p 89.
5. Washington to Congress 14 December 1775. Ibid p 89.
6. Duffy, J, 1952, Smallpox and the Indians in the American Colonies. Bull Hist Med, vol 25, pp 324-341.
7. Stearn, EW, Stearn, AE, 1945, The Effect of Smallpox on the Destiny of the Amerindian. Bruce Humphries Inc, Boston, pp 44-45.

8. Washington Order from Headquarters, 13 March 1776. As quoted in Gibson,op cit. p 90.
9. Washington to Congress 19 March 1776. Ibid
10. ibid p. 91.
11. Fenn, EA, 2001, Pox Americana. The Great Smallpox epidemic of 1775-82. Hill and Wang, New York, Chapter 2: Vigilance.
12. Gibson,ibid p96
13. ibid p 97-98.
14. ibid p 98.
15. ibid pp 98-99.
16. ibid p. 99.
17. ibid p. 99.
18. ibid p. 130.
19. ibid p. 131.
20. Thursfield, Hugh, 1940, Smallpox in the American War of Independence. Annals of Medical History, vol 2, p 312.
21. Gibson, op cit pp 131-137.
22. Thursfield, op cit pp 317-318.

Chapter 24

1. Buchan, William, 1772 Domestic Medicine or, a Treatise on the Prevention and Cure of Diseases by Regimen and Simple Medicines. 2nd ed. As discussed in Chapter 20.
2. Blake, JB, 1959, Public Health in the Town of Boston 1630-1822. Harvard University Press, Cambridge, MA, p 244.
3. ibid, p 115.
4. Anonymous, 1803, Gentleman's Magazine, vol 73, p 213.
5. Howlett, J, 1781, An Examination of Dr. Price's Essay on the Population of England and Wales. Maidstone, p 152. As quoted in Razzell, P, 1977, The Conquest of Smallpox, Caliban Press, Firle, Sussex, p 92.
6. Razzell, P op. cit
7. ibid.
8. ibid.
9. ibid.

10. Holingworth, TH, 1964, Population Studies, vol 18, issue 2, The Demography of the British Peerage: Supplement. November 1964, pp 52-70.

11. Phadke, AM, Samant, NR, Dewal, SD, 1973, Smallpox as an Etiological Factor in Male Infertility. Fertility and Sterility, vol 24, pp 802-804.

12. Wrigley, EA, Davies, RS, Oppen, JE, Scholfield, RS, 1997, English Population History from Family Reconstitution Studies 1580-1837. Cambridge University Press, Cambridge.

Chapter 25

1. Baron, John, 1838, The Life of Edward Jenner. Henry Colburn Publisher, London.

2. Pearson, George, 1798, An Inquiry Concerning the History of the Cowpox. Printed for J. Johnson, London, no 72, St. Paul's Churchyard, pp 84-85.

3. Baron, op cit p 3.

4. ibid p 47.

5. Pearson, George, 1798, An Inquiry Concerning the History of the Cowpox. Printed for J. Johnson, London, no. 72, St. Paul's Churchyard.

6. Jenner, Edward, 1801, On the Origin of the Vaccine Inoculation. Printed by D.N.Shury, Berwick Street, Soho, London, p. 1.

7. Moore, James Carrick, 1817, The History and Practice of Vaccination, J. Callow. London, p 2.

8. Fewster's letter is in Pearson, "An inquiry.." pp 84-85.

9. Jenner, Edward, 1799, Further Observations on the Variolae Vaccinae or Cow Pox. Printed for the author by Sampson Low, no. 7 Berwick Street, Soho, London. Most of this piece is a discussion of "spurious cowpox". Several letters in Pearson op cit confirm this fact.

10. Jenner, Edward, 1798, An Inquiry into the Causes and Effects of the Variolae Vaccinae, a disease, Discovered in Some of Western Countries of England particularly

Gloucestershire and Known by the name *The Cow Pox.* Sampson Low, p 19.

11. Crookshank, EM, 1889, History and Pathology of Vaccination. KHK Lewis, London. Chapter 7, pp 250 -266.
12. Woodville, William, 1799, Reports of A Series of Inoculations for the Variolae Vaccinae, or Cowpox. James Phillips and son, George Yard, Lombard Street, London, pp 57-59.
13. Report from the Committee on Dr. Jenner's Petition, respecting his Discovery of Vaccine Inoculation, 1802. Ordered to be printed. House of Commons, p 7.
14. Dixon, CW, 1962, Smallpox. J&A Churchill, London, p 250.

Chapter 26
1. Pearson, George, 1798, An Inquiry Concerning the History of the Cow Pox. In Crookshank, EM, History and Pathology of Vaccination. HK Lewis, London, vol 2, pp54-55.
2. Creighton, Charles, 1894, A History of Epidemics in Britain. Cambridge University Press, Cambridge, vol. 2, pp 590-592.
3. Fenner F, Henderson DA, Arita I, Jezek Z, Ladnyi ID (eds), 1988, Smallpox and its Eradication, WHO. Chapter 27, pp 661-663 and 682-685.
4. ibid 667-668.
5. ibid p 1032.

Appendix 1
1. Woodville, William, 1796, The History of the Inoculation of the Small-pox in Great Britain, vol 1. Printed- and sold by James Phillips, George Yard, Lombard – Street, London, section II. pp 33-52.
2. Pylarini, Jacobus, 1716, *Nova et tuta variolas excitandi per transplantationem emthodus; nuper inventa et in usum traacta: qua rite pereacta immunia in posterum praeservanter ab hujusmodi cntagio corpora.* Phil Trans vol 29, no 347 pp 393-399.

3. Kittredge, GL, 1912, Some Lost Works of Cotton Mather. Proceedings of the Massachusetts Historical Society, pp 418-440.

4. Scheuzer, JG, 1729, An Account of the Success of Inoculating the Smallpox in Great Britain for the Years 1727 and 1728. London. The letter from Cassem Aga is published as an appendix to this paper.

5. Jurin, James, 1723, A Letter to the Learned Dr. Caleb Cotesworth containing a Comparison between the Dangers of Natural Smallpox and that Given by Inoculation, pp 25-31.

6. The letter was written in 1721, a ninety year old would have been born in 1630. Assuming that his mother was inoculated before him this takes the practice back to about 1600 or before.

7. Timonius Emanuel, 1714, An Account of History, of the Procuring the Small Pox by incision, or Inoculation: as it has for some time been Practised at Constantinople. Being the Extract of a Letter from Emanuel Timonius, Oxon and Patav. M.D. F.R.S dated at Constantinople, December 1713. Phil Trans, vol 29, pp 72-82.

8. see ref 4 above

9. Needham, Joseph. 2000, Science and Civilisation in China, vol 6, p 6, edited by Nathan Sivin. Cambridge University Press, Cambridge, pp 134-149.

10. op cit pp 156-161

11. op cit 169-174

12. Coult, R. 1731, Operation of Inoculation of Smallpox as performed in Bengal.(letter from R. Coult to Dr. Oliver Coult in An account of the disease of Bengal (dated 10 February 1731) reprinted in Dharampal, 1971, Indian Science and Technology in the Eighteenth Century. Impex.India, Delhi, pp 141-143.

13. Howell, JZ, 1768, An Account of Inoculating for the Smallpox in the East Indies. Printed for T. Becket, and P.A.Q. de Hondt, near Surrey Street in the Strand.

14. Hopkins, DR, 1983, Princes and Peasants. University of Chicago Press, Chicago, among many others.
15. Wajustyk, Dominic, 1987, A Pious Fraud: The Indian Claims for pre-Jennerian Smallpox Vaccination. In: Meulenbild GJ, Wajustyk D, eds. Studies in Indian Medical History 2nd edition. Groningen (also Dehli 2001) and Personal communication 8 January 2012.
16. Miller, Genevieve, 1957, The Adoption of Inoculation for Smallpox in England and France. The University of Pennsylvania Press. Philadelphia, p 86.
17. Moore, James Carrick, 1817, The History of the Small Pox. Printed for Longman, Hurst, Rees, Orme, and Brown, Paternoster-Row, pp 224-225
18. Maty, M, 1768, A Short account of inoculating the Small pox on the coast of Barbary and at Bengal in the East Indies. Extracted from a memoir written in Dutch by the reverend Mr. Chais at the Hague. Phil Trans, vol 58, pp 128-131.
19. Boylston, Arthur, 2012, The Origins of Inoculation. JLL Bulletin: Commentaries on the History of Treatment Evaluation. www.jameslindlibrary.org.

Made in the USA
Lexington, KY
12 July 2013